D1367360

the roots of the ego

the roots of the ego

A PHENOMENOLOGY OF DYNAMICS AND OF STRUCTURE

Carl Frankenstein, Ph.D. Professor of Special Education at the Hebrew University, Jerusalem

76494

The Williams & Wilkins Company

Baltimore ● *1966*

Library of Congress Catalog Card Number 66–24502

Printed and Composed at
The Waverly Press, Inc.
Mt. Royal & Guilford Avenues
Baltimore, Md.   21202   U.S.A.

ERRATUM

The references on this erratum sheet were inadvertently omitted from Dr. Frankenstein's bibliography. Please place this sheet between pages 280 and 281 to complete the reference section.

110. Reich, W.: *Der Triebhafte Charakter.* Wien, Internationaler Psychoanalytischer Verlag, 1925.
111. Reik, T.: *Geständniszwang und Strafbedürfnis.* Wien, Internationaler Psychoanalytischer Verlag, 1925.
112. Riesman, D. a. o.: *The Lonely Crowd.* New Haven, Yale University Press, 1950.
113. Rothschild, P. S.: *Das Ich und die Regulationen des Erlebnisvorgangs.* Basel, S. Karger AG, 1950.
114. Schilder, P.: *Brain and Personality.* New York, International Universities Press, 1951.
115. Sheldon, W.: Constitutional factors in personality. In *Personality and the Behaviour Disorders*, edited by J. McV. Hunt. New York, Ronald Press Company, 1944.
116. Spencer, H.: *The First Principles.* Chicago, Rand, 1880.
117. Spitz, R.: Hospitalism. In *The Psychoanalytic Study of the Child*, Vol. I. New York, International Universities Press, 1945.
118. Spitz, R.: *A Genetic Field-Theory of Ego Formation.* New York, International Universities Press, 1959.
119. Stephens, W. N.: *The Family in Cross-Cultural Perspective.* New York, Holt, Rinehart and Winston, 1963.
120. Szondi, L.: *Schicksalsanalyse.* Basel, Benno Schwabe and Company, 1948-1956.
121. Tillich, P.: *The Courage to Be.* New Haven, Yale University Press, 1960.
122. Watts, A. F.: *The Language and Mental Development of Children.* London, George H. Harrap and Company, Ltd., 1957.
123. Wechsler, D.: *The Measurement of Adult Intelligence.* Baltimore, The Williams & Wilkins Company, 1950.
124. Werner, H.: *Comparative Psychology of Mental Development.* Chicago, Pollett, 1948.
125. Whyte, W. H.: *Organization Man.* Harmondsworth, England, Penguin Books, 1961.

This book is dedicated to the memory of my teacher and lifelong friend, ERWIN LOEWENSON (1888–1963). Through his writings and his friendship he has proved that, in action and in contemplation, man is committed to the essence of being.

Introduction

Any analysis of the ways in which the environmental conditions of ego development produce definable forms of behavior should be based not only on a definition of these results and these conditions but also on an attempt to make the *structural* conditions of human existence and development understandable.

This is the purpose of the present book. Obviously, the outcome will not be a purely psychological essay, since its aim is recognition and definition of the transpersonal roots of man's observable behavior rather than a description and comparison of correlations between isolated factors and results.

The book deals not only with constitutional factors, but also with processes of structural differentiation as a condition of individual development, with categories of experience as the basis of environmental determination, with life tendencies and principles. It speaks of an inner non-ego (meaning: affects and patterns, the unconscious and the organism) and an outer non-ego (meaning: the physical and the human environment) as primary realities with which the ego is confronted and to which it is normally bound in polar relationships. In other words, it emphasizes the transpersonal aspects of man's existence before analyzing the meaning of developmental phases and causal factors.

But even when these phases and factors are discussed in this book, our analysis will *not* be based on individual case histories but rather on a phenomenology of essentials and a construction of ideal types. We believe that a definition of essentials must precede any meaningful statement about phases, causes, and forms of normal and abnormal behavior. Observation and induction are legitimate instruments in the study of behavioral sciences only when their data have first been clearly delineated from each other on the levels of manifestation and cause, but not when they are used as auxiliary methods of quantitation, that is, for the purpose of eliminating individual essentials.

We shall try to show that the phenomenological and the psychodynamic approaches, far from being alternative, are in fact complementary, provided we do not identify the second concept (that of psychodynamics) with the narrow meaning it has in psychoanalysis (reduction of manifest behavior to—mostly unconscious—mechanisms of defense), but include in it the changing relationships between structural agents, tendencies, modalities.

Similarly, not only relational but cognitive functions as well must be included in any truly dynamic theory of behavior, which should aim at discovering those elements that are common to both types of functions rather than trying to explain one as the epiphenomenon of the other.

This analysis of the ego is meant to be an introduction to a theory of deviations from the norm of behavior. It will be the purpose of a second volume to analyze cultural varieties of what we shall define and describe as "externalization," that is, different forms of "living from without." It is therefore only logical that in this discussion of environmental causes of development emphasis will be laid on negative more than on positive factors. Where environmental conditions are positive, that is, conducive to the emergence of normal internalizaton of concepts and values, constitutional variables account for the different behavioral outcomes. Where the configuration of environmental conditions is negative, that is, detrimental to normal development, their causal weight increases.

The reader will find in the theses and reasonings of the book a variety of influences. *Wertheimer's* Gestalt theory has left its imprint on the configurational method applied in this book to causal interpretation. *Piaget's* analysis of ego functions; *Freud's* discovery of the ego's defenses against the unconscious; *Erikson's* reinterpretation of the psychoanalytical theory of the stages in man's development; the studies of the effect maternal deprivation is liable to have on the intellectual and the relational abilities of the child; *Jung's* dynamic typology and, in particular, his distinction between the personal and the transpersonal unconscious; *Buber's* philosophy of the dialogue—these are the main roots from which the present study has grown.

Believers in the sanctity of specialization and of adherence to one school of thought will probably reject our seeming eclecticism. But in the end, it is precisely this seemingly eclectic, but in actual fact selective and configurational, approach to the interpretation of human behavior that makes possible a unified and unifying theory of man, comprising the areas that are commonly considered areas of exclusive competence of the psychologist, the psychiatrist, the anthropologist, the sociologist.

CARL FRANKENSTEIN

Contents

PART 2: Environment and Development

Basic Concepts

1

Elements of Structure Analysis

1. Differentiation

In the psychology of human development, concepts such as Piaget's "undifferentiation" (106) or Szondi's "adualism" (120) are being used to describe a primary stage in which the boundaries between the stimulus-sending environment and the stimulus-receiving organism are not yet clearly established. Neither of the two is yet definable as subject or as object, categories that are meaningless until we can speak of perceivable and perceived intentionality in the stimulus-receiver and in his reactions to the stimulus-sender. What the outside observer, including the human stimulus-sender himself, knows to be intentionality remains for the infant in this primary stage of undifferentiation a process within the unity field of his existence.

This is only another way of saying that the primary stage is characterized by the absence of polar relationships between a self-identical, identifiable, reacting and integrating ego and an independent non-ego, which could be experienced by the ego as both a subject (that is, as the *bearer* of intentions) and an object (that is, as the possible *aim* of the ego's intentions). This is the unity stage, a basic concept in any biological, psychological, and psychiatric discussion of the primary child-mother relationships and of their relevance for the development of the child.

There are, however, two facts that make the, *prima facie* convincing, term "unity stage" questionable: even before birth and much more so, of course, after the child's separation from the maternal womb, his existence becomes conditional on the separation of uncontrollable factors of excitation, which separation institutes what we might call the *dynamic* polarity between tension and rest. Without this dynamic polarity neither development nor experience would ever become possible. Unity therefore does not preclude tension and change but, on the contrary, is forced into differentiation by this inherent dynamic polarity. We see in this process a manifestation of the normative interaction between the two basic life tendencies, that toward expansion and that toward what we shall call "staticness" (see pp. 7 *ff.*).

Our second reservation regarding the concept of unity stage is based on the complex meaning of the term non-ego; it is not identical with the environment but includes the inner world of archetypes, that is, of the constituents of human experience (78); it includes our inherent mental and physical dispositions, endowments and deficiencies, thresholds and reaction patterns; it includes our instinctual drives; it includes our repressions, that is, what we later call, with Jung, the "personal unconscious." In other words, we must distinguish between an outer and an inner non-ego (see pp. 35 ff.). The latter is no less autonomous than the former in its directedness toward, its impact on, the developing mind. In fact, it is through the autonomy of this inner non-ego that the environment is at all capable of making its imprints on the growing mind, of producing what we call meaningful stimulations, long before structural polarization has taken place, long before an ego operates in reaction to stimuli coming from the non-ego, assimilates them, and organizes the ego system.

We maintain, then, that the *inner* non-ego is the structural precondition of man's ability to experience the *outer* non-ego, the environment. In this way, the very possibility of differentiation, that is, of the unity stage coming to an end (of transcending itself), becomes comprehensible: *it is because the inner non-ego "belongs" existentially to the growing ego and functionally to the outer non-ego (the physical and social environments which are its fields of application), that the ego can at all emerge, first as an object of the inner, than as a subject vis-à-vis the outer non-ego.* It is through the non-ego's autonomous intentionality that the growing ego learns intentionality, learns "meaning" and "being meant." The organism with its unknowable physiology and its unforeseeable manifestations, the instinctive drives in their relatedness to needs and need-satisfaction, the feelings connected with recurring events and images, and, above all, the structurally given categories of experience force the ego into crystallization. Human existence is one of contrasts and contradictions: of tension and satisfaction, of part and whole, of remote and near, of emptiness and fullness, of absence and presence, of expulsion and intake, of closure and intrusion, of differentiation and synthesis, of things paternal and things maternal. These opposites structurally precede and make possible (constitute) experience, and particularly so that of polarity, which leads to the emergence of an ego standing *opposite* an all-embracing non-ego.

The term non-ego, then, denotes all those factors and forces that, while obeying their own inherent laws, are related to that agent of organization that we call ego, related in a way which the latter increasingly experiences as intentional. The fact that we use here a negative term (non-ego) indicates, of course, the bias implied in the topic of our discussion (which is: the development of the ego). It would perhaps be more appropriate to use the more neutral term, "reality," bearing in mind, of course, the existence of an outer, environmental, and an inner, psychic, reality. In this case, however, the use of the opposite term, ego, would become questionable.*

Primarily, not only the environment but also the transpersonal unconscious (96), or what we have suggested (32) should be called the depth zone of the psyche (see pp. 36 ff.) is undifferentiated from what later emerges as the ego. While the absence of clear-cut boundaries between the *environmental* stimulator and the stimulated organism is expressed in such terms as "homogeneous matrix" (Spencer (116)) or "global mass activity" (Werner (124)) or "indissociation" (Piaget (106)), the non-differentiatedness between the inner non-ego and the (later) ego is, as a rule, being overlooked by the psychologists of human development. Even Jung, to whom we owe the discovery of the "reality of the soul" (75) and of the autonomy of the transpersonal unconscious, has not given much thought to the developmental aspects of this discovery. (The only attempt to apply Jung's theses to the genesis of consciousness and to the development of the child has been made by Neumann (99). Our own position, as we shall try to show in the following analysis, differs from Neumann's in that we propose to emphasize the external forces and factors of determination (the outer non-ego) in configuration with their archetypal corollaries (the inner non-ego), whereas he tries to reconstruct the empirical development of the child as a replica of archetypal history).

Differentiation between non-ego and ego, that is, the emergence of the ego as a relational pole to the non-ego, goes on, we maintain, on the internal and the external level simultaneously. At the same time, however, the non-ego, as well, emerges as a relational pole to the emerging ego, and again in the two dimensions, that of the environment and that of the psychic structure. Or, to put it differently: the inner non-ego— that is, the universe of the individual's structurally given categories of experience, patterns of reactions, instinctual and affective tendencies, and organic dispositions—passes through a process of differentiation or separation from the environmental conditions in which it is embedded, at the same time as both the inner and the outer non-ego become intentionally directed factors of determination and objects of intentional relatedness for the *thereby* emerging ego.

In addition, the universe of the inner non-ego as well as that of environmental determinants undergoes a continuous process of internal

---

* Unless we would have recourse to a neurostructural theory of the type suggested by Rothschild (113), in which both the ego and the environment are represented in the structure of the brain, the ego through what he calls the "*Körperpol*," the environment through his so-called "*Weltpol*." But there is no place in this model for what we have called the *inner* non-ego.

differentiation and organization, to the extent that the boundaries between the growing ego and the non-ego (in its different aspects) become more firmly established. The truth of this statement can be proved *e contrario:* wherever a process of temporary or permanent dedifferentiation takes place, as a result of later frustration or traumatization, not only the frontiers between the ego and the environment, between the ego and the unconscious, or between the ego and the organism, but also the demarcation lines between different ego functions, between different contents of consciousness, between different areas of environmental occurrences and appearances, between different affects, phantasies, imaginations, between the personal and the transpersonal unconscious, etc., are bound to become blurred.

Thus, we can say that the *process of differentiation,* which leads from the unity stage of nondifferentiatedness to separation between the ego and the non-ego, also leads to a state of differentiatedness within the ego and within the non-ego. At the same time, we may add, the *process* of differentiation produces differentiation as an ego *activity,* its possible objects being the ego itself, the non-ego in its various connotations, and the relationships between ego and non-ego. An ego capable of active differentiation is called a *differentiated ego,* one of the main symptoms of this differentiatedness being a sense of nuances. (Reversely, an ego *not* capable of active differentiation is called undifferentiated or primitive, in both the developmental and the pathological sense of the word.)

The more differentiated the ego is, the more strongly developed will be its ability to experience the non-ego as well not only as differentiated but also as actively differentiating. It would, of course, not be correct to define differentiation or lack of differentiation in the external non-ego as an exclusive function of the ego's differentiatedness or lack of differentiatedness; there are objective factors at work as well that determine the degree of the non-ego's differentiatedness or nondifferentiatedness, quite independently of the ego; and the latter's development toward differentiatedness is determined to no small extent by the objective non-ego conditions (primitive patterns of culture being a good example for the objective limits to the individual ego's development toward differentiation).*

Although the process of differentiation between the ego and the non-ego is a precondition of ego development, it would be erroneous to see the non-ego as constant and only the ego as changing. The non-ego, too, at least the inner non-ego, grows in the process. We are used to seeing habit formation, the emergence and entrenchment in the personality of

---

* Differentiation of the inner non-ego is primarily a function of the ego's readiness to communicate with it, to understand its intentions, and to react to them. It would therefore be more correct to speak in this case of the ego's openness to the inner non-ego than of the inner non-ego's differentiatedness (see pp. 29 *ff.*).

cultural patterns, stereotypes, self-images, the processes of repression, defenses, and reaction formations as part of the history of the ego only. And we forget that the individual, while assimilating, and familiarizing himself with, the outer non-ego through such processes and operations, *causes* the emergence, within the ego, of many uncontrollable elements of behavior, on which he then depends no less than on his constitution, his congenital disposition, and his environment. In other words, assimilation of the outer non-ego through habits, stereotypes, patterns of thinking and feeling, repressions, reaction formations, and defenses, far from being symptomatic of differentiation, rather indicates a kind of dedifferentiation and deprives the ego, in part at least, of its relational and intentional spontaneity and vigor. Thus, it increases the area of the inner non-ego with which the ego then has to cope by way of self-distantiation, that is, by renewed and ever more complicated processes and activities of differentiation.

We shall come back to the problem later, when discussing the meaning of internalization and of ego and non-ego relationships (see pp. 29 *ff.* and particularly pp. 35 *ff.*), and again in Chapter 5, "Structurization" (see pp. 60 *ff.*).

We now return to the question of how the ego can be imagined to emerge from that primary unity stage of nondifferentiatedness, which we can call with equal justification a pre-ego stage and a non-ego stage.

We define the ego as the coordinator of heterogeneous and divergent contents of consciousness; as the agent controlling and integrating into relative unity the sensorimotor, emotional, intellectual, and all other ego functions; as the agent responsible for determining reactions in a more or less uniform manner, for raising defenses against dangerous impulses; in other words, as the agent for establishing and maintaining the individual's identity and for guarding continuity in change and diversity.

This agent is the outcome of a long process of development. It grows *through* the gradual (active) transformation of the physical and social environment into contents of knowledge and consciousness, but also into cognitive, moral, emotional, and relational functions and into factors of structural determination. But the very processes and acts of transformation *require* the existence and operation of such an agent, at least in a nuclear form, supposed to operate already in the primary cell from which the individual develops. As in the case of many concepts of psychological interpretation, that of ego, too, has a threefold connotation: it means a modality, a structure, and a dynamic force. It is the last aspect that may help us understand its emergence as a modality and as a structure.

2. The Life Tendencies

In most theories of human behavior and development we find, in one form or another, the claim that the life process is regulated by two contradictory tendencies, though they are, as a rule, believed to be held together by a unifying principle such as the law of compensation, the law of constancy, the so-called Nirvana principle, etc.

Compensation, for instance, may be held responsible for the return of an injured organism to integrity (57a), or for the return to homeostasis, once the latter has been disturbed by extrinsic or by intrinsic factors of change (16), or for overcoming feelings of inferiority by "overdoing it" (2). In Freud's earlier theory of the pleasure and reality principle (45) the supremacy of the former and the auxiliary function of the latter are evident (the reality principle being little more than the guarantee for more secure, albeit delayed, pleasure-gain). In Freud's later, more genuinely dualistic, Eros-Thanatos theory (47), it is the return to the anorganic state that is defined as the ultimate aim of life; the life instinct, though coexistent with the death instinct from the moment of conception, is inferior to the latter, delaying "rather insensibly," says Freud (46), "the ultimate aim of life."

Freud's claim as to the dualistic character of his conception of life and development, in contrast to what he calls Jung's basically monistic libido theory (47) is unconvincing: true enough, in each phase of his thinking, Freud uses some kind of dichotomy; but the fact that in each of these theories one principle or instinct is accorded dynamic superiority over the other—pleasure over reality, object over ego, Thanatos over Eros— shows that his conception is basically a monistic one.

Jung's theory (77, 78), on the other hand, contains many more elements of truly dualistic interpretation, not only in his typology but also in his philosophy of integration or in his conception of the structural opposition between consciousness and the unconscious. True enough, the former is being defined as a derivative of the latter (or, better, of the infiniteness of the psyche); and the dynamic processes going on between the two areas are subject to the law of compensation (meaning here the correction of partial and therefore negative forms of existence). But the way to wholeness or to the "Self" (in Jung's language) is progressive and not regressive, hence *requires* the continued existence of the ego as the center of communication with the outer and the inner world, with the consciously mediated environment and with the unconscious, the reality of the soul; *requires* active confrontation and dialogic relationship.

A truly dualistic theory of man should be based on the assumption of two equally essential life tendencies which normally operate in opposite directions while being related to each other. We suggest that these two mutually opposed and interrelated principles be called the life tendencies toward staticness and toward expansion. The first life tendency aims at systematization and balance, the second one at change, growth and transformation, at the formation of new states.*

The aim of life is *not*, as Freud has claimed, the return to the anorganic state, but is, on the contrary, "the creation of ever more complex organic and psychic systems out of simple units. Their creation goes through two phases: expansion and systematization. The process of expansion and transformation can, it is true, be achieved only through a (relative) negation of what exists; but as long as the negation is subject to its structural aim (integration) it does not contradict the second life tendency, that toward staticness, since this tendency too, is normatively experienced in actual life only as a tendency toward the *formation of new systems* and never, because of the eternal processuality of life, fully achieves its aim. The libido feeds both life tendencies equally. This, however, means that the tendency toward staticness is not identical with the striving of the organism toward death, and the tendency toward expansion is not identical with the erotic tendency to continue life; *both function by interaction in order to achieve the life aim which is the formation of complex systems more highly integrated*. Both tend toward the elimination of the separateness of elementary units, the second by way of *polarization* and the first by way of *systematization*. Polarization means: elimination of separateness through relating contradictory elements to each other, thus preparing and making possible the coming into existence of new systems; systematization means: elimination of separateness through forming new systems from mutually related elements. Only when the two tendencies function in isolation, without interaction, does the tendency toward staticness degenerate either into regression or into petrification (under the direction of a perverted pleasure principle, as it were); and the tendency toward expansion becomes a destructive and aggressive tendency toward a blind conquest of life (under the direction of a perverted reality principle, as it were).

"Life admits of no resolution of the essential tension between the two principles either by means of fleeing into staticness or by means of aggressively negating an existing actuality; the tension can only be resolved *by acquiescence in the process of transformation accompanied by a tendency toward systematization, toward the formation of new systems"* (29, pp. 315 *ff.*).

"The fact that individuals differ in the degree of integration and interrelatedness of these two life tendencies may of course be due, at least partly, to congenital predispositions. There can be no doubt, however, that early childhood experiences finally determine the individual's ability to give up staticness for the sake of expansion and growth, while at the same time trusting that every expression of the growing ego's boundaries tends toward systematization and thus leads back to staticness, though always on a higher level of development and structurality. The

---

* The discussion on pp. 9 to 11 is largely quoted from our earlier essay on anxiety (29) and our book, *Psychopathy* (34).

most important environmental factors in the development toward this interrelatedness of the two life tendencies is the infant's experience of regularity in the sequence of tension and need-satisfaction. It is in this way that the child learns not to fear or avoid the necessary 'interruptions' of staticness but to trust in the return of staticness; out of this trust, he becomes more and more able and ready to leave staticness on his own and to seek expansion of his narrow boundaries. And it is in this way that staticness becomes the basis of the first feelings of identity, that is, of the ego, whereas interruption of staticness through tension and growth becomes the basis of the experience of otherness, of the non-ego.

"Thus, we may say that the interrelatedness of staticness and expansion based on the experiential interrelatedness of tension and satisfaction makes possible the foundation of the ego as the organizing center of consciousness, or facts and functions, of knowledge and feeling, of action and affect, past and present, because it is on the basis of this interrelatedness of the two life tendencies that the polarity between ego and non-ego can be experienced" (34, p. 5).

We shall come back to this issue later, when discussing the impact of the primary child-mother relationship on the development of the ego and on differentiation (see pp. 149 ff.). Here suffice it to add another quotation from our previously mentioned study (34), in anticipation of our later analysis:

"Structural polarization (between the ego and the non-ego) depends on the extent to which constitutional and environmental factors allow for the experience of regularity in the sequence of stimulation and rest, that is, for the experience of energetic polarity as rhythm rather than as contradiction.

"Normally, the experience of this rhythmic sequence leads to an association of rest and staticness (need-satisfaction) with ego feeling, and of stimulation and change (tension) with non-ego, that is, to the emergence of a primary feeling of identity and nonidentity. The fact that, in the unity stage, subject and object are not yet differentiated from each other does not mean that they are identical with each other, but rather that they do not exist as such. Identity and nonidentity become possible only as a result of the polar organization of reality.

"The interaction of the two life tendencies finds its expression in the primary process of differentiation. Normally, it is this interaction that leads not only to a first separation of what later crystallizes as ego and non-ego but also to their interrelatedness; not only to differentiation but also to polarization. We can understand why, at least in human beings, differentiation normally appears as polarization, when we consider that it is rooted in the mother-child unity, the interruption and the restitution of which are the prototypical manifestations of the two life tendencies. Hence the link, in the infant's development, between being separated (from the mother) and being separate (vis-à-vis the non-ego), between separation and helplessness, between helplessness and otherness; hence the link between being united (or reunited) with the mother and being whole, between wholeness and staticness, between staticness and omnipotence, between omnipotence and egoity. But, since the child-mother unity, which for the child is the existential root of staticness, contains at the same time the mother's intentionality, the child comes to experience staticness as relatedness; and since the temporary interruption of the unity, which for the child is the source of the experience of otherness, change and expansion, contains that same element of material intentionality, the child (normally) experiences expansion as coming not only from without but also from within the unity situation, as expansion of the growing ego's functions and not only as change imposed" (34, p. 129 *ff*).

3. The Categories of Experience

Thus, the ego comes into existence. We maintain that *it is the very intentionality of the environmental and particularly the maternal non-ego that forces the ego into development and crystallization.* Intentionality is an ego modality. The reactions elicited by the operations of the non-ego in the growing organism and its ego nucleus are, then, likely, by way of induction, as it were, to show a similar intentionality, that is, to be purposefully directed toward a specific aim, be it something within or something without. But while the non-ego's *intention*, according to its inherent tendency toward expansion, is *change* to be produced in the (intended) organism and its behavior, the nuclear ego's reactional intention is, according to its inherent tendency toward staticness, *systematization* of the changes elicited by the non-ego.

But does this not mean that we are begging the question? So far, we have ascribed ego modality to the non-ego, and we have presumed the preexistence of an ego nucleus capable of reacting to the non-ego's intentions and, more, of systematizing the changes elicited. If we were concerned, as behaviorists are, with the question of how environmental influences and intentions produce increasingly systematized reactions in the organism acted upon by the environment, it would be sufficient to add at this stage of our discussion that a prolonged process of ever-repeated intentional impacts followed by induced imitations and "identifications"* is needed to bring about a *system* of reactions. But it would be rather arbitrary to call this system an ego, that is, to identify it with that *structural* agent of direction and coordination in which we see the precondition of dialogic relationships, of polarity, of continuous differentiation. The ability to experience the reality-inherent dualism between "intending" and "being intended," between stimulation and reactions,

---

* The word "identifications" is put in quotation marks to indicate that in the pre-ego stage of development, as discussed here, the term means a process and not an activity.

as a structural dualism between ego and non-ego, cannot be explained satisfactorily as the result of a continuous process of conditioning unless we content ourselves with using the concepts as *façons de parler* only.

We are concerned here not with an ability to *experience* reality as divided into an ego and a non-ego, but with the differentiation process as such, in the course of which *boundaries emerge* between the structural agent of organization and relationship (the ego) and the inner and outer reality contents with which that agent is confronted and which it is challenged to transform into contents of consciousness and into ego functions. *It is this very emergence of boundaries that causes the organizational force—the nuclear ego—inherently active in the human organism as such, to grow into an independent structural agent of coordination called the ego.* For, the concept of "boundaries" is both a structural and a behavioral concept, indicating both delineation and transcendence. Only where boundaries exist can life processes be experienced as originating somewhere beyond, as "coming from" somewhere, as connecting something outside with something inside.

The emergence of such structural boundaries depends, as we have already mentioned (p. 11), on the intentionality of an external, particularly of the maternal, non-ego, but no less, we now add, on the intentionality of the inner non-ego, that is, the structurally given categories of experience. With regard to the first condition, what we have said about the connection between the primary mother experience and ego feeling (p. 11) may suffice here, particularly since we shall come back to the subject later, when discussing the primary phases in the mother-child relationships (see pp. 15 *ff.*). It is the regularity of significant occurrences and, through it, the expectation of changes as something coming from somewhere in space and in time, that produce spatial and temporal dimensions (at least operationally), thereby breaking up the primary unity feeling* and preparing the ground for differentiation and boundaries.

But the dimensions of space and of time are not the result of maternal regularity, are not produced by processes of conditioning; they are structurally given conditions of experience and, as such, are parts of man's inner non-ego, the autonomously intentional unconscious.† Although these structural conditions would never produce experience without operating through the medium of empirical occurrences (in our case, the actuality of maternal behavior), the latter would never produce the dimensions of space and time as organizational forms of experience but

---

* What Neumann (96) has called "uroboric" and Freud (49) "oceanic."

† In this context, Kant's argumentation (81) against the English empiricists is still valid, though he would not agree to our or, rather, Jung's translation of the terms "constituents" or "categories" into concepts of a structural and dynamic theory of human behavior and development.

can only transform them into dynamic forces of development and ego formation.

Thus, the category of space is represented in (and by) the inner non-ego through the images of "near and far," of "contained and alone," of "contact and emptiness"; the category of time, through the images of "staticness and movement," of "halt and flux." In other words, the categories of experience are relational categories from the very first second of life on. Hence, they enable the organism to experience the external non-ego as a likeness, a replica, of the inner non-ego, even though the environment may not always supply sufficient confirmative experience. (There is, of course, a minimum of environmental confirmation for the structural categories of experience to become operative, a minimum depending, incidentally, less on outer reality than on the constitutional conditions with which the individual is born.)

We suggest that the categories of time and of space are primarily one and that they are split into separate categories in the course of development only, through the actual life process. It is the very contradictoriness of human existence that produces the separation of space from time. Were there nearness, containedness, contact only, were there farness, isolation, emptiness only, there would be no time-experience (which requires the element of change). Were there "halt" only, staticness only, space would become meaningless, since tridimensionality presupposes movement; it would be correct to say the same, however, if there were "movement" only, since placeability, this second element of space, requires limitation. The primary oneness of the space-time category in which "near" and "now" are identical, as are "movement" and "far," and which could best be described as "approximation" and "withdrawal," is gradually being replaced by separate space and time dimensions, to the extent that the living organism encounters the mutually related contradictoriness of existence.

There are, of course, many more categories of experience at work from the beginning of life on, all represented by living and activating symbols of universal validity, all entering our consciousness much later, all determining the individual's reaction to external stimuli from the start. We have chosen those of space and time because of their intimate link with the emergence and crystallization of the ego.

It is needless to add again that the actualization of the structurally given categories of experience and their image-representations depends on certain constitutional, maturational, and experiential factors (see Chapters 6, 9, and 10). But without the categories of time and space in their dichotomous manifestations (and without their intentionally) polarity and tension would never become possible modes of experience. It is due to these categories that the regularity in the sequence of excitation and rest, this basic human condition, becomes a personal (and interpersonal) experience: stimulation becomes tension, rest becomes elimination of tension, because, and to the extent that, the infant comes to experience both as caused or as elicited by, as emanating from, an intentional non-ego, a world beyond, which is both outside and inside, both environment and structure. Without the experience of regularity and sequence, expectation would never become possible, and without expectation no relational structure would ever emerge. But without the preexisting modes of spatial and temporal experience, *regularity* could not be experienced and its place would be taken by disconnected experiences whose contradictory character would not even become "experience." The humanization of biological and physical stimuli, so vital for the infant's development, depends on the inner no less than on the outer non-ego.

Here we come back to the subjective aspect of the emergence and the growth of the ego. Tension becomes increasingly associated with non-ego and staticness with ego and identity. Tension is liable to produce in the infant a feeling of being exposed to unknown, alien, influences. These influences, irrespective of whether we describe them as coming from the environment or from the organism (as we say in the language of a later phase of development), are, for the infant, not only *representations* of the outside, the non-ego, but they also *constitute* it in his growing consciousness. It is, as we have already said (p. 10), the temporary interruption of staticness, it is tension, that becomes the basis of the experience of otherness, of the non-ego. Reversely, it is in, and through, the elimination of tension, that is, in and through his return to staticness, that the child comes first to experience selfhood and identity. Awareness of the non-ego is essentially associated with change and tension; ego feeling is essentially associated with staticness, and staticness with a stage either before or after separation, duality, otherness, tension. Experiencing the regularity (the regular sequence) of tension and staticness is not only the basis of spatial and temporal dimensionality and, thereby, the basis of breaking up the primary unity feeling (see p. 12), but also of differentiation and polarization—which we shall discuss later in the developmental meaning of the terms.

We shall in Chapter 2 analyze the mother experience of the infant in its normal and normative form, in its relationship to the growth of the ego. We shall then proceed to an analysis of what we call the *paternal principle of differentiation and internalization*. The differential meaning of the mother and the father—both as persons and as principles of development—for the male and the female child will then be discussed briefly.

2

The Mother and the Father

1. THE MOTHER EXPERIENCE OF THE INFANT

The primary mother experience is no less decisive for the development of the ego than are the congenitally given elements of constitution. (The latter crystallizes into what is later the individual's "final" constitution under the impact of the former.) For the purpose of describing this development analytically we distinguish between three phases (although we should add, in order to avoid semantic misunderstandings, that the term "phases" does not so much signify here parts of a temporal sequence as it means elements of a structural condition which we prefer to *describe* genetically). These phases are: "the mother as part" (MaP), "the mother as the absent one" (AM), and "the mother as the near one" (NM).

The first phase coincides with that in which subject and object are not yet clearly differentiated. The "other" does not yet exist as such, but is identical with the ever-recurring tension which, in turn, results from the ever-recurring interruption of staticness. Even this formulation is somewhat anachronistic, as the association of excitation and rest with tension and satisfaction, the transformation of the biological into the human dimension, is not yet completed in this phase (*cf.* p. 10 and p. 14).

But the mother is "part" of the child only as long as the latter is at her breast, in her arms, or at least in some kind of communicative contact with her. This unity is again and again interrupted by each period of time between the end of a contact situation and falling asleep as well as between awakening and the return to the unity situation.

If the infant's needs are satisfied adequately, the first form of interruption does not have a negative effect (does not disturb his return to staticness) but rather operates as a positive factor, insofar as it helps to keep alive the experience of staticness for a small but slowly increasing period of being awake; interruption of the unity situation then only strengthens and furthers the development of ego and consciousness.

The second type of interruption, on the other hand, does not, as a rule, fulfill a positive function at this first stage of life, where it is always connected with the experience of "absence," of "want," irrespective of

15

the extent of preceding satisfaction. This connection will, of course, be all the more evident when the primary needs of the infant have remained unsatisfied (for reasons to be sought in the psychosomatic structure of the child and/or of the mother). In this case, the remainder of the unresolved tension institutes, as it were, the experience of "something" withholding satisfaction, that is, of otherness as opposed to the nuclear feeling of egoity.

This is the first meaning of the second phase which, as we said, is that of the mother as the absent one. A feeling of helpless dependence and, with it the experience of the non-ego, emerges, which at first, we now understand, must have negative qualities only.

At the same time, however, it is precisely the intensity of that experience of absence which helps transform the second phase into the third, in which the absent mother will be more and more experienced as independent, that is, not as *non*-ego but as an other ego. This third phase is that of the mother as the near one whose regular return can be expected. This means that from now on the return to the unity situation with the mother will be experienced with increasing clarity as dependent on the return of some "other" ego *to* the child. It is obvious that this is the basis of relationality and polarity.

The psychological, pediatric, and psychiatric studies of "maternal deprivation" (12, 56, 117)—the term meaning, of course, primarily the *child* being deprived of the mother—has proved that most relational pathologies of later years—with their well known symptomatizations in the areas of thinking, feeling and behaving as well as of physical growth and well-being—are rooted in this third of the three primary phases, that is, in the experience of the mother as the near one.

No interpretation of normal and disturbed behavior in later years would be adequate that would try to reduce those later results to the quality of the infant's primary mother experience only, without asking how the latter itself is determined and supplemented by a number of internal and external factors.

We know that the most important of these determining factors are the somatic structure of the child, his innate abilities (including his potential level of intellectual functioning), the intensity of his love-needs, his level of tolerance for pain and frustration, his thresholds of perception, his type-conditioned patterns of reaction and other constitutional factors, the degree of tension or harmony in the parental milieu, the emotional and intellectual patterns prevailing in the child's home and culture, the quality of the mother, and the quality of other environmental factors.

But among these determining factors should be included also the essential experiences of the first and second phases, that of staticness *following* the adequate termination of a unity experience, and that of the absent mother, that is, of otherness as against the nuclear identity feeling. Without the first experience, the development of time consciousness and identity, and without the second, the differentiation of reality, the development of structural polarity would be delayed, disturbed, or even prevented. Without the first experience the mother would remain too long and too exclusively tension-related; a feeling of incompleteness and the experience of reality as "outside only" would become increasingly dominant. Without the second experience, that of the mother as the absent one, the relational ability would remain impaired, because the experience of return (to the mother, and later, of the mother), that basis of relationality and polarity, presupposes the experience of absence.

It is self-evident why cases of the first type (of defective MaP experience) will always occur more frequently than those of the second type (of defective AM experience): the fundamental biological conditions of human existence account for the prevalence of the experience of tension and explain why the experience of staticness is endangered by the very fact of life. It would, however, be wrong to conclude that the third phase experience, that of the mother as the near one whose return can be anticipated, was less dependent on the second than on the first phase.

It is the artificial distinction between quasi-separable phases that is liable to distort the problem here under discussion. In reality the two phases and their essential experiences are not independent, but are interconnected and interdependent, in time and in structure. The experience of absence becomes meaningful for the emergence of that nearness only in configuration with, and on the basis of, the degree to which, and the manner in which, staticness had been experienced before. Absence (AM) may further the process of differentiation and polarization when it is supplemented (preceded) by that feeling of basic trust (23) that stems from an adequate experience of the mother as part (MaP); it may, however, have precisely the opposite effect, that is, it may prevent differentiation and polarization, when it is not based on and linked with such an experience and the resulting trust and courage, or when it is too extreme. Similarly, wholeness (MaP) may paralyze the process of differentiation and polarization when it is not supplemented (followed) by absence (AM), irrespective of whether this lack of supplementation is a result of too much of the first experience or too little of the second.

We may, then, distinguish between the following constellations: $MaP < AM$; $MaP > AM$; $AM < MaP$; $AM > MaP$. The signs for "more than" or "less than" mean in our context: "more than" or "less than" is conducive to the emergence of that precondition of normal development which is the experience of the mother whose return can always be expected, the mother as the near one (NM). We could express their normal constellation by using the formula: $MaP \cong AM \rightarrow NM$.

Approximate equality ($\cong$) is, of course, relative to the needs of the individual.

2. DIGRESSION: DEFECTIVE MOTHER EXPERIENCE

We shall now try to relate what we have said in the foregoing paragraph to a number of pathogenic conditions. We shall discuss these conditions in greater detail in a subsequent volume; what we intend to make clear here, at this early stage of our analysis, is the central role of this environmental yet structure-determining factor in any theory of behavior.

Let us first consider the cases in which the experience of the mother as part (MaP) is in excess.

(a) Sometimes, constitutional lack of sensitivity to frustration may account for an abnormally weak experience of the absent mother (AM). Here belong those children in whom the life tendency toward staticness is so strong that they do not depend on the basic experience of MaP in order to maintain their feeling of staticness when they are left to their own resources. Here belong further those feebleminded children of the good-natured variety whose low sensitivity to being left alone is a function of their low intelligence. Here belong certain children with strong extravert tendencies and at least normal intelligence who are able to feel protected not only by the mother but also by the perceivable environment. And finally we find in this group a certain variety of psychopaths in whom nondependence on the quality of the mother experience is a symptom of their incorporative tendencies (34).

(b) While in the first group the excess of the MaP experience is primary, in another group this excess is a result of environmental restriction of the AM experience. Here belong, first and foremost, the cases in which the infant is overprotected by a guilt-ridden or overanxious mother (90). Other instances of insufficient opportunity to experience the absent mother (AM < MaP) can be found in certain cultural conditions, as described by anthropologists (23, 93) and sociologists (17, 18, 40).

All these conditions have one element in common: that the child is not growing up sufficiently prepared for the unavoidable encounter with frustration. Life situations in which he is forced to act and to react in isolation, no longer protected by the illusion of being contained in the maternal environment and of being familiar with the world outside, find him defective in his ability to differentiate, though in various forms. The need for differentiation may produce discomfort (as in the extravert), anxiety (as in the overstatic), aggressive denial (as in the overprotected), or it may remain unfelt (as in the cultural variety and in the mentally defective). To the extent that the need for differentiation is felt at all, it is being felt as something imposed from the outside, as ego-alien.

In most of these cases, it is true, the ego will nevertheless in due course of time become separated from the non-ego. But polarization, that is, bilateral relationships of mutuality, interdependence, and exchangeability of the subject-object positions, is liable to be defective: it will mostly be devoid of the quality of inner experience, of self-involvement and self-consciousness. One could in the end speak of "externalized polarization."

This concept, too, has a different meaning in the different constellations mentioned above: whereas in the feebleminded the ego becomes part of the non-ego, exactly the opposite is true for the psychopath; whereas overstaticness may limit the ego's responsiveness to the communications of the non-ego, extraversion may produce a kind of pseudo-responsiveness in which the ego does not match its receptiveness with activity; whereas the overprotected child in our society may come to see the non-ego as a kind of ego extension, so that he will later expect the non-ego to behave as though it were not an independent reality, the child whose culture fails to supply him with sufficient opportunities to experience the environment as limiting and frustrating will grow up to continue a life pattern of primitive externality of behavior and thinking.

We shall now consider the reverse pathology, predominance of the experience of the absent mother over that of unity with the mother. It may again be due either to constitutional and organic conditions (MaP $<$ AM) or to a severely traumatic environment (AM $>$ MaP).

(c) A child may be constitutionally oversensitive to such an extent that he will feel frustrated, unless he receives an extra amount of love and care. Congenital defects in intelligence, aggravated by a low level of frustration-bearance or by strong aggressive drives may produce a general feeling of frustratedness. Similarly, congenital organic defects, in a sensory organ, in sensory screening, in the basic metabolism, in the homeostatic function, in general vitality or otherwise, may limit the child's ability to experience the mother as part, that is, staticness, irrespective of the objective quality of maternal care.

(d) On the other hand, a constitutionally normal child may be exposed to maternal deprivation either in an institution with its typical impersonality of routine care; or in a family where poverty prevents the parents, and particularly the mother, from relating to the infant in a manner conducive to differentiation and polarization;* or in a family where severe parental pathologies counteract the development of a constitutionally normal ability in the child to relate to his environment; or in a culture which prefers impersonality to the establishment and development of strong personal ties between parents and child (this

* To be discussed in a subsequent volume.

may be the case on different levels of cultural differentiation, in a highly sophisticated society as well as in a rigidly patterned primitive group); or under certain social conditions in which parents keep, as it were, at a distance from their child and do not allow themselves to become involved in their parental function.

All these conditions produce one common result, the emergence of an ego nucleus which will later be constricted in its synthetic function *vis-à-vis* the non-ego. The weaker the primary unity with the mother, the greater will be the danger that the process of polarization will be disturbed and perverted. For true polarization, as we have pointed out (p. 7), presupposes the simultaneous development of two poles which, though interrelated and interdependent, must be identifiable independently, both functionally and structurally.

A persistent preponderance of the experience of absence over that of wholeness (AM > MaP) is liable to turn the whole reality into an undifferentiated "otherness that is outside." In this pathological situation, too, different as it may be in essence from that of feeblemindedness, the ego remains part of the non-ego, by way of returning, as it were, to the primary stage of nondifferentiatedness (pp. 3 *ff.*).

There is, of course, an essential difference between the primary and the pathological forms of nondifferentiatedness: the latter are preceded by a successful differentiation between subject and object; consequently, the non-ego character of reality can be experienced as "otherness" and "outside" by an already existing nuclear ego. When we say that in this situation the ego as well has non-ego character, we mean to say that, to the extent that it exists and operates, it does so not as a subject of synthesis but as an object only of what happens. In the MaP > AM constellation, differentiation between the ego and the non-ego happens, we have said, as a result of tension processes; in the MaP < AM (or the AM > MaP) constellation, the reality itself remains outside and happens.

3. THE MATERNAL PRINCIPLE

We shall now relate what we have said about the normative mother experience to the question: in what specific way do normal mother-child relationships in the first phases of development determine that sense of basic trust and security on which normal intellectual and emotional growth depends?

When favorable conditions of environment and constitution produce a more or less equal degree of intensity of staticness and tension, each of these two contradictory experiences supports the other and both become internalized. Properly speaking, it is true, the term internalization applies to a later phase of ego development only, when experience is not only ego-*related* but has become already an object of ego-*consciousness*.

But at a preliminary and preparatory level even the earliest experience of the infant can be called internalized, provided, we should add, that a relatively equal intensity of both experiences (of staticness and of tension) renders possible an at least partial coexistence of the one with the other, that is, at the time the other occurs.

This is only another way of saying that the other as the absent one becomes the mother as the near one to the extent that the contradiction between staticness and tension loses of its absoluteness and reality loses of its threatening character. The causal equation can, of course, be reversed as well: nearness further weakens the absoluteness of the contradictory experiences and the threatening character of reality. More specifically: the experience of the mother as the near one provides the growing time-consciousness with the experience of small time-spans, an indispensable precondition of normal intellectual and relational development: time-consciousness is capable of expansion only if and when contradictory experiences approximate each other (until they are finally related to each other) through the force of what might be called the aftereffect of engrammation.

But maternal nearness, that expression of normal and normative child-mother relationship, has yet another effect on the infant's perception and conception of the world and, through it, on his development. We have mentioned so far the relatively equal intensity of contradictory experiences, their gradual transposition from the biological to the relational level, the growth of time-consciousness and trust. We have said that nearness includes, is a synthesis of, wholeness and absence; in other words, that the mother normally fulfills her double function as an agent of protection and stimulation simultaneously. Thereby, the mother causes not only the time-span between contradictory experience to narrow, but also limits the infiniteness of possible encounters with the world of objects and processes by endowing them with maternal character. The infant's world is normally a mother-world.

Thus, waiting for the returning mother (which gradually changes into "expectation") helps expand not only the child's time-consciousness but also his object-comprehension and his reality-orientation, because the ever-recurring experience of the returning mother brings in its wake ever-increasing familiarity with the many situations in which this return may occur. In this way, again, the non-ego becomes less threatening and less traumatic. This process of gradual maternalization facilitates acceptance of otherness and thus strengthens the ability and readiness to differentiate. In other words: not only the basic *categories of experience* (identity and separateness, wholeness and deficiency, staticness and tension) originate in the primary relationships of the child with his mother, but also the very process and activity of *acquiring experience,* that is, the *paternal principle of differentiation and internalization.*

4. THE PATERNAL PRINCIPLE

We have so far discussed the primary conditions of internalization as if they could be reduced to elements of the mother-child relationship only. We shall now try to supplement our interpretation by an attempt to analyze the role of the father in the early stages of the child's development.

Although the functions of the father depend more than those of the mother on cultural conditions, so that we can distinguish between various types of paternal functioning in various cultures, social subgroups or historical periods, at least one common element can be discovered in almost all of these culturally different types: *the primary externality of the father image.*

What is the meaning of this concept?

The normal sequence of contradictory mother experiences stimulates, so we have said, the process of differentiation between subject and object; the non-ego becomes acceptable as the "other ego" to the extent that it is impregnated, as it were, with the maternal quality of nearness. In other words: the mother must enter outside reality in order to fulfill her structural function.

The father, on the other hand, *is* outside. From the beginning of life onward he represents otherness, the non-ego. Hence, he becomes an object of inner experience only after the process of differentiation has advanced to a point where the non-ego, as the "other ego," emerges as relational pole to the ego.*

He may be "expectable" (at least in the personalistic family of our culture where his regular appearance is part of the life pattern), but his "expectability" does not by itself mean identifiability, because at this early stage of development the manifestations of the environment are recognized and identified only to the extent that they have been transformed into parts of the ego.

This then is the way in which the father, too, becomes identifiable. We call the transformation of emotionally relevant figures in the family environment into parts of the child's inner life and structure *introjection,* as against the more general term, internalization, which includes *all* transformations of environmental contents into internal contents, through perception, apperception, and conceptualization as well as through the formation of value patterns and feeling patterns.

---

* It has been said that the words for "father" are the first class names, while the words for "mother" are the first individual names in the children's languages all over the world (122); in other words, that the father figure is being experienced as impersonal, as a transferable quality, in contrast to the personal uniqueness of the mother.

The processes of introjection and internalization are motivated by the structural tendency to transform into freely available ego property all that is experienced as—actually or potentially—wanting. Internalization and introjection eliminate the feeling of being separated from the outside object and thus protect against the feeling of want.

This feeling and its elimination in the processes of internalization and introjection, however, mean something different when they relate to the mother and when they relate to the father. It is the mother's function to become the near one by ceasing to be part of the child. Normally, she becomes the near one *not* by way of introjection—at least not in the first phases of life—but by way of the child experiencing her regular return. In other words: *to the extent that she ceases to be part of the child, she moves away from him.* In contrast, the father must *become* part of the child's inner reality by losing his character as "the stranger," the "one who is far away."

Moreover: in contrast to the *processuality of the absent mother becoming the near one, the transformation of the father as the stranger* who is outside and remote into part of the child's inner reality cannot be interpreted as the result of a process but must be understood as the result of *internalization as an activity.*

This ability presupposes the at least nuclear existence of an ego as the center of consciousness, which as such is intentionally directed toward an independent non-ego. This implies that any internalization, hence also any introjection, is *preceded* by the experience of the mother as the near one, since this experience is the indispensable condition of drawing the frontiers between the ego and the non-ego, of polarization and of relatedness.

In other words: we do not accept the psychoanalytic reduction of internalization to oral incorporation (27, 69, 84). In oral satisfaction (that libidinal equivalent of the experience of the mother as part) the life tendency toward staticness finds its expression: absence of tension between ego and non-ego is its central characteristic. Incorporation, on the other hand, means changing and expanding the existing ego frontiers. It presupposes the experience of a separated "outside" non-ego, that is, tension (though tension to be overcome). It is the opposite life tendency, the one toward expansion, that finds its expression in these incorporative tendencies, toward intake and integration of environmental stimuli as well as toward incorporation of the parental figures.

We therefore speak of *paternal internalization* as against *maternal unity.* It is the father who symbolizes separateness, distance, strangeness, as well as the (mental and structural) activity required for their elimination.

Internalization as action, not as process, presupposes not only separateness but also separation, that is, differentiation. Not only must the non-ego objects of internalization be identifiable, that is, differentiated from each other, *the growing ego must also be capable of active identification and differentiation. This is what we suggest should be called the paternal principle of differentiation and internalization.* It is a condition of ego development, no less essential than the primary child-mother relationships. We maintain that in order properly to understand the structurizing effect of the latter we must see it in configuration with the former.

The paternal principle operates from the beginning of life, although it manifests itself as active differentiation in a later phase of development only. Its expressions are: the engrammic readiness of the organism which is a precondition of learning, the polarization between ego and non-ego (p. 3), and the child's ability to expect the mother's return (p. 16). This, however, means that without the operation of the paternal principle—as a basic factor of human structure—the MaP and AM experiences could not lead to that of the mother as the near one; nor would that primary sense of trust and security emerge which, in turn, is a precondition of the gradual enlargement of consciousness through the conquest of ever-widening areas of otherness. On the other hand, the paternal principle of active differentiation and internalization fulfills its function only to the extent that the experience of the mother as the near one has emerged. *Thus we can say that the paternal and the maternal principles are interdependent.*

Another way of expressing this interdependence is to say that growth and development are fed from two sources, from the experience of the non-ego as near and secure, and from the active intake of the separated non-ego; that relatedness and thinking, relational abilities and intelligence, are interlinked. The term paternal principle means, in short: *self-distantiation of the ego from the non-ego, for the purpose of internalization and self-enlargement.*

It would, of course, be wrong to conclude from what we have said so far that only the father is an object of introjection. The mother, too, normally becomes part of the child's inner reality, though only after fulfilling her structural functions as the near one, that is, as the object of expectation and relationship, her functions of impregnating reality with maternal character, and of producing basic trust and, through it, furthering relational ability, growing, and mobility. Where she fails to fulfill these functions, the process of internalizing her image will be defective, too, both dynamically and materially (contentwise).

The introjection of the father, on the other hand, will be defective in the first years of life only to the extent that the paternal principle of differentiation is structurally defective, but not as a result of defective relationship with the personal father (who becomes causally relevant for the child's development at a later stage only).*

This defectiveness of the paternal principle, however, is not only a subject of individual pathology but also of cultural anthropology. We know that socialization does not always, not in every culture, make use of introjection (9, 18, 23). It is known as well that even where a culture upholds the ideals of introjection, large subgroups are unable to live up to these expectations of the general culture, and the father remains "outside" (17, 93, 112). In these cultures or subgroups the father is being experienced so intensively as the stranger, the one who is outside, that only absolute subordination is considered adequate behavior; otherness and externality are *not* being eliminated through introjection but are maintained either through a tradition of heteronomy (subordination under the father as representative of law and value, of truth and tradition) or in the very externality of behavior and thinking.†

Where the culture emphasizes the primary externality of the father without using introjection as a step toward structurization, the resulting quality of mental processes will clearly reflect that basic attitude: all ego contents and functions will then show the stamp of strangeness and externality, even though the mother may have been successful in giving her child a basic sense of trust.

We agree with Parsons (103) when he says that the distribution of functions between the father and the mother is not, as certain anthropologists (for instance, Mead (93)) claim, culture-conditioned but is universally valid, although the way in which these functions operate may be different from culture to culture. But we do not accept Parson's model of interpretation (paternal instrumentality *versus* maternal expressivity) which, we believe, remains too closely connected with the dimension of sociological description. We have tried here to define the *structural* meaning of the father and the mother; this is why we have used the concepts of paternal or maternal *principles,* meaning both structural agents and categories of experience, rather than the individual experience of the personal father and mother figures as analyzed by psychoanalysts.

* Structural factors may be specifically correlated with the maternal and with the paternal principle. Thus we may say that the constitutionally given intelligence furthers paternal internalization much more than those processes that are set in motion through the child-mother relationships and produce the basic sense of trust and security of feeling. Reversely, the constitutionally given level of balance between contrasting functions and tendencies exercises a much stronger and a much more decisive influence on the emergence of the experience of nearness and trust than on the quality of stimulus reception and integration. Of the four functions in Jung's typology, sensation and thinking could be defined as paternal, feeling and intuition as maternal. Introversion helps the maternal way, extraversion the paternal way (at least as long as we remain within the limits of normality).

† This will be described and analyzed in Volume 2.

Our analysis of the structural, the transpersonal meaning of the mother and the father, that is, of the maternal and the paternal principles, would not be complete without a discussion of the problem of sex differences as a factor of structural, transpersonal determination in the development of the ego.

5. SEX DIFFERENCES AS STRUCTURAL DETERMINANTS

The ways of internalization and introjection are different for the male and the female child, the son and the daughter. They are, of course different in each culture, in each socioeconomic group, in each historical period as well. But, whatever the impact of these differentiating trans-individual factors may be, the sex-conditioned ways in which the male and the female child experience the mother and the father can be described, so we claim, as structurally different.

This is true even with regard to those cases in which individual pathologies (which may be rooted in the child or in one or both of the parents) have reversed the structural significance of the parental figures. It is this very reversal of structural roles that prove our claim, *viz.*, that the father and the mother have a structurally different meaning for the male and the female infant.

According to psychoanalysis, sex-conditioned differences between the son's and the daughter's perception of the father and the mother do not appear before the phase of oedipal involvements. Whatever differences do exist in the pre-oedipal phases of development are explained as epiphenomena of physiological peculiarities and of the libidinal strivings accompanying them (42, 50).*

Even Klein's thesis (84) of a pre-oedipal beginning of introjection and superego formation does not necessitate the presumption of sex differentials in the way the male and the female infants experience the parents. Here, one of the essential differences is in evidence between psychoanalytic personalism and Jung's transpersonalistic approach (77, 78), particularly as represented by Neumann (96–98). Our own structural analysis differs both from the personalistic interpretation as offered by psychoanalysis and from Jung's concept of an archetypal reality.

The primary MaP and AM experiences, that is, the experiences of

---

* Although Freud believes that in the pre-oedipal phases the father is little more than an "inconvenient rival" in the boy's as well as the girl's struggle for the total possession of the mother, he recognizes the fact that the girl's animosity never reaches the degree of intensity that we find in the boy at this stage of deevlopment. Here, it would seem to us, he should have added that this difference indicates the operation of certain pre- (or trans-) experiential, that is, structural, factors of determination and differentiation—factors which psychoanalysis consistently overlooks.

Similarly, the fact that the oedipal conflict is solved differently by the girl and by the boy—an important point in the psychoanalytic theory of development—does not lead psychoanalysts to conclusions beyond the dimension of personalistic interpretations.

unity with the mother, of wholeness and staticness, on the one hand, and of separation, of deficiency and change, on the other, are universal, independent of sex. But the ways in which the ego emerges from the first experience and the non-ego from the second experience are different for the male and the female infant: we maintain that, in a rationally or empirically inexplicable manner, *the infant is structurally conditioned not only by the two primary mother experiences but also by the fact of sexual difference from, or identity with, the mother.*

It would, of course, be absurd to speak of some kind of conscious awareness of this difference or equality, but there does operate, it would seem, a potential tension factor which limits the male infant's ability to experience unity and staticness and the female infant's ability to experience otherness and differences.

With regard to the male child's development we could say that "otherness," which we have suggested should be defined as "paternal," is already present in his maternal experience. This is only another way of saying that the paternal principle of differentiation operates from the beginning of life on, long before the personal father, in his characteristic "outside-otherness," can be experienced, and certainly long before he elicits reactions.

Thus, the early ego development of the male infant is structurally determined by the fact that the experience of staticness—which, as we have said (p. 10), is essentially connected with identity and ego feeling—already contains in his case elements of nonidentity and non-ego. The unavoidable AM experience of absence, deficiency, change, and tension only increases the male infant's sensitivity to the non-ego. Hence, he reaches the third phase, that of the mother as the near one whose regular return can be expected (NM), not only through the experience of her regular return—no doubt a universal condition of trust and expectation—but also through his own active differentiation, which in turn is an outcome of the coexistence of identity and nonidentity in the first phase, that of the MaP experience.

The "otherness" of the mother explains why in the early life of the male infant the basic sense of trust is not "a fact of nature" but must be realized, time and again, must be maintained, always anew, against that "otherness" of the mother.* This structurally conditioned "otherness" may be held responsible for the fact that normally objectivity and differentiation develop earlier in a male child than do relational abilities.

For the daughter, on the other hand, the mother, because of their sexual identity, continues to represent staticness, even when she has ceased to be "part" (MaP) and has become the near one whose regular

---

* To paraphrase Ortega y Gasset's words: trust is not a *factum* but a *faciendum*.

return the infant expects (NM). For the girl the non-ego remains therefore so much associated with the ego that the ability to distantiate herself from reality and to differentiate between subject and object, between
different situations or different events, is liable to develop more slowly,
to remain for a longer time incomplete, or to decrease more easily (by
way of regression) whenever negative—external or internal—conditions
favor tendencies toward staticness.

The positive equivalent of this weakness of differentiation is intuitive
nearness to the unconscious and empathetic connection with the human
environment, those two characteristics of female psychology. Hence relational abilities develop with greater ease than objectivity and differentiation, which require separateness and separation, that is, a strongly developed paternal principle.

(It should be self-evident that these structural equations can be modified or even reversed by individual factors of determination such as
congenital abilities and type-conditioned propensities. But extreme predominance of a sex-contrary structural tendency endangers the child's
normal development no less than any other constitutional defect.)

3

Internalization: Ego and Non-ego

1. THE EGO-NON-EGO CONSTELLATIONS

We have so far tried to identify some of the structural roots of the ego. Obviously, no such analysis can ever dispense with genetic concepts, although they may be only borrowed from developmental psychology, may have been translated, as it were, from the language of empirical observation into that of structural analysis.

When speaking of internalization, this basic concept in every theory of human development, we have in mind that slow process, leading through many phases, of taking in, remembering, comparing, relating to each other, and organizing stimuli "coming from without"* from the non-ego, and making them into freely available contents of consciousness, while at the same time transforming them, in part at least, into structure and function. Growth of consciousness, learning of skills, transfer of learning, on the one hand, crystallization and change of the congenitally given constitution, canalization (see p. 62) and structurization, on the other hand, are examples for these two aspects of internalization. It should be studied as a process and as an activity, in fact, it is both, process and activity.†

So defined, the study of internalization should be divided into five parts: (a) the structural constellations between ego and non-ego; (b) the inner non-ego; (c) the environment, that is, the external non-ego, in its many facets; (d) the developmental conditions; and (e) the actual process of transformation and structurization. This seemingly logical sequence, however, is by no means the ideal way of presenting the problems of internalization, since the discussion of every single aspect actually presupposes a prior discussion of the others. We shall therefore proceed less systematically, even at the risk of being unable to avoid repetitions.

The conditions of internalization are: first, a readiness of the organism to receive imprints from the non-ego, that is, from the internal and the

---

* However, *cf.* the analysis of "the inner non-ego" on pp. 35 *ff.*

† In this respect, processual theories, behaviorism for instance, are as one-sided, as, let us say, metapsychological theories, trying to explain psychic processes as manifestations and results of purposefully acting agents.

external environment (plasticity); second, the hierarchical and functional organization of the organism, that is, its structure; and third, assimilatory and coordinating strength of the ego. In other words: internalization, being identical with an attempt to the ego to overcome the dangers inherent in differentiation, is structurally based on, and expands, the normative interdependence and interrelatedness of the two life tendencies, that toward staticness manifesting itself in the growing ego's organizational strength and that toward expansion manifesting itself in the plasticity, the openness of the organism. Every transformation (of a stimulus into a memory trace, of concrete objects or events into a generally applicable concept, of a human being into a relationship-partner, of experience into feelings and attitudes, of parental commands and prohibitions into contents and guiding forces of the conscience, of the body into an element of identity) requires the cooperation of both life tendencies.

This cooperation, hence also the proportion between the ego's openness and organizational strength, varies, of course, from individual to individual (according to constitutional givens called reaction-type, thresholds of frustration-bearance, endowments and deficiencies); it varies within one individual under the influence of life events, developmental and, particularly, maturational, changes, etc. For the purpose of our analysis it may be sufficient to point out four ideal types of structural constellations:

(a) When the ego's organizational strength is—constitutionally or developmentally—weak or weakened and its receptiveness *vis-à-vis* the non-ego, its readiness to receive and to accept directives from the environment, the unconscious, or even the own organism and to react to them adequately is equally weak, we find that type of constitutional apathy that, from the beginning of life on, slows development. Here we find the feebleminded variety of abnormal weakness of differentiation (which is *not* due, as the schizophrenic variety, to *absence* of boundaries between the ego and the non-ego but is due to not seeing them, not feeling challenged by their implications). Here we find general weakness of structurality (a concept to be explained later) if both life tendencies are equally weak; existential (not reactive) rigidity if the life tendency toward staticness is dominant; automatic reactions if the opposite tendency prevails.*

We should be careful not to include at this stage of our analysis cases of defensive resistance against the non-ego (as we find them, in later phases of the individual's development, in reaction to anxiety), since defensiveness presupposes a relatively high degree of organizational ego

* We presume that these prevalences are due to certain organic (cerebral) conditions.

strength, in any case higher than the one characteristic of the structural constellation here analyzed.

(b) This leads us to the second constellation, that of a relatively high degree of organizational ego strength and a low degree of openness and receptiveness *vis-à-vis* the inner or the outer non-ego. Again, we are not concerned here with those cases in which organizational strength *produces* nonreceptiveness as a defense but rather with the constitutional condition of primary egocentricity which precludes genuine communication with the non-ego.

We should bear in mind what we have said about the different connotations of the concept of non-ego: the degree of openness and receptiveness to the external non-ego (the material and the human environment) may be much lower than to the inner non-ego (the unconscious), and in fact is so as a rule in the introvert type, whereas the opposite is true in extraverts.* Not only what Jung calls the attitudinal type, but the functional preference, as well, determines the area of the non-ego to which the growing ego may be relatively open while being rigidly closed to another one. Although it may be questionable whether the functional preference, that is, the primarily sensory, intuitive, evaluational or cognitive approach to reality, is innate or results from education and development, there can be little doubt that at least in the extreme cases it can be observed from a very early phase on. We must therefore be careful not to generalize prematurely but to differentiate as clearly as possible between the various manifestations of *partial* openness and receptiveness to the different areas of the non-ego.

In the constellation here discussed, that of relative organizational strength in conjunction with a relatively low degree of openness to the non-ego, the results will therefore not be uniform: sensory acuity may, even in this constellation, keep open some avenues of contact with the material, emotional acuity—with the human surroundings, in contrast to the other functional propensities which may help to keep open contact with the inner world of images and imagination. But we are speaking here of those cases in which the ego's readiness to be stimulated, directed and determined by the non-ego, is structurally weak and in any case significantly weaker than its tendency and capacity to organize contents and functions into systems. The latter tendency and capacity will then only support the functional preferences, help them develop into constitutional reaction patterns, to the detriment of all other possible orientations. The one-sidedness thus produced causes a secondary expansion of the non-ego, that is, of the reality areas that are "not reachable." Failure to adapt to changing conditions, to assimilate new experiences, as a rule accompanies in this constellation the basic egocentricity.

* One could almost say: by definition.

(In the first-mentioned constellation, on the other hand, the ego's organizational weakness is liable to cause an early extinction of such functional preferences as might have been in operation originally—as structural determinants—and apathy will soon produce dullness in all respects.)

But the relative structural weakness in the individual's receptivity to the non-ego may, as we have said, relate to the *inner* non-ego only (in extraverts) or to the *outer* non-ego only (in introverts). In the first case, the result will be a structural predisposition to dominate the environment, in the second, an obsessional tendency to live without environmental contacts, as if inner images could replace them as sources of stimulation.

(c) What will happen, we should now ask, when a relatively weak ability of the ego to organize and systematize its contents and functions appears together with a strongly developed receptivity toward the non-ego? If the receptivity is of the introvert variety and the individual is open to the communications coming from the inner world of the unconscious more than to those coming from the physical and the social environment, the danger of being invaded and drowned by uncontrollable forces from within is obvious, since the ego's organizational ability is defective, according to our present presumption. If, on the other hand, the openness is of the extravert variety, the result is likely to be a predisposition to react nonselectively to environmental stimulations.

We should beware of interpreting these conditions solely by reducing them to the dominance of one life tendency over the other. Openness is not identical with expansion, since the first implies passivity, the second activity (intake); organizational strength is not identical with staticness, since the first implies change (transformation, systematization), while the second indicates absence of change, at least when we think of a condition of *predominance* of the tendency toward staticness. Hence, we find cases of predominant staticness that preclude neither openness, at least to the *inner* non-ego, nor weakness of the ego's organization ability (for instance, certain psychoses). On the other hand, we find behavior units in which the life tendency toward expansion predominates, such as certain psychopathic states (34) which preclude neither absence of communicative contact with the non-ego, at least with the social environment, nor a well-functioning organizational ability of the ego.

These conceptual differentiations are far from being purely academic. We shall try to show, when discussing the role of typology in the interpretation of ego development and personality normal and abnormal, that without such (and other) distinctions typology is bound to become a meaningless abstraction and generalization (*cf.* Chapter 6, "Etiology," particularly pp. 94 *ff.*).

(d) The combination of ego strength and openness to the non-ego is the norm of behavior, provided it is based on a relative equivalence of the two life tendencies. If either one predominates to such an extent that their normative interrelatedness and interdependence is disrupted, then each of the two elements of the structural constellation is liable to turn into a negative factor: the organizational ability may serve both— staticness and expansion (as an instrument of systematization or incorporation), and openness (as a supplier of material to be systematized or incorporated). Individual cases of pathological behavior belonging to the same clinical picture differ from each other not only as the result of constitutional, experiential, and maturational factors but also as a result of the degree of the ego's organizational strength and of its openness to the non-ego, irrespective of whether these enter the individual equation as structural determinants or as the intermediate results of partial developments.

It is obvious that no behavior pattern, no individual pathology, and no clinical picture can be explained or classified meaningfully through an analysis of the relationship between these structural factors only (ego strength, openness to the inner and the outer non-ego, the two basic life tendencies, type conditions). They must always be interpreted as reflecting the operation of a variety of differently configurated constitutional, developmental, and experiential factors. On the other hand, no ego analysis would be complete without taking into account these structural factors and constellations.

We have said that internalization is based on the normative interdependence and interrelatedness of the two life tendencies, that toward staticness manifesting itself in the growing ego's organizational strength and that toward expansion manifesting itself in the plasticity, the openness of the organism (p. 30). In other words: internalization requires cooperation between the two life tendencies. Whenever the latter is disturbed or defective, internalization processes will be made difficult, or they will be distorted or prevented.

2. AUTONOMY AND INTERNALIZATION

We are now going to discuss the relationship between ego and non-ego under another aspect, that of autonomy. Although we shall have to come back to this concept in various contexts in the course of our analysis (and particularly so in Chapter 8, dealing with the phases of development), a preliminary discussion of autonomy would seem indispensable, since it is the ultimate criterion for an adequate transformation of non-ego into contents and functions of the ego, called internalization.

It would be absurd to describe the process of ego formation as if it implied a gradual shrinkage of the non-ego. The latter is identical with the infinity of all possible realities. Although normally an ever-increasing non-ego "area" becomes an *object* of ego experience, becomes known, becomes related to a specific ego situation, these transformations are ultimately changes of ego modalities only: they indicate the ego's growing ability to recognize the non-ego as such, to relate to it and to differentiate between old and new, between equal and different.

But this does not mean that the antithesis "ego-non-ego" is identical with the antithesis "subject-object." Ego and non-ego are *both* subject and object in relation to each other. It is true that, normally, the ego becomes more and more an autonomous subject, relating to, dealing with, and experiencing the non-ego as object—but as an *autonomous* object, that is, in a sense, as a subject, too. It is a mistake of rationalistic interpretation of life to speak of autonomy and heteronomy from the point of view of the ego only, as if the latter's autonomy could ever eliminate that of the non-ego. *True ego autonomy does not mean independence, but it does mean awareness of the non-ego's autonomy; it implies recognition and acceptance of heteronomy as one of the essentials of human existence.* On the other hand, the concept of heteronomy implies not only the ego's dependence on the non-ego, but also the existence and the development of the ego as a separate unit of the psychic structure, that is, to some extent, the recognition of the heteronomous object character of the non-ego.

In other words, autonomy means that the ego is capable of guarding its subject position as an object of the autonomous non-ego. We have said that normally organization and synthesis—the functions of the ego as the center of consciousness—are related to, and dependent on, its readiness and ability to be receptive *vis-à-vis* the non-ego. This dual character of the ego, however, reflects and indicates a similar duality of the non-ego: it is, on the one hand, the *object* of the ego's intentionality, and it *aims*, on the other hand, at this ego in its actuality, in its changes, in its development (it "intends" the ego). *The simultaneity and exchangeability of these subject-object positions is the structural condition of normal development.*

In order to understand the meaning of internalization in the light of this statement we must take seriously the concept of simultaneity: it is not sufficient to recognize the indisputable fact that every ego and every non-ego is at one time *determined*, at another *determining*. The actual basis of autonomy is the experience that what determines the ego at any given moment is, in this moment, *being* determined both by outside factors and by the ego itself; and whenever the ego tries to determine, to influence, to change (or even only to use) any part of the non-ego, it should not lose awareness of its own dependence, in this very moment of activity, on inner and outer factors of determination, including the

presently determined non-ego itself. Neither the illusion of absolute freedom nor that of absolute dependence allow for autonomy. The illusion
of omnipotence and the feeling of impotence are equally indicative of
heteronomy. Exclusive identification of the ego with its subject position or
its object position, one of the criteria of classification in any phenomenology of behavior disorders, also precludes adequate internalization just
as disruption of the normative interrelatedness of the two life tendencies
does.*

An ego unable to experience itself as a subject of determination will
never be able to internalize the non-ego; but unless this subjectivity is
accompanied by a feeling that internalization is *not* there to "eliminate"
the non-ego, that its transformation into concepts, values, feelings, relationships or inner tensions *requires* relating these results of internalization to their non-ego sources and representations, internalization will
never be genuine. In the first case, that is, when the ego is incapable of
experiencing itself as a subject of determination, reality, including the
ego itself, remains "outside," as we have tried to show in another study
(33). In the second case, internalization, to the extent that it will take
place, is bound to be irrealistic and, thus, to produce another type of
pathology.†

3. The Inner Non-ego

Here, however, we must again differentiate between the inner and the
outer non-ego and ask ourselves how what we have said about the
simultaneity and the exchangeability of subject-object positions (as the
essential characteristic of autonomy and as the prerequisite of genuine
internalization) applies not only to the physical and the human environment but also to the inner non-ego, the universe of instincts, drives,
impulses, affects, feelings, of the personal and the transpersonal unconscious (32, 78, 96).

Whereas it is self-evident that in order to make ego formation and ego
development possible, separation between the growing ego and its environment must take place, and that, consequently, internalization means
a process of transforming external objects into internal contents, separation from the *inner* non-ego and internalizing the inner non-ego seem
to be self-contradictory concepts. How can we imagine the emergence of
dialogic relationships between the ego and the unconscious as being
comparable to those between the ego and the physical and human en-

---

* This does not mean, of course, that both pathogenic conditions are identical. Predominance of the tendency toward staticness, for instance, one of the possible causes of
that disruption, is compatible with the ego's identification with either its subject position or its object position. So is the reverse predominance.

† We shall elaborate on these subjects in a subsequent volume, in which some cultural
and individual varieties of externalization will be discussed.

vironment, relationships in which not only the ego but also the non-ego, the unconscious, is both a subject acting on the ego and an object of that ego? And does it make sense at all to speak of internalizing an inner non-ego?

We refer to what we have said at the beginning of our analysis: that the inner non-ego (at least that part that we have called the constituents of experience) is a precondition of experiencing the environment, including the mother; that it belongs existentially to the ego, which at first is its object until it becomes a subject *vis-à-vis* the external non-ego; that its intentionality gradually imparts itself to the thus growing ego; that primarily the inner non-ego is no more separated from the ego than the environment (pp. 4 *ff.*).

All these statements refer, of course, to the transpersonal unconscious only at the hypothetical stage of development that Neumann (96) calls the "uroboric phase" when its contents, the archetypal categories of experience, do not yet appear as identifiable and describable images. If we take seriously the central idea in Jungian psychology about the categorical meaning of the archetypes, we are forced to assume the existence of a primary stage in man's development, right after birth, at which the so-defined unconscious not only forms part of the ego nucleus but is, in fact, identical with it.

Separation sets in through the experience of external realities and primarily, of course, the mother. Neumann speaks of a process of "personalization" (99)* that *leads* to the discovery of the parents as persons and to the establishment of relationships with them, and particularly with the mother, as described in Chapter 2. It is precisely because the mother is experienced at first archetypally, that is, transpersonally, that differentiation between the inner non-ego and the growing ego takes place under the reality impact of maternal care and contact; in other words, their non-ego character establishes itself to the extent that the ego emerges and develops. It is in and through this process of primary differentiation, brought about by experience, that the archetypes of the transpersonal unscious, the categories of experience, become identifiable as images.

As such, however, they are threatening in their separateness, just as the external non-ego, the environment, becomes dangerous through its being separated from the ego. And just as we have defined the function of internalizing the outer non-ego as a way of overcoming its dangerous separateness, so the inner non-ego, too, becomes an object of internalization: the growing consciousness starts to face the phantasies and images, in which the transpersonal is taking shape, as realities no less real than the external environment. The growing ego feels more and

* The term "secondary personalization," as used by Neumann, is misleading since it could be understood as meaning that it is preceded by a phase of "primary" personalization.

more challenged to confront them, to listen to their communications and to speak to them; the ego becomes increasingly familiar with those strange and yet real images of the inner non-ego, learns how to live with them, and, later, how to adapt them, in part at least, to outer realities, or how to project them onto these realities.

These are the viscissitudes of the inner non-ego at the beginning of life: after a primary unity stage in which the inner non-ego is identical with the ego nucleus (and no difference exists between the inner and the outer non-ego), comes the first stage of differentiation between the non-ego and the ego, on the one hand, and between the inner and the outer non-ego, on the other (see pp. 5 ff.), by means of personalizations. This process makes possible an increasingly conscious communication between the ego and the inner non-ego; in the end its image manifestations (by themselves resulting from the impact of reality-experience on the preexisting archetypal contents of the transpersonal unconscious) become familiar enough to be connected with objects and events in the environment. This could be called a process of *primary projection* as against the later process of *secondary projection* which is one of the defenses against guilt and anxiety originating in the personal unconscious from conflicts between incompatible impulses and tendencies.

Communication with the inner non-ego is a truly dialogic process, to the extent at least that the growing ego not only listens to the images of the transpersonal stratum of the mind but also experiments with them, provoking them thereby into different manifestations. Thus, the ego is indeed an active partner, a subject, in its dialogic relationship with the inner non-ego, and not only an object of that non-ego's manifestations, directions, communications. And the inner non-ego, the autonomous depth zone of the psyche (32), reacts to the ego, is an object of the latter's experimental activities.

It goes without saying that this is the description of a normative development only, of an ideal type. In reality, the process is far from being as clearly divided into phases of primary differentiation, communication, primary projection, and internalization. And even to the extent that these processes do take place, the phasic achievements are partial only.

This, however, means that the process of internalization cannot be made comprehensible, unless we see the object of internalization, that is, the non-ego, as dynamically changing and growing no less than the internalizing ego itself. It may, of course, be argued that reality—meaning both the universe of external phenomena and events and the universe of the soul—is infinite and therefore cannot grow. But from the point of view of the ego in its efforts to internalize the non-ego, it is correct to say that this non-ego grows through the very acts and processes of internalization; differentiation, this precondition, concomitant, and result of internalization, makes visible and identifiable ever new and added aspects and manifestations of reality. Moreover, some forms of assimilating the outer non-ego (through habits, stereotypes, patterns, repressions, reaction formations, and other defenses) increase the area of the inner non-ego, the unconscious (as we have mentioned above, see p. 6). It is this latter aspect that we should keep in mind when discussing the processes of internalization.

The here-considered inner non-ego is no longer identical with the transpersonal unconscious but emerges and grows, as the *personal* unconscious, through the unavoidable partiality of the ego's success in its efforts to internalize the physical or social non-ego and to establish truly dialogic relationships with it. But the emergence and growth of that personal unconscious proves the never-ceasing need for differentiation from, and communication with, the inner non-ego. Internalization is neither identical with structurization, as we shall try to show later (see pp. 42 *ff.*), nor with "making conscious" what had not been conscious before, as certain personalistically and rationalistically oriented schools of psychology and therapy claim; it means, in the here-considered context of drives and affects, of defenses and patterns, exactly what it means when its object is part of an external reality or of the transpersonal reality: transformation into freely available ego contents and ego functions whose free availability depends on the ego's dialogic relationship with them as well as with their external reality representatives and sources.

Drives or affects can be considered internalized when the ego recognizes their autonomy and is ready to accept their manifestations as objective realities (that is, as parts of the non-ego), while at the same time, and through its reactions to them, experimenting with the variety of their possible manifestations. Drives or affects are not internalized, as long as the ego feels itself to be their aim and object only, or, what is the same, accepts them as parts of itself, without differentiation. In other words, relating oneself to the inner non-ego, as if it were an objective reality only or part of the self only, proves *non*-internalization.

The same holds good for habits, reaction patterns, stereotypes, and self-images, for man's identity with traditions and cultural patterns, for reaction formations and other defenses against inner contradictions and unbearable tensions.

Whatever the way may be that leads to the formation of habits, reaction patterns, stereotypes, and self-images (and we shall come back to this question in Chapter 5, on structurization), their very resistance to relativization, objectivization, revision, and adaptation to differing and changing reality demands proves, so it would seem to us, precisely the opposite of what we are inclined to think: it proves their *non*-ego character. Man's tendency uncritically to identify with these parts of his ego system— more, to *define* his identity through them—is evidence for the absence of differentiation, autonomy, internalization and dialogic relationship. When discussing the essence of structurality and structurization we shall see that these parts of the inner non-ego, too, may become objects of internalization, and again through conscious confrontation with their objective (that is, transindividual) meaning, through "conversing" with them, as if they were capable of answering questions concerning their origin and their hidden meaning (and, in fact, they do give us those answers, if only we know how to ask the proper questions). This, how- ever, means that we must be ready and willing to distantiate ourselves from them to such an extent that we will no longer feel threatened with partial or total annihilation, when we dare to question their role as parts of our identity; we must accept their emergence as unavoidable, we must recognize their existence as objective realities, but only in order to internalize them by way of relating to them critically, autonomously, dialogically.

Man's dependence on traditions, beliefs, cultural patterns is more easily recognized as proving their non-ego character than are his habits and personal reaction patterns; it is the fact that the former are shared with many which accounts for our relative readiness to accept them as transindividual realities, and to relate to them as to possible objects of internalization.

Internalizing traditions, beliefs, and cultural patterns implies con- scious identification with their constituent elements, and ego involvement in their realization. Although the individual is not free to decide on his own or even to bring about changes—although he feels bound to the directions implied in the traditions and beliefs, to the culture-inherent patterns of thinking, of evaluating, of feeling (which to him are parts of an absolute non-ego)—he may learn how to relate himself to this non-ego in a polar relationship. We can speak here of *internalized heteronomy*, which presupposes the discovery of the ego as *partner* of the tradition and the pattern. Internalizing the cultural non-ego means, then, that the ego ceases to feel (and to be) contained in it as part, as instrument, as object only. And once again, we must understand the concepts of polarity and of dialogue literally: man must come not only to accept, and to react to, those parts of the inner non-ego, but also to ask what traditions, beliefs, and patterns have to say in answer to his questions. Internalizing these transindividual aspects means not only reacting or adapting one- self to them but also, and primarily, provoking the cultural non-ego into adequate reactions to the changing needs of the individual.

And finally there is the personal unconscious, as it emerges from repressions, defenses, and positive or negative character formations. Regarding this form of the inner non-ego as an object of internalization is bound to lead to the problem area of structurization, changeability, reversibility, on the one hand, and to analyzing the essence of the unconscious (or better, the "reality of the soul"), on the other. Separate chapters will be devoted to each of these two problem areas. It will, therefore, be sufficient here to apply what we have said about dialogic relationships between the ego and the non-ego as a precondition and a symptom of internalization to this area of the inner non-ego as well.

The disappearance of stimuli that fail to cross the threshold of perception and never become objects of consciousness (although they may leave mnemic imprints, as can be proved by experiments with hypnosis) may be due either to a process of mechanic pressure or to some sort of screening. We are inclined to regard the latter as indicating a psychic activity, rooted in, emanating from, directed by, an agent of selection and coordination, an agent that knows the needs of the organism and is capable of protecting it. And we ascribe similar knowledge to that inner agent of selection and protection called the ego, when, later, certain impulses, affects, feelings, desires, attitudes, or memories are found to be incompatible with an already established system of internalizations, and the ego decides to eliminate them by way of suppression or repression. The same knowledge finds its expression in the mobilization of defenses meant to maintain the protective selections and eliminations (those additional repressions, those displacements, denials, reaction formations, projections, etc. described as defense mechanisms in the psychoanalytic literature).

But the final result of these ego interventions is, paradoxically, the emergence of a system of character traits, attitudes, reaction patterns, and strivings which, though firmly entrenched and clearly represented in man's consciousness, are often experienced as foreign bodies, as parts of an *alter-ego*, as unaccountable, that is, as *non*-ego. This inner contradiction—which has given rise to a number of attempts in analytic ego psychology to interpret the genesis of structures dynamically—again becomes meaningful when we regard it as indicating a disruption of the (normal) interrelatedness of the two life tendencies (staticness predominating over expansion), or as symptomatic of the absence of truly dialogic relationships between the ego and its systematizations.

True enough, such a disruption of normative interrelatedness is the necessary concomitant of any process of selection and of mobilizing defenses; but on the other hand, it is precisely this unavoidable deviation from the norm that *requires* a later (re-) establishment of dialogic relationships between the ego and the personal unconscious for the purposes of internalization. And here again, internalization does *not* mean "making the unconscious conscious" (*cf.* p. 38), but means recognizing its non-ego character; confronting it both as an object of genetic analysis and as a subject of communications; manipulating it, experimenting with it by questioning the ego character of its manifestations; asking whether this or that trait, attitude, pattern, or striving is really "mine," is really an expression of my self; and waiting for the answers, that is, for the subsequent behavior manifestation which may reveal its non-ego character and thus make possible change and transformation, or which may prove its ego character by its inner consistency.

Thus, a genuinely polar (dialogic) relationship between the ego and the inner non-ego, in each of the meanings here discussed, prepares the way for internalization, that is, for transforming it into an integral part of the ego system; and this transformation, in turn, makes possible more truly polar relationships between the ego and its internalizations.

4

The "Reality of the Soul"

1. STRUCTURE AND INTENTIONALITY

The analysis of the concept of inner non-ego in its double connotation, of the personal and the transpersonal unconscious, requires a digression into the metaphysical aspects of the problem. Following Jung—and quoting him (75)—we speak of "the reality of the soul" of which the inner non-ego is but a segment, related to the ego as to the agent of experience and reaction. We believe that our later analysis of the process of structurization (character change, identity formation, emergence and crystallization of constitutional determinants, therapy-induced reversal of developmental pathologies, etc.) will be more meaningful if preceded by the presently suggested speculations on the dynamics and the structure of the psyche.*

We need not analyze here in detail the often discussed differences between the Freudian and the Jungian conceptions of the unconscious. According to psychoanalytic personalism, the unconscious is but a result of repression, hence differs from consciousness in the mode of organization only, is accessible to energetic-mechanistic categories of interpretation (tensions producing discharge, forces realizing themselves), and is not reality-related. According to Jung, on the other hand, even the personal unconscious, resulting from repression, seeks reintegration with the ego not as the result of energetic processes, but because it obeys the universal laws of compensation and the life-inherent tendency of the psyche to realize itself ever more completely.

True enough, the energetic-mechanistic conception of the "chaotic" unconscious, as formulated by Freud and his followers, strangely contradicts their personalistic interpretation of the *contents* of the unconscious and their finalistic interpretation of its *realization tendencies*. The unconscious, says psychoanalysis, uses its archaic modes of operation to overcome the ego's resistance to being penetrated by unconscious drives; time and again, the unconscious is being presented as a sly strategist who knows well how to cheat the ego, which, in spite of its elaborate

* This chapter is based, in part, on our earlier paper on the unconscious (32).

42

defenses, appears not to be too intelligent and efficient in its struggle against the former. But even when we do not accept the frequently offered excuse, namely, that these strategic manipulations are mere *façons de parler*, convenient for the purposes of teaching but not to be taken seriously (that is, realistically), there can be little doubt that psychoanalysis, at least of the Freudian blend, is basically nonfinalistic, in contrast to analytical psychology which speaks about "communications" to the ego, for instance through a dream series or through other spontaneous experiences coming from the unconscious. Here, the assumption of unconscious *intentionality* cannot be avoided.

An intention, however, cannot be imagined but as "being had" by some inner agent comparable to the ego. Intentionality is essentially an ego category; whether we speak of the ego's function of synthesis or of its responsibility for growth and change or for screening and defense, we cannot make its modes of operation comprehensible unless we presume underlying intentions. This, however, means that the hypothesis of intentionality in the unconscious as it manifests itself in dreams, phantasies, or spontaneous creations requires a revision of our basic concepts of psychological interpretation.

Jung rightly points out the paradox implied in the assumption of "a consciousness within the unconscious" (76), the latter concept being by definition the negation of the former. But it would not be justified to use this conceptual incompatibility as an argument against the assumption of intentionality in the unconscious. *The term "unconscious" designates both a modality and a reality. Intentionality, it is true, contradicts a mode of existence characterized by the absence of consciousness; it does not contradict, however, existence per se, neither material nor human.* But in order to make the concept relevant and usable for the interpretation of ego development, we must think of the reality in which intentionality is supposed to operate, "the reality of the soul," not in negative terms (such as "the un-conscious"), but, *as of an individually limited segment of the transindividual infiniteness of the psyche.* Infiniteness precludes, of course, structure, and the psyche cannot be compared to the ego, as it manifests itself in the individual personality. Intentionality, on the other hand, being a category of relatedness, presupposes a structural organization in which it is meaningful to speak not only of intentions but also of agents of intentions. It is for this reason that we interpret growth and development as processes going on, within the infinite reality of the soul, between the two agents of intentionality, the ego and the depth center of the (individually segmented) psyche.*

---

* Jung calls this agent the "Self" (as against the ego) and emphasizes its transindividual and universal character, which actually precludes speaking of "my" and of "your" Self. In the Self, he says, the "total psyche" is "centered." But strictly speaking, we should not go on from here and call the Self "the center of the psyche": while "*being* centered" is

These speculations belong to the field of metaphysics (though they are equally applicable to the problems of mass and energy in physics). We summarize and enlarge our constructions as follows:

(a) The ego is the center of consciousness, emerging from the total psyche through a process of self-limitation, of partial transformation of energy into structure, and therefore continues to operate in the service of both life tendencies, that toward staticness and that toward expansion. Its responsibility for coordination, control and systematization is a continued manifestation of the process that led to its structural emergence; its responsibility for channeling the total psyche's tendency toward enlargement and reintergration ("return to the Self," in Jung's terms) is an expression of the dynamic infiniteness of the total psyche.

(b) The latter relates to the individual ego through the medium of a specific point of energetic concentration, which we have called, for lack of a better term, the depth center. It is a center only with regard to a specific individual ego, to which it relates intentionally. In other words, in any given moment, the total psyche (like the outer non-ego, the physical and social environment) becomes intentionally relevant for the ego not in its infiniteness but in a certain, concretely defined, segment only.

(c) The depth center always aims at bringing the ego to a higher level of integration, to greater completeness. For this purpose, it uses the contents of the personal unconscious in conjunction with archetypal images, with transpersonal contents (as they emerge spontaneously). Thus, the former are likely to become the "bearers of the message," the vehicles of communication from the depth zone of the psyche, in addition to conveying their personal message of attitude-change required (35).

(d) What we have said about the structural constellations between the ego and the non-ego in general (see pp. 29 ff.), applies, of course, to the relationship between the ego and the depth zone of the psyche as well, though the ego's function is here one of reacting more than of answering, of organizing more than of experimenting.

(e) The modality of unconsciousness in the personal meaning of the term (being eliminated from, and not belonging to, the ego area) indicates a low degree of openness in the ego to the communications from the psyche. The processes of distortion, defensive systematization, and pathogenesis, which form the main subjects of the psychoanalytic study of the unconscious, therefore indicate a negative constellation only.*

(f) Development and change may take place within the ego system without affecting its structure, or may produce structural transformations.

---

still a dynamic concept, "center" is a static, a structural concept. The infinite may be "centered" in certain "points of energetic concentration," but once we imagine them as structurally definable "centers," they cease to be "of" the infinite.

* This means that we regard as erroneous the subsumption of seemingly or genuinely *positive* solutions, such as sublimation, under the general concept of defense mechanisms.

The essential difference between these two forms of change is not adequately defined as one between degrees of radicality; it rather indicates different forms of relationships between the ego and the non-ego. In transformation, the ego becomes the aim and object of the depth zone (or better, of the center of the depth zone); in nonstructural changes (which take place constantly), the ego is exposed to the influx and influence of the external non-ego. It is this external non-ego to which the ego reacts as the center of its field of contents and functions, trying to change them or its own modes of operation (assimilation). Even the admission to, and incorporation in, consciousness of unconscious material (that is, of contents, feelings, strivings, suppressed or repressed, which form part of the area of our past or future experience) does not, as a rule, require radical transformation. The latter always presupposes the intentional intervention of a reality experienced, in the very moment of its intervention, as transcendent, as absolutely superior, as unknown, though at the same time as demanding from the ego readiness to cooperate in the internalization and realization of its intentions.*

(g) In those processes of development and change that can be interpreted as essentially resulting from the impact of enrivonmental forces on inner factors of organization, the experience of "being self-determined" prevails over the feeling of "being meant," that is, of being called upon to serve the intentions of an ego-transcending reality. These are the cases in which the ego succeeds in experiencing its *own* actions and reactions as intentional and as responsible for the processes of development and change going on and controlled within its area of contents and functions. It may well be that this ego feeling (of autonomous intentionality) is based on an illusion and that the changes initiated, if not by the environment, then at least by the personal unconscious, are indeed *beyond* the ego's responsibility, are in fact results of ego-*transcending* forces of determination and therefore produce radical transformations; but the very fact that the ego remains capable of *feeling* itself "intending" rather than "intended" can serve as a criterion of differentiation between ego-transcending transformation and ego-inherent developmental changes. We shall see later that this distinction is of the essence for an understanding of the meaning of what we call structurization.

(h) The concept of "center" implies relatedness of an agent of intentionality, of selection and differentiation, of coordination and synthesis, to a subordinate field of contents and functions. Now, while this hierarchical conception of psychic reality makes sense when we speak of the ego as the center of consciousness, it would seem to be at least problematical to speak of a similar relationship between the depth center and

* We shall have to keep this essential difference in mind when discussing the meaning of structurization (Chapter 5).

the total "reality of the soul." This is why we have introduced the concepts of ego-related segments and of specific points of energetic concentration (see point (b) on p. 44). We shall try to describe and analyze the ways in which this specific depth center functions in regard to its object, the ego structure, by comparing them with the methods of selection and coordination characteristic of the ego in its relationship to the environment and its inner representatives, on the one hand, and to the personal unconscious, on the other. For this purpose, however, we must once again return to an analysis of the ways in which the ego deals with *its* fields and particularly with the personal unconscious (patterns of reacting, of thinking, of feeling and of evaluating, defenses, character traits, etc.).

2. The Personal Unconscious

The ego area contains not only what, at a certain moment, is conscious but also all that is capable of becoming, or of being made, conscious without producing a radical change in the personality. The very fact that the ego refuses to accept a certain content (a memory, a striving, a feeling, an attitude, etc.), thereby forcing it into repression, proves, paradoxically, that it belongs to the ego system and does not transcend it. This would seem to be a valid statement, although we know (or, at least, are being told by Freud) that the unconscious takes part in the process of ego contents being repressed—in other words, that repression is the result of both an ego activity and the retractive power of the unconscious (43).*

The personality-determining influence of repressed contents and tendencies grows to the extent that the control contact connecting them with the ego grows weaker, that is, to the extent that the contents sink deeper into the unconscious and thereby become parts of the non-ego. The earlier the developmental stage during which repression takes place and the more violent the rejection preceding it, the more radical will be the personality changes that may follow it. And yet: even the most radical changes remain reversible, to the extent that the *ego* was responsible for the repression and the reactive systematization following it. Although the repressed contents and tendencies themselves may become unrecognizable as the result of their being subject to what Freud calls "the primary process," that is, as the result of ever-decreasing reality control over them, none of those changes (in the repressed material as well as in the personality affected by repression) is a *structural* change, none requires the intervention of an ego-transcending "agent of intentions" to eliminate

---

* That the unconscious is here conceived of as being in existence *before* repression takes place does not contradict our earlier claim regarding the basically personalistic and genetic nature of psychoanalytic theory, since its pre-individual roots are being defined as "archaic rests," that is, as the result of phylogenetic experience and repression in "archaic persons."

them (if, for some reason, their elimination should be considered indicated, desirable, necessary).

If the soul were identical with the areas of consciousness and the personal unconscious, says Jung (76), the concept of "ego" would be sufficient to explain the vicissitudes of personality development; the ego would then represent the individual in its totality. Even in those processes that lead to the (seeming) disappearance of ego contents in the unconscious, the ego is a participant; similarly, it is a partner in those processes, in the course of which repressed contents make themselves felt, in one way or another, in our consciousness, as associations, seemingly senseless mistakes, phantasies, neurotic symptoms, or even as dreams; for, in all these manifestations of the unconscious the ego continues to participate. Although the degree of consciousness is low when ego material sinks into the unconscious or reappears, the ego remains responsible for the compromise form in which the unconscious manifests itself; when the ego feels itself being subjected to processes beyond its control, it is precisely in this experience that its subject modality expresses itself as responsibility for unity and integration, that is, as synthesis.

This synthetic function of the ego, claims psychoanalysis, accounts for the fact that we *experience* energetic processes of libido discharge (leading to one of the many uncontrollable, spontaneous, manifestations of the unconscious), as if they had intentional character, whereas the intentionality is but a later addition, a kind of distortion, produced by the ego. In other words, as long as we remain in the area of the personal unconscious, of repressions and their symptomatic effects, we remain also in the area of the ego.

The fact that repressions, as a rule, result in the emergence or in the reinforcement of certain patterns of behavior and thinking or of character traits proves that the very life tendency toward staticness that is responsible for the acts and processes of repression also accounts for their structural aftereffects. The same applies to the reverse process, that leading to reintegration of repressed material and tendencies in the ego system of consciousness: even if, as the result of such reintegration, certain patterns or character traits undergo more or less radical changes, even if certain defenses which had produced or reinforced these patterns and traits become superfluous and meaningless (to the extent that the ego learns how to give up its resistance to the previously repressed and unconscious contents and strivings)—even then the processes of change are going on *within* the ego system and do *not* indicate the activity of an ego-transcending agent of intention, that is, the participation of what we have called the depth center in the psyche.

But the astounding adaptability of the unconscious contents and strivings to the actuality of the ego system cannot be reduced to the ego's synthesis function alone. It would seem to us that these unconscious contents and strivings have a kind of knowledge about the structure and the ever-changing actuality of the ego system, which allows them to find exactly the most convenient points of entrance and the methods capable of opening the doors and of joining the ego system. This knowledge, we claim, is a derivative of the depth center: *the state of unconsciousness apparently brings the personal unconscious under the impact of the transpersonal unconscious.*

Here we refer to what we have said at the beginning of this chapter about Jung's conception of the "reality of the soul": according to him, we said, even the personal unconscious, resulting from repression, seeks reintegration with the ego *not* as the result of energetic processes (obeying the laws of pressure and counterpressure, as it were) "but because it obeys the universal laws of compensation and the life-inherent tendency of the psyche to realize itself ever more completely" (p. 42). In other words, ultimately the intentionality of the ego in its selective, repressive, and system-forming functions as well as in its normative function of keeping itself and its system open to the communications of the inner and outer non-ego, the environment, and the unconscious, is an offshoot of the tendency of the total psyche to realize itself ever more completely, the ego being the reality organ of the total psyche. At the same time, however, the ego is the aim and object of the total psyche.

What does this mean for an understanding of the differences between the modes of operation of the ego and the depth center?

3. The Modes of Operation: Knowing and System Formation

We define consciousness as modality, by saying that a certain fact belongs to the ego system, that the ego is able to know and understand it, to use and manipulate it. But when we use the term of consciousness topically, as an area, we include the ego among its possible objects. The second meaning of the concept, however, only reflects an inadequate and inaccurate way of speaking: consciousness as an area of contents is identical with the ego as a system of contents and functions. Instead of defining the ego as both bearer and object of consciousness, we should define it as the synthesizing and differentiating center in an area of contents and functions which as a rule are characterized by the modality of consciousness. The fact that the ego can become its own object (in the reflective acts called ego-consciousness), the ability of the ego to operate as subject and object simultaneously, that is, to transcend itself, and the fact that the ego system is changeable—all indicate that it is but an offshoot of the total psyche, emerging from it, as we have said (p. 44), though a process of partial transformation of energy into structure, and not losing its original energy character, as it were, even after it has taken on the form and function of a system, a center of organization.

We have suggested the use of the concept of depth center in order to make comprehensible the dynamic and dialogic relationship between the ego and the "reality of the soul." The term depth center means that part of the total psyche that is relevant for the formation and the transformation of the ego system; we need the structural terminology (area, center) in order to explain the process of growth and change as being based on polarity.

The concept of relevance has three aspects: the *emergence* of (potentially) comprehensible and meaningful psychic contents; the *provocation* of specific (adequate or inadequate) *ego reactions;* the initiation of a *dialogic process* between the ego and the psyche. Not every possible content is relevant for each individual at any moment. When we apply this seemingly trivial statement to the outer non-ego, chance is the factor determining the emergence of a certain fact at a certain moment, and the ego's reaction is determined by the inner constellation of its functions at the moment of occurrence. But when we have in mind the emergence at a specific moment of a content that belongs to the "reality of the soul," to the inner non-ego, selection must precede the occurrence, and the occurrence must have been determined by an intention in order to make it meaningful and relevant. The reaction of the ego will then be a response, adequate or inadequate, but in any case setting in motion a dialogic process whose aim is transformation (though the aim may be missed when the response is inadequate).

This dialogic process presupposes, according to our construction, a knowledge about the structure and the ever-changing actuality of the ego (p. 48), one of the functions of the depth center, just as knowing the environment is one of the basic functions of the ego. And just as knowing the external reality implies knowing the ways and means of reacting to it, of interfering with it, of manipulating it, of changing it—so the structure knowledge of the depth center implies knowing the ways and means of changing and enlarging an existing ego system, selecting the functionally and structurally indicated communications and channels of realization.

Comparable to the ego's task (and ability) to coordinate and synthesize (that is, to bring into a system) a variety of divergent contents and functions, is the second function of the depth center, that of bringing about, compensatorily, the structurally necessary, that is, the normative, changes, whether through the ego or by way of enforcing them from without, as it were (sometimes even disrupting thereby the ego system).

But although both—knowing and system formation—seem to be comparable to their counterparts in the ego, we must not overlook the essential differences between the two levels, the ego area of consciousness and

the depth zone of the psyche: whereas in the ego knowing and systematization are two separate functions, sometimes even isolated from, and
unrelated to, each other, they are identical with each other in the depth
center. What is the meaning of this identity?

Conscious knowledge is characterized by the rational ego-relatedness
and the categorial hierarchy of its contents. This definition does *not*
apply to the intuitive, and certainly not to the instinctual, the organic
or the telepathic forms of *knowing*. By *intuition* we understand: knowing
whole-contexts in which the possible appears as reality-inherent; it is a
knowledge that does not emerge from discursive rationality but from
synoptic receptivity, a knowledge more object-related than ego-related.
Telepathic knowledge, in addition to being receptive and object-related,
is independent of the temporal, spatial, and causal conditions of reason.
Instinctual and *organic* knowledge differ from both previous forms insofar as their contents do not necessarily persist as such, that is, as known
and knowable facts even after having entered consciousness, but undergo
an immediate transformation into reactive, systematizing or integrating
activities of the organism. In intuition and telepathy the ego is called
upon to take cognizance of what it has seen or recognized, although it
often does so rather incompletely and after a long delay only, and fails
to revise its customary positions in the light of the intuitively or tele-
pathically mediated experience. Instinctual and organic knowledge, on
the other hand, is identical with the system-forming functions of the
organism, it occurs within the organism without conscious elaboration,
and at least at the beginning, without ego participation.

Let us now compare the knowledge of the depth center about the ego
structure with those forms of nonrational knowledge. With the instinctual
and organic variety it has the identity of knowledge and systematization
in common, the knowledge manifesting itself primarily as a tendency of
the psyche to realize itself in a specific ego system, as transformation. With
telepathic knowledge it has the lack of dependence on the spatial,
temporal, and causal categories of experience in common. With the
intuitive variety it shares receptivity and object-relatedness. But in all
these forms of knowledge the object of knowing is the non-ego in one of
its meanings, whereas *in the knowledge of the depth center, the object is
the ego structure in its changeability*. Whereas the forms of irrational
and rational knowledge have separateness and consecutiveness of knowledge and systematization in common with each other (although the
order may be different), knowledge about the ego structure in its changeability manifests itself only in the process of interference.

It is this identity (simultaneity) of knowledge and action that turns
every statement about the modes of operation of the depth center into a
speculation about transcendence; the maker of the statement, the ego,

that is, a specific part of the total psyche, here attempts to make a statement about itself not as an object of itself (as in the acts of self-reflection) but as an object of the psychic reality that contains and transcends it—obviously not a rational or empirical procedure. On the other hand, it is an empirical experience that makes such self-transcending statements at all possible: the experience of the ego that it can become the object of an inner non-ego without losing its ego character.

Let us now try to re-formulate what we have said so far: we have called the ego an offshoot of the total psyche, or rather, of the depth center that "intends" the realization of the future ego. The ego is contained in the depth center and develops out of it as the agent of realization, the representative, of the total psyche in the universe of empirical facts and relationships. Its function of systematization and synthesis requires specific modes of operation, and the latter determine the conception not only of reality but also of the ego structure.

The function of the depth center, on the other hand, is not system *formation* but system *change*. Hence, it relates directly to the ego system and only indirectly, through the ego, to the contents of experience, to which it adds new contents from within autonomously. But even these new contents will have to be assimilated and integrated by the ego, which establishes the associations between them and external experience. In other words: the ego as the agent of systematization is, structurally, the "organ" of the depth center, while the ego system is its object.

This structural relationship between the ego and the depth center accounts for the latter's independence of the temporal, spatial, and causal categories of experience. It can rely on the ego with its categories of experience and its reality-related and reality-conditioned modes of operation for the purposes of its self-realization. The way in which the depth center knows the ego is not comparable with the way in which the ego knows its objects, since it does not precede systematization as an eliciting factor or follow it as an integrating factor; its way of knowing can be defined rather as apperception of the ego's structural dispositions and growth potentials, or, in other words, of that part of the reality of the soul that is relevant for the ego in its specific actuality. In this apperception, potentials are represented as realities, the future as present. This is why the structural knowledge analyzed here is comparable with those irrational modes of knowing that we have mentioned above, intuition and telepathy, instinctual and organic knowledge (and this, incidentally, is the reason it usually expresses itself through symbols).

4. THE EGO AND THE PSYCHE

It can be argued against our construction that it is based on a fallacy, that there is no intentionality in organic or in mental processes, in de-

velopment or in pathology, all of which can be explained adequately as
the outcome of energetic processes only, with compensation being one of
the central concepts of interpretation. Since without the assumption of
intentionality structural concepts, too, are redundant (as there is then no
need for assuming a "bearer" of intentions), the model suggested here
becomes meaningless. That Cannon (16), when analyzing homeostasis,
found it necessary to speak of the "wisdom" of the body, can hardly be
used as a counter-argument, since the expression could be understood
as a mere *façon de parler*.

It would seem that it is indeed difficult to prove the need for structural
concepts and for the presumption of intentionality, although we believe
that with their help more phenomena of human existence and development become comprehensible in a more or less unified manner (see also
Chapter 6, "Etiology").

Specific claims, however, against the presumption of intentionality in
the unconscious can be refuted. It is claimed, for instance, that there
should be more frequent manifestations of such intentionality, and that
they should be more systematic if a structural center, as bearer and guide
of these intentions, were in operation. This claim, however, can be
countered by saying that it is the fault of the ego when intentionality is
not perceived as such or when the impression of lack of inner logic,
consistency and order is created. Were it not for the estrangement and the
recession of the ego from its matrix, the total psyche, the abstractive
(logical) mode of operation, characteristic of the abstracted ego, would
not have emerged as opposed to the symbol methods of the unconscious
and the depth zones of the psyche, and the latter would not be experienced as unsystematic. It is only the extreme specialization of the ego in its
reality-relatedness that limits both the ability accurately to recall spontaneous manifestations of the total psyche and the understanding of their
meaning and of the communications implied in them. Whenever the ego
returns or is brought back, at least to the periphery of the psyche, and
the separation is, at least partly and momentarily, eliminated, the abstractive mode of operation loses its absolute validity, and transpersonal
experiences become possible that are convincing in their unambiguity and
clarity of meaning.

Here we come back to our discussion of the different structural constellations between the ego and the non-ego, and we shall now try to relate what we have previously said (see pp. 29 *ff.*) to the different relationships between the ego and the personal and transpersonal unconscious, or
better, the depth zone of the psyche. We also refer to our genetic analysis of primary differentiation between the ego and the transpersonal non-
ego (pp. 35 *ff.*). What we have in mind here is a different aspect of the same
problem: that of the "return of the ego"—an aspect of great importance

for an understanding of the problems of structurization and reversibility, to be discussed in Chapter 5.

What we have said about the ego's organizational strength and its openness to the non-ego in general appears now as its ability to experience the intentions of the psyche, the "reality of the soul," its tendency toward structure change, and as readiness to operate as the organ of realization of the depth center, the representative of the psyche. This ability and this readiness presuppose, of course, another ability and readiness in the ego: to *see itself as transitory* and not as final and self-identical. Such a conception of the ego of itself as final, indicating, as it does, a radical abstraction (isolation) of the ego from its structural matrix, is liable to lead to a pseudo-causalistic perception of reality: whatever happens may then be perceived as belonging to an external level of existence, unrelated to the ego, intentionless. The feeling of transitoriness, on the other hand, requires *responsibility for the assimilation and systematization of change-factors* in order not to degenerate into passiveness and apathy. But without that feeling of transitoriness, this very responsibility becomes a pathogenic factor, as can be proved through an analysis of a number of individual and social disorders in our Western society.

Here we find those individuals (and groups) whose naive identification of reality with their conceptions of reality, whose belief in their ability to determine their fate alone and whose blindness even to the most obvious personality discontinuities and contradictions are often matched by their excellent reality orientation, their efficiency, and self-confidence. High intelligence may delay their defeat, but only at the cost of inner tension, psychosomatic suffering, or character neuroses and of escape into a "life from without."

That same rigid self-identification may, however, appear in individuals who are not capable of organizing their ego contents and ego functions as effectively as those in our first group. Their ego weakness may be due to structural deficiency, but it may also be the result of an autonomous irruption of the total psyche into their consciousness, that is, of an unprovoked, spontaneous emergence of unassimilable contents, whose energy charge is too much for the unprepared ego. It is obvious that this process is liable to set in motion a vicious circle of structural weakness, increased assailability by the inner non-ego (often enough, incidentally, by the environment as well), and a secondary weakening of the structure and the organizational competence of the ego. The inevitable outcome of this constellation is an inadequate reaction to the spontaneous and uncontrollable manifestations of the psyche, whether it will take the form of projective aggressiveness, of hysteric conversions, of compulsive self-constriction, or of anxiety and its secondary elaborations.

Making such an ego aware of the existence of an objective and autonomous psychic reality and of its dependence on that reality would not be sufficient to safeguard its integrity; on the contrary, it may only serve to replace rigid self-identification by a feeling of helplessness and absolute dependence. Simultaneously with producing that awareness and thereby eliminating rigidity, educational and therapeutic interventions must strengthen the ego's organizational ability. We claim that the ego must fulfill its synthesis function in two directions and on two levels simultaneously, once the contact with the unconscious and with the depth zones of the psyche has been established: as the coordinating center of consciousness and as the—active and reactive—organ of realization of these depth zones.

We should bear in mind that a combination of weak ego synthesis and openness to the total psyche is indeed a most dangerous condition. Here we may recall what we have said (see p. 32), when discussing the third ego-non-ego constellation, about the danger of being invaded and drowned by uncontrollable forces from within (in the introvert) and about the predisposition to react nonselectively to environmental stimulations (in the extravert).

Giving up one's identity, either as the result of a developmental crisis or under the impact of consistent external pressures, does not, of course, mean readiness for communication with the "reality of the soul"; on the contrary, this readiness essentially requires identity or, at least, a quest for identity. Identity should not be confused with rigid self-identification, it is essentially a dynamic concept, indicating "sameness in variety" (25). Identity proves itself only in and through change and growth. Normatively, then, identity and openness to the inner and the outer non-ego are interdependent. Where the ego is not ready for the latter, either structurally or developmentally or pathologically, true identity cannot emerge either; its place may then be taken by that pseudo-identity that appears as rigid self-identification.

It is in the light of these facts that we understand the dangers inherent in a combination of openness to the inner non-ego with ego weakness (manifesting itself equally in organizational incompetence and in rigidity, in multiplicity of self-definitions and in resistance to change). Openness is, in this combination, a negative and, at least potentially, destructive factor; it means that contents from the depth zone of the psyche are free to enter the ego area of consciousness without being channeled by the depth center, this specifically ego-related and ego-intending representative of the total psyche; it means nonintentional irruptions "from without," irruptions that bring about not a revision of ego positions or growth and enlargement of the ego structure but—almost inevitably—

destruction,* unless indiscriminate reactivity neutralizes, as it were, this danger of destruction, particularly in the extravert.†

Here again, the questions of reversibility, structurality, and structurization arise. Are the constellations that we have mentioned structural givens, in the meaning of congenital dispositions and tendencies? Or should we define them as the more or less irreversible end products of a long process of conditioning, development, structurization? But before trying to answer these basic questions of any theory of development, we shall once more try to compare the essential differences between those elements of experience that can be subsumed under the concept of "personal" and those that Jung and Neumann have called "transpersonal." It is through such a distinction that we hope to be able, in later stages of our analysis, to make comprehensible not only the differences between various units of (normal and abnormal) behavior, but also the dynamics of structurization.

5. THE CONCEPT OF TRANSPERSONALITY

Jung distinguishes between those psychic processes and phenomena that cannot be explained through reduction to personal, ontogenetic experience (including earliest events that never crossed the threshold of consciousness and later experiences, conscious or repressed) and what he calls the "archetypes of the collective unconscious" (including or being identical with the symbol-represented categories of experience). We have mentioned that the universe of these transpersonal contents forms part of the "reality of the soul," constitutes what we have called the depth zone of the total psyche. It manifests itself in the phenomena of inspiration and creativity, of telepathy and prophecy, in phantasies and dreams. But whatever these manifestations of the depth zone may be, the ego can experience them only in the form of more or less comprehensible *contents*. In what way, then, do the contents of personal experience differ from those of transpersonal experience?

The first difference could be defined as one between *degrees of essentiality*. A comparison of various phantasy or dream materials may help us understand this difference. The more the autonomous reality of the psyche is responsible for the emergence of these materials (rather than the ego in its relatedness to external experiences), the more convincing will be the transpersonal symbol character of the emerging images, the stronger will be the feeling of essentiality. Even apparently personalistic and purely empirical contents may then be experienced as symbolizing

---

* Some neurotic and psychotic processes are due to such "transpersonal irruptions" (whatever personal traumatizations may have paved the way for them, or may have followed them as reinforcing factors).

† Psychopathy (34) is a different unit of behavior: instead of "openness" to the non-ego there is use and abuse of the non-ego; instead of ego weakness there is ego-inflation.

transpersonality, as expressing structure and laws of existence. In those phantasies and dreams, on the other hand, that owe their emergence simply to a decrease of ego controls, the evidence-feeling of meaningfulness is absent; they give the impression of resulting from automatic association processes; seemingly transpersonal contents may then be found to be but personal contents in disguise, as a rule connected and connectable with the latter by some sort of external association only.

Between these two extremes can be found all those phantasies and dreams whose contents belong to the area of personal, ontogenetic experience, whereas their meaning has been determined selectively by the intentional activity of the depth center, dependent, of course, on the cooperation of the ego. Here, the depth center transforms ontogenetic contents into symbols of structural constellations and processes, using them for its compensatory tendency toward self-realization.

If this is the case, we must distinguish not only between personal and transpersonal *contents* but also between personal and transpersonal *levels of meaning*, the second being a function of the extent to which the ego is open to the depth center and its communications while, at the same time, being ready and able to function as the center of systematization and adaptation: the transpersonal level of meaning can be discovered in transpersonal as well as in personal contents, though interpretation will be needed to bring home to the ego the implied communications from the depth zone of the psyche.

No amount of interpretation, however, will be capable of convincing an ego which is *not* ready for dialogic relationships with the unconscious and the depth-zone that a transpersonal level of meaning exists at all. Not only do we then find those superficial dreams that may indeed simply be the product of automatic (quasi-mechanical) associations—and need no interpretation; under these conditions the very process of remembering the dream communication will be so partial and so distorted that neither personal nor the most evidently transpersonal contents will convey the experience of essentiality.

Sometimes, the consciousness may be invaded by undistorted dreams utterly strange and incomprehensible, so that the ego does not even feel itself upset or threatened and remembers the most meaningful contents in every detail. It seems that at least some nuclear form of contact with the depth center, some intuitive knowledge about the structural superiority of the transpersonal contents and the danger of changes in the ego system that may be brought about by them, must be present to provoke resistance, which will then manifest itself in distorted and partial reproduction of those contents. Where not even this nuclear knowledge is present, the result may be an undistorted, purely transpersonal dream or phantasy—utterly irrelevant for the ego both structurally and emotionally.

This would seem to prove the reality character of the psyche, precisely because such invasive dreams do not leave experiential vestiges, and the ego is not involved either before or after the emergence of those undistorted transpersonal images. Here we can identify a third criterion of differentiation between personal and transpersonal contents: whereas the degree of essentiality and the evidence-feeling in the experience of essentiality both belong to the level of significance, the difference between the *intensity of the effect* of emerging contents belongs to the level of reality.

Transpersonal contents are the forms in which the constituents of the psyche express structural processes, constellations, and factors. As symbol contents they become the vehicles of the ego's self-experience; as autonomous forces they become determinants of structure, factors of change, of development, of integration. Their effect transcends the level of experience, is felt—and provable—on the objective level of structure and change.

Here, a short digression into the question of the functions of the dream may be allowed in support of our concept of the "reality of the soul."

A dream may reflect an inner change which, though already having taken place, may not yet have been noticed by the ego, at least not clearly enough, and may therefore not yet have led to structurization of the changed attitude, feeling, quality, or insight. A dream may indicate that an inner change has begun to take place and that the new position requires attention, support, encouragement, training. It may emphasize that certain affect-tensions have actually outlived themselves so that new attitudes have become possible. It may correct certain patterns of evaluation, so that the dreamer may recognize how a strongly posited or negated quality or attitude in fact essentially depends on another reversely evaluated quality or attitude. A dream may also bring about (revive) a forgotten or repressed causal connection between a present ego position and past life events (and not only serve as association-eliciting material in an analysis). Also, correcting a false interpretation suggested by the analyst belongs to this group of dream functions.

This finalistic conception of the dream essentially differs not only from Freud's monistic conception of the dream as "guardian of the sleep" (45) but also from other theories in which the productions of the unconscious are being interpreted and understood as mental processes requiring cognitive associations through consciousness; we maintain that at least certain dreams and phantasies not only *reflect* actual processes of change, produced in the ego structure by the forces of the inner and the outer non-ego, but also *produce* these changes.

Our definition of dream functions can perhaps serve as a criterion for comparing the essentials of personal with those of transpersonal contents. Experience shows that both fulfill the functions we have mentioned, though their capability of determining and bringing about radical structure changes is different indeed. Personal contents lend themselves less than transpersonal elements to symbolic expression; it is pre-cisely this mode of self-manifestation through living and creative sym-bols that makes experience of the depth zones of the psyche and their contents possible and effective, contents that take on, in reality-related, personal experiences, the form of abstract, conceptual summaries of reality only. This is the reason personal elements of experience (though often enough participating, as it were, in the symbolic image manifesta-tions of the transpersonal reality of the soul) are less effective in bring-ing about structure changes. The more the self-experience of the ego relates to—and is mediated through—the *personal* contents of experi-ence, the more is the effect of change processes liable to remain restricted to personal problems only, and the more it will depend on rational elaborations. Important as such processes are for the normative expan-sion of the ego, their objective significance for the ego-containing and ego-transcending reality of the inner and the outer non-ego is obviously more restricted than that of experiencing transpersonal contents, what-ever the empirical result of the latter may be in the life contexts of the affected individual.

Through the experience of transpersonal contents the laws of human existence become accessible as possible objects of both understanding and manipulation or self-adaptation. In this way, inner changes will be ca-pable of effecting objective reality transformations. The ultimate criterion of "intensity" and "meaningfulness" of personal and transpersonal con-tents is the effect they may have on reality beyond the limits of the individual, that is, their objective power of determination. It is the autonomy of the transpersonal contents of experience, as against the dependence of personal contents on external realities and ontogenesis, that accounts for the essentiality of the former and their possible effect on structurization and on structure change. *

---

* By way of summing up what we have said in this chapter on the essential differences between the concepts of the unconscious and the depth zone of the psyche, we should ask how the ego's relationship to both and how the autonomy of each *vis-à-vis* the ego can be described. The ego feels the unconscious either as a part of its identity without becoming aware of its essentially non-ego character (*e.g.*, in reaction formations), or it feels the unconscious as an essentially foreign body without becoming aware of its ego roots (*e.g.*, in psychoses). It must learn to see it not as part and not as stranger, but as non-ego which is in communication with the conscious; it must become increasingly aware of the challenge that is implied in this communicative relationship.

The ego feels the depth zone of the psyche, if at all, as non-ego and normatively, tries to understand its communications, that is, to discover within itself the corollaries of the transpersonal contents of that non-ego, symbols recreated by the ego. The unconscious acts upon the ego through forgotten or repressed experiences, that is, from within, and tries to change it. The depth zone of the psyche, or better, the depth center, acts upon reality (containing the ego) through its transpersonal contents that have never been part of conscious experiences, though it may use personal experience for the purpose of its realization.

In fact, structurization should be defined as the process in the course of which the contents of transpersonal experience cease to be experienced as such, become increasingly personalized, and thereby turn into forces of crystallization. If this definition is accepted, then we will understand that the reversal of structurization, including structure changes, requires a prior revival of the experience of these transpersonal elements that have lost their experiential character in the very process of structurization.

This will be the subject of the following chapter.

5

Structurization and Reversibility

1. Transformation of Experience into Structure

The concept of "structurization" has several connotations, one of which is: the developmental process producing that modality of mental phenomena that we call "structuredness": in a structured whole all parts are interdependent, while the whole and its parts are interdependent as well, both statically and dynamically, in space and in time. In a structured ego each of its reaction patterns, its qualities, and its modes of operation owes its emergence to the participation of all others, with the ego serving as agent of coordination and integration; each is capable of undergoing changes without losing its identity as reaction pattern, quality, or mode of operation of that specific ego. In this sense, the process of becoming structured presupposes—and furthers—differentiation (as analyzed at the beginning of the present study).

Lack (or loss) of structure, on the other hand, manifests itself in the replacement of dialogic relationships between ego and non-ego by unilaterality of determination (either through the ego alone or through the non-ego alone); it manifests itself in the ego's weakness to coordinate its functions and the contents of consciousness, to relate them to each other and to itself, so that each is liable to become automatically processual instead of being indicative of an intentionally guiding identity force.

Two other meanings of the concept, which we intend to analyze here, are: the transformation of experience and reaction into a meaningful whole-context, called structure (constitution, pattern, identity, etc.), and the transformation of an existing structure under the influence of internal and external factors of determination.

Here we have in mind the process in the course of which experience gives up part of its energy charge to the crystallization of structures that are not extant at birth, although some dispositional basis must be present in order that transformation may take place at all. Thus, congenitally given liabilities and assets tend to become not only more pronounced through their application to ever-changing task situations, but also more typical, that is, more specialized, more one-sided. Jung's functional types are a good example: it is most unlikely, and we should not assume, that functional preferences (such as sensation, intuition, thinking, and feeling) operate as selectors of experience from birth on, though constitutional assets and liabilities certainly participate in their crystallization as type patterns. Even attitudinal types, for instance, extravert or introvert tendencies, even the predominance of one of the two life tendencies, that toward staticness or that toward expansion, even the constitutional degree of integrational powers are not finally given at birth but go through a process of structurization, that is, in this case, of growing "finalization" (which term originally indicates that a certain pattern turns into an exclusive mode of operation or that a certain quality loses its quantitative mobility).*

On the other hand, a congenitally given disposition may *not* develop into a corresponding type pattern, when organic or environmental conditions are extremely prejudicial to its dominance: early illness and loss of vitality may not allow an innate extravert tendency to develop and to establish itself structurally; an extremely stimulating environment may be obnoxious to the crystallization of innate introversion; certain forms of organic or environmental frustrations may counteract innate functional assets; etc. In all these cases we find a phenomenon similar to what Sheldon (115) calls "the dyscrasias or incompatibilities between morphology and manifest temperament." Constitutional hyperactivity, as a rule connected with certain pathogenic cerebral or glandular conditions, in a physically handicapped child, sudden changes in a child's endocrine economy in contradiction to congenitally given extraversion or introversion, environmental starvation of innate tendencies—all these and similar conditions operate *against* structurization in the second meaning of the concept.

And yet, even in this (perhaps not at all exceptional) case of inherent contradictoriness, a transformation of experience into structure does take place: though the result may be a self-contradictory, tension-charged pattern of reaction, it will be a pattern, it will operate as a specific selector of experience.

In later phases of development we speak of "becoming," of personality integration, of identity formation, when we have in mind the long process, in the course of which a variety of qualities, endowments and deficiencies, reaction patterns, tendencies and preferences become increasingly interrelated and ego-related, that is, come to form a whole, a structure. This structure, though capable of growth or of shrinkage, of changes in emphasis or in intensity, will remain self-identical (and therefore identifiable). The forces and the elements that go into its building

* It would, of course, be a hopeless endeavor later to isolate from each other congenitally given nuclear elements of constitutional tendencies, preferences, assets, and liabilities, on the one hand, and modifications or reinforcements that may have taken place during the phases of plasticity in infancy and childhood, on the other hand.

are no longer those single and repeated experiences and reactions whose transformation into fixed qualities, patterns and tendencies is the primary stage of structurization, but are the results of those primary structurizations. And just as experience gives up part of its energy to the structure it helps build, so the results give up part of their energy in the process of identity formation.

This transfer of energy, incidentally, may explain the fact that only an existing structure has the dynamic power to meaningfully determine behavior and development, that is, also, to structurize. Structurization is not a process of coagulation or of consolidation, of freezing, as it were; it is not comparable to mechanical association based on contiguity and coherence; in brief, it is not a process of conditioning.

Murphy (95) compares conditioning with what he calls, following Janet, "canalization." The latter term designates a process leading to the formation of preferences and patterns. What is canalized, he claims, cannot be extinguished like the results of a process of conditioning; it is permanent, even though it may be overlaid by something more powerful. The process implies the consolidation of responses into a structural pattern. It is not a sequence of repeated stimulations, each reinforcing the results of the preceding ones, but is, to use Allport's expression (6), "progressive" and requires ego involvement; or, as we would prefer to say, it requires active selection, creation, and self-transcendence.

These, however, are characteristics of structurization. It presupposes the existence of an agent of selection, of coordination, of synthesis, operating in a reality that aims at enlargement and not only at systematization (although the latter is the existential precondition of the former); it presupposes a readiness, on the part of the agent of synthesis, to be imprinted, impressed, directed, changed by this reality (within and without), that is, to transcend itself, in the very acts of structurization. We use the concept dynamically, as indicating an activity rather than a process (although it is unavoidable to describe structurization as a process), whereas Murphy's concept of canalization is indeed a processual one, and its results are conceived of as static.

This basically nondynamic conception is reflected, for instance, in the fact that Murphy analyzes canalization and the formation of individual patterns, intrinsically connected with it, without mentioning the phenomenon of repression. And yet, every process of canalization implies the exclusion from consciousness (by way of suppression or repression) of all those negative evaluations, all those unlived tendencies and qualities, all those neglected feelings that are considered negative, remain unlived, must be neglected in order to make the canalization possible, and then form what Jung calls the "personal unconscious." In other words: every patternization, every preference formation, is accompanied by an opposite canalization, which, however, does not, as a rule, result in the emergence of a structured pattern but remains a dynamic tension factor operating from the unconscious against self-identification with the established pattern.

We shall see later that this process supplies one of the conditions of structure change. Here, we are concerned with the opposite aspect of repression, that is, of *experience sinking into the unconscious. We maintain that this seemingly negative process is one of the preconditions of structurization:* Whatever contents of personal experience, of imprint and reaction, remain in our consciousness can become part of a determining structure only when some of the energy vested in the process of canalization is set free for the activity of structurization. Without this partial liberation of energy such processes as getting used to a certain mode of behavior or even the growth of consciousness may become explicable, but not the transformation of experience into structure.

This energetic explanation is almost identical with the psychoanalytic principle of the shifting or transfer of libido cathexis. We may be able thus to account for the fact that the ego system of consciousness is constantly exposed to attack and is therefore forced into using defenses, which, in due course of time, become consolidated into structural patterns, to use Murphy's above-quoted expression. But it does not account for the fact that in the very process of structurization principles of organization participate which do not originate in the area of personal— remembered or repressed—experience.

Here we recall what we have said in the preceding chapter about the relationship between the personal and the transpersonal source of the inner non-ego. *We claim that the process of experiences sinking into the unconscious (das Unbewusst-werden) is a necessary precondition of structurization, because it activates the depth center of the psyche with its categories of experience, those principles of selection and organization in any act of structurization* (including the very act of "experience being made").

But we must add that this "sinking into the unconscious" leads to structurization (in the meaning of the concept here under consideration) only, if the *depth-center of the psyche is allowed by the ego nucleus and, later, the ego, to select and to determine selectively and intentionally what contents of experience shall become structure.* Hence, structurization, in the second meaning of the term, depends on the existence of a more or less normative constellation between ego and non-ego. *In other words: only to the extent that there is polarity between the constituent areas and agents of reality, can structurization take place;* disturbance of polarity, due either to a structural deficiency or to developmental deviations inevitably restricts structurization, the results being disorder and insufficiencies in the processes of internalization, of identity formation, of determination from within. The fact that the causal order implied in this statement can also be reversed (structurization being responsible for growing polarization), far from contradicting it, only comes to support its validity: every result of a causal process becomes an additional cause; this, as we shall try to show in Chapter 6, is one of the basic principles in the interpretation of human development and behavior.

Thus, we interpret structurization not as a process in the course of which experience gradually consolidates (or coagulates) into a pattern, but as the result of a polar (dialogic) relationship between two agents of change and synthesis, between what we have called the depth center and the ego; that is, as the result of an organizational activity. If so, we understand that it requires not only a normative relationship between ego and non-ego, but also one between organizational ability and readiness for change, between the two basic life tendencies. Structurization, far from being an expression of the life tendency toward staticness, reflects the normative interrelatedness of the latter and that toward expansion; it forms not only the basis of selection (*via* pattern formation) but also of integration (*via* identity formation). Without this normative interrelatedness of the two life tendencies, there can be no true structurization, and its place is taken either by diffuse reactivity or by petrification, by lifeless rigidity, as in processes of habit- and pattern-formation, which owe their change-resistance to associative adhesion rather than to their rootedness in, or their connectedness with, a personal identity. This is why we may call habits and patterns collective rather than individual, their individual differences being nonessential.

They may, however, become parts of the identity, by way of active confrontation with the ego, and as parts of an inner non-ego with which the ego enters into dialogic relationships (see p. 38). In this way, habits and patterns of long standing may become interrelated, just as value and concepts, knowledge, attitudes and qualities, acquired through identification with adults, may become internalized. But would it be correct to call this process structurization? Are those possible objects of internalization by themselves structures (and not only *parts* of our personality structure which grows and crystallizes through their internalization)?

If we were concerned with the philosophical aspect of the problem, at least of values and concepts, it would make sense to speak of, and to analyze, their structure and their universal, transindividual validity. But since we speak here of their intrapsychic equivalents and representations, that is, of their functions as contents of consciousness (along with attitudes and qualities) it would seem to be more adequate to apply the term structurization not to the process during which habits and patterns (or, for that matter, concepts and values) become objects of inner self-confrontation and of polar relationships, but rather to the very process of identity formation and their causative role in the process.

We have mentioned, at the beginning of this chapter, the concept of structuredness, meaning a modality of mental phenomena, their inter-relatedness and "whole-relatedness." In this sense a habit or a pattern, a quality or an attitude, a value or a concept can be called structured, to the extent that it becomes connected with the individual's identity, that is, with the ego system, whereby it becomes personally tinged without losing its transpersonal meaning.

Here, a short digression may be permitted to explain the concept of identity.

2. Identity and Identification

Erikson, the psychologist of identity *par excellence*, defines it as same-ness in change, as "the accrued confidence that one's ability to maintain inner sameness and continuity . . . is matched by the sameness and con-tinuity of one's meaning for others" (24). It develops out of a gradual in-tegration of all identifications, in all stages of development. Identity, thus defined, is almost synonymous with personality structure, though it has a more dynamic and a more functional connotation, depending on whether we emphasize sameness, the *feeling* of sameness, the recognizable Gestalt, or the ego activity constantly required for the formation and maintenance of inner unity.

We have already said that identity presupposes differentiation and polarization between ego and non-ego, as a basis for the recognition of individuality and otherness. It is obvious, then, that the term should not be used to define or circumscribe that primary unity stage preceding polarization: Identity can emerge only after that unity stage has come to an end. (Needless to add, we also reject the interpretation of later identity disorders as regressions to primary nondifferentiation).

Even less acceptable seems to us the use of the term "primary identifica-tion," in which Freud sees the basis for the gradual emergence of ego and superego (45). For, identification always implies an at least partial loss of identity, a more or less temporary replacement of one's own identity by that of the aim and object of identification. ("Primary identification" therefore is a *contradictio in adjecto,* since identification by definition cannot be "primary.")

Identification is more than imitation (although the latter is one of the indispensable techniques of the former). Imitation allows the ego to remain conscious of its being different from the object of imitation. One may be tempted to say that imitation is to identification what sup-pression is to repression. Identification is never imaginable on a purely conscious level. Although at least the ideological variety may give this impression, a closer and deeper analysis easily reveals that the *conscious* part of the identification process often rooted in rational imitation only of certain concrete of symbolic manifestations—is not sufficient to bring about genuine identification, but will at best produce what might be called *identity extensions* (the ego being responsible for selecting the objects of identification).

We repeat: identification presupposes identity, to be given up partly in the very act of identification, in order to be re-found, or better, reconstructed, afterward, that is, in the process of gradual assimilation of new contents. If so, we cannot accept Erikson's thesis according to which identity owes its emergence to a gradual integration of all identifications, in all stages of development, although it certainly grows in functional applicability and intensity through each identification (irrespective of the latter's objective value). How, then, does identity emerge?

We suggest the following answer: Sameness is one of the categories of experience; it is present and operates in the life of every individual from the start, independently of environmental and organic stimulations and reactions; in fact, it participates in constituting the experience character of those stimulations and reactions. Sameness is the categorial expression of the life tendency toward staticness. Where the latter is structurally weak (as in psychopathy), sameness will be slow to emerge and identity will remain dependent on the constant intake of every thing non-ego. When the life tendency toward staticness is overstrong (as for instance in infantile autism), sameness will be experienced to the exclusion of otherness, differentiation will be delayed or even impeded, and, as a result, identity will be dependent on the constant suppression of otherness (34). It would therefore seem correct to say that *identity owes its emergence to the category of sameness, which is represented, in the life space of the infant, by the basic experience of the "mother as part."* Identity grows and crystallizes through constant exposure to otherness (non-ego) emerging from the basic experience of the "absent mother," and through ever-repeated acts of identification with that non-ego.

3. NEGATIVE STRUCTURIZATION

We now return to the main subject of our analysis, the concept of structurization. We have so far discussed the first and the second of its connotations: the meaning of structuredness and the transformation of experience into structure. It now remains to analyze the concept in its third connotation, that of radical changes taking place in an existing structure—be that a congenitally given disposition or tendency, be it a reaction pattern which may have emerged and crystallized under the influence of early experience.

How do we explain those processes of structure change that take place at the beginning of life, in reaction to environmental frustrations or stimulations, long before we can speak of the ego as an "agent of selection" (see p. 63)? What happens to the institutionalized child in the first months of his life, or what happens to the infant born with certain structural predispositions for psychopathic reactions which may crystallize into an irreversible constitution in reaction to negative experiences with the mother, or what happens through early experiences to the psychosomatic diatheses of any infant? Should we not regard these changes as proof that structurization does not depend on the selective activity of an ego or, at least, an ego nucleus (in polar relationship to a depth center of transpersonal determination)? Or must we exclude all these (and other) transformation processes from a discussion of structurization?

When one of the two life tendencies is so much stronger than the other that they cease to be interrelated and dependent on each other, we say that the integrative powers of the growing ego nucleus are defective, either congenitally (structurally) or following a severe, usually organic, traumatization at the time of, or shortly after, birth (cf. p. 64).

When the tendency toward staticness is not strong enough (or is, at any rate, definitely weaker than the opposite tendency), ego feeling, as just mentioned (p. 66), is liable to depend on the constant incorporation of everything non-ego. The result will be psychopathic inflation, if certain forms of earliest frustration act upon a child whose ability to experience anxiety is structurally weak (cf. 34). Here we see a psychopathic constitution (which for all practical purposes will remain irreversible) emerging in the first years of life. And yet, it would seem open to question whether this should be called a process of structurization. True enough, the psychopath does not depend on the quality of his environment, after his earliest traumatic experience with a rejecting, an indolent, a "disappearing," an overindulgent mother has determined his capacity for anxiety and his mode of dealing with the non-ego. Moreover, the psychopathic pattern of behavior is no longer connected causally or otherwise with those earliest frustrations at the hands of an incompetent mother. Should we not, then, see in this independence a sign of experience being transformed into structure, that is, of structurization?

But structurization is not identical, as we have already pointed out, with coagulation, consolidation, or freezing, with the processes of what Murphy (95) calls "canalization" (see p. 62). A certain mode of operation, a certain pattern of behavior, emerges in reaction to, or in protection against, negative experiences, which without such protective pattern would be liable to destroy the organism, particularly at an early age when the ego is not yet fully available as agent of screening and coordination. But this fact alone does not prove structurization. On the contrary: the very prevalence of the life tendency toward expansion—one of the essential characteristics of the case here under discussion—or, correspondingly, the very weakness of the tendency toward staticness, delays or even prevents processes of genuine structurization, including, paradoxically, that of ego formation. An ego that depends for its existence on constant incorporation of the non-ego is not and never can become a structure; it is, as it were, permanently in flux (a pattern without identity).

We have devoted another study to an analysis of the essential elements of psychopathy (34). We have discussed there the meaning of ego inflation and of absence of anxiety and have tried to show that only an ego that has not gone through a process of structurization can be inflated. Here, where we are not concerned with the pathological aspects of the problem, we shall limit ourselves to pointing out the essential difference that exists between structurization and those processes of early consolidation of (irreversible) patterns of behavior, of which noncongenital psychopathy is one of the most extreme examples. What can we learn from this example for the understanding of the essence of structurization?

It depends, as we have said above (p. 64), on a polar relationship between ego and non-ego, between an independent agent of selection and organization, on the one hand, and an equally independent source of stimulation and partner of relatedness, on the other; it depends on the preservation of the content-character of experiences that have been transformed into structure. We shall return to this point when discussing the question of reversibility of structurizations and structure changes. When those contents (belonging to the external *and* the internal non-ego, the environment *and* the "reality of the soul") cease to be reachable, can no longer be brought back to consciousness, even with the aid of depth analysis, irreversibility, far from indicating structurization, becomes symptomatic of lifelessness. Again in other words: *structurization is there to help growth;* in its negative manifestations, such as the early consolidation of a psychopathic constitution, it *prevents* growth (though growth may still take place, upon the initiative, as it were, of the constitutional pattern).

Let us now briefly consider the opposite constellation, that of a prevalence of the life tendency toward staticness, though again not for the purposes of a detailed analysis of the relevant pathologies but only with a view to clarifying the concept of structurization.

Staticness-predominance finds its expression in constitutional inability to separate, and keep alive separation, between subject and object, and between ego and non-ego, leading to a variety of pathologies, of which psychotic elimination of the boundaries between ego and non-ego (26) is only the most dramatic case. Even more relevant for our present discussion are those many examples of finalization that clinical observation and analysis offer us: processes which make, for instance, psychosomatic dispositions and symptom manifestations into an almost irreversible system of somatic behavior, which account for the final transformation of neurotic defenses into character systems, which help childhood neuroses grow into adult systems, etc. All these developments could be understood as cases of "functional autonomy," in Allport's meaning of the term (6): the results of a developmental process losing connection with their experiential roots, becoming aims in themselves, determining the individual's future behavior (which, incidentally, explains why any purely reductive method of therapy, aimed at discovering and gaining conscious control over the experiential roots, is bound to fail).*

We claim that these are, again, cases which, far from proving structurization, should be classified as examples of perverted structurization, as it were. To the extent that deficiencies of the psychosomatic, the character-neurotic, or the neurotic variety become final, irreversible, systematized, they prove a structural prevalence of the tendency toward staticness. An approximate equivalence of the two life tendencies, on the other hand, makes such finalization (systematization) problematic, if not impossible, since it will always be counteracted by an opposite tendency, that toward change, or, at least, by a tendency to experiment with other, even with opposite, attitudes and behavior.

The prevalence of staticness, as it manifests itself in the finalization of pathologies, contradicts rather than explains structurization; it accounts for the processual character of personality development around the neurotic syndrome, for its ever-growing functional autonomy. The latter comes to replace the normative structural relationship between a traumatized ego and a specifically traumatizing environment by a pseudo-relationship between the ego as coordinator of reactions and defenses and those reactions and defenses as integral parts of its system. It comes to interrupt the communicative contact not only between the ego and the outer non-ego, but also between the ego and the inner non-ego, the personal and transpersonal unconscious; which, again, explains the rigidity and lifelessness of the finalized neurotic.

To avoid a misunderstanding: the prevalence of staticness as condition of finalization must not always be a structural tendency, present from the start; it may also be the result of a circular process of canalization, in the course of which the tendency toward staticness grows stronger;

---

* Changes from early observable deficiencies into later normalcy occur as well; but it is understandable why they are being overlooked, as a rule: the early deficiencies are likely to be interpreted as symptoms of immaturity only, that is, as developmental pre-stages of normalcy. And yet, there is no reason whatsoever for reserving the concept of structure change to the above mentioned negative instances only.

certain patterns of reaction and behavior, through their canalization, restrict and slowly eliminate the opposite life tendency, that toward expansion—thereby making finalization of psychosomatic, character-neurotic, and neurotic symptoms easier and more effective. (Whether and to what extent a structural predisposition must be there to favor such secondary restrictions of the life tendency toward expansion is a question that cannot yet be answered empirically.) It may be that the well known difference between neurotic and character-neurotic syndromes with regard to their therapeutic accessibility (the latter being as a rule much more rigid than the former) should be interpreted as a difference between degrees of structurality in the prevalence of staticness.

Another case of negative structurization is that of the decrease of physical and mental abilities in a child growing up in an institution or under the impact of extreme poverty and educational neglect. Here, it is the element of continuity in an impersonal mode of living that is causally responsible for the deterioration processes; mental abilities, the readiness and willingness to establish meaningful contacts with the environment, and organic vitality are bound to sink to a lower than congenital level of functioning, when they are not being fed and supported by more or less constant maternal contacts (cf. Chapter 2). This decrease, which may become irreversible to the extent that it starts early and is not being compensated by strong factors of integration, is adduced as an example of (negative) structurization because the process affects the total personality of the child and not only this or that function.

And yet, what is going on here is not adequately described as a process of structurization, of experience being transformed into structure and structural determination. The functional self-restriction resulting from the atmosphere of impersonality in an infant's home or a hospital manifests itself as a nonstructured personality, as absence of integration rather than as avoidance of initiative. There is still less intentionality in the emergence of the devitalized personality than in that of the character-neurotic personality, where defensive avoidance and reaction formation account, at least at the beginning, for the emergence of the behavior patterns, although their finalization is again processual rather than intentional (p. 69). The irreversibility of the damage caused to congenitally given abilities by the impersonal atmosphere of early institutional care should not make us interpet the process as structurization.

It is easier to avoid this interpretation in the case of the child who grows up under the impact of extreme poverty and educational neglect, that is, under the impact of a cultural variety of externalization.* Shrinkage of potentially normal or even above normal intellectual and relational abilities is a much slower process here, because the multitude of

* This will be analyzed in a subsequent volume.

environmental figures in the early and later life of the child growing up under conditions of externalization compensates, to some extent at least, for their *impersonality*. Externalization, we shall see, contains many elements of conditioning, among them that of changeability (through reconditioning or through extinction); hence, the slower pace of finalization. But the damage caused to intellectual and relational abilities by consistent externalization, not checked by educational intervention, becomes, nevertheless, for all practical purposes, irreversible after adolescence.

It should be by now be obvious why this process is, again, not one of structurization. Still less than the developmental conditions so far mentioned does the loss of potentials under the impact of social and educational deprivation reflect a process of functions becoming increasingly interrelated and ego-related (see our definition of identity formation, p. 61). On the contrary: absence of Gestalt character, of interrelatedness, and ego-relatedness, characterizes the externalized personality and accounts for the devitalization and the loss of functions. Neither would it be correct here to speak of "experience sinking into the unconscious," one of the dynamic preconditions of structurization (p. 62) or of ego selection and polarity (p. 63). Personality shrinkage in externalization excludes identity formation (pp. 65 *f.*).

4. Reversibility of Structure Changes

Irreversibility by itself is not a sufficient criterion of structurization. On the one hand, nonstructurized results of habit formation and even of conditioning may become irreversible; on the other hand, the results of structurization, at least in the first meaning of the concept (a process producing the modality of structuredness) are reversible. Moreover, the experiential roots of structure, the personal or transpersonal contents of experience, even after having been transformed into structure, remain reachable (though probably not in every stage of development and not in their entirety and certainly not through the conventional means of analysis only); inasmuch as they *are* being reached by the ego, their structurized counterparts can at least be modified by educational or therapeutic interventions, or spontaneously. And the results of structurization in its third connotation (change of structurally given qualities and tendencies), brought about by environmental stimulations and frustrations, are often irreversible although the process of change had not been one of genuine structurization, as we have tried to show in the foregoing paragraph.

The question of reversibility is of particular theoretical and practical importance when we think of the last-mentioned group of structure changes, the one that includes reactive character formations, the finalization of psychosomatic patterns or neuroses, psychoses, and psychopathic states. To what extent and under what conditions can education, can therapy, can the life process itself reverse what environmental factors, in configuration with certain constitutional dispositions, have done to the congenitally given structure of the individual? (We shall concentrate our discussion at this stage on negative changes only.)

The first law of reversibility says that when structure changes emerge in the earliest stages of development, in the first six to twelve months of life, they are much less amenable to change than when they emerge later. Changes that take place in the pre-ego phase grow, as it were, into the emerging ego structure, so much so, in fact, that it will be almost impossible later to distinguish between congenital dispositions and subsequent changes. (The finalization of the congenital constitution through first-year reinforcements and modifications,* the—hypothesized—crystallization of the noncongenital forms of psychopathy (34), the devitalization brought about by earliest institutional care are some examples.)

The second law, which supplements the first, says that *the chances of reversal are better when later traumatization has not yet operated long enough to produce a pattern of behavior and a system of reactions and attitudes that are in themselves sources of direct or indirect, normal or abnormal, satisfaction:* If, and to the extent that, the child is allowed to become addicted, as it were, to his overcompensations or defenses, to his aggressiveness or fearfulness, to his compulsions or apathy, to his ineffectiveness—if, and to the extent that, the child comes to derive from them a secondary sense of security and identity—the chances of reversal decrease.

In other words: the later in the child's development traumatization starts, the longer is the period required for the production of irreversible structure changes, and the better are, as a rule, the chances of reversal. This is only another way of saying that later traumatizations, to the extent that they are not based on earlier ones, do not produce structure changes but operate as factors of negative conditioning only, whose effects can be extinguished, counteracted, eliminated by way of reconditioning.

One of the best examples for this case is the gradual intellectual impoverishment resulting from lack of educational stimulation, activation, and guidance; under such conditions, an originally normal intelligence and mental initiative may begin to shrink at school age only, and yet reach a hopelessly low level of functioning until the age of puberty or adolescence; it may then become increasingly difficult to rescue the

---

* The transition from modification to radical change cannot be as clearly defined as one would wish to be able to do for the sake of conceptual exactitude and clinical investigation.

drowning intellect, particularly when the individual ceases to be an object of planned and systematic attempts at reconditioning or rehabilitation. The stimulus-monotony of an average adult environment then completes what inadequate schooling has begun, and the result is an irrevocable, irreversible damage.

Here, however, a *third law of reversibility* should be mentioned: reversibility depends not only on the starting age of traumatization and not only on the length of the period during which damaging factors are allowed to affect the individual, it also depends on *the intensity, that is, the radicality of these factors and the exclusiveness of their operation.* Intensity is, of course, not objectively measurable, it is determined by subjective factors, such as the individual level of frustration-bearance and of love-needs, thresholds, integrational abilities, the presence or absence of compensatory factors in the environment, etc.; in fact, so much so that the objective degree of radicality becomes almost unrecognizable. This factor is so complex that it would seem advisable to break it down into a number of subfactors of determination, lending themselves to the formulation of a series of additional laws.

Thus, *a fourth law* can be formulated: *reversal of structure change presupposes a number of environmental conditions.* The reversal must be expected by the environment to such an extent that the individual considers it an achievement worth the effort. The environment must provide the instruments of change of which the individual can then avail himself. The environment must be prepared to take a moratory attitude toward the changing individual and his achievements, must be ready to accept partiality and graduality of reversal as natural and as necessary. Where such an attitude is absent, where the environment is intolerant and absolutistic or indolent, or where the treatment tools that may be required to bring about changes are not being provided by the environment, changes tend to be much less reversible even in such cases in which the individual may be prepared for reversal. In other words, a dynamic, generally change-oriented environment is conducive to reversal of structure changes, and a static, generally *fatum*-oriented environment is prejudicial to such reversal. (We are not speaking here of the rare cases of spontaneous reversal or of maturational processes going on in the second half of life, and which are discussed on pp. 182 *ff.*)

The following laws refer to the *inner* conditions of reversibility.

The *fifth law* says that *reversibility depends on the cooperation from within of specific abilities making possible achievement and integration in certain fields of functioning that are not directly affected by the traumatization.* This is sometimes formulated as *the law of compensation.* But what we have in mind here is not so much the role of certain assets as counterweights to the liabilities of structure damage, as it is their

restitutional function: the very fact that certain areas of the total personality are not, or not yet, affected by the structure-changing (or func-
tion-changing) traumatization, helps to reverse the damage caused by the
latter once appropriate therapeutic, educational or otherwise rehabilita-
tional actions are undertaken.

The *sixth law*, too, refers to an inner condition of reversal: *The ego
must be structurally open to the non-ego.* The life tendency toward
staticness must not be in excess, since an overdose of staticness makes it
impossible for the ego to feel itself as object of the non-ego,* hence, also,
to feel itself potentially different from any of its given conditions and
manifestations. "Being open" and "being an object" mean, in the context
of the problem of reversibility discussed here, two qualities: man's ability
to distantiate himself from his conditions and his readiness to react to
communications coming to him from the outer and the inner non-ego,
the environment and the unconscious. Without such dialogic relationships between the ego and the non-ego, reversal of structure damages
becomes impossible.

When the human environment, for instance, loses its object character in processes of projective distortion, character formations based on
such distortions are no longer amenable to correction, because communication channels between the ego and the world have been blocked.
Therapy can actually be defined as the attempt to reopen those channels,
to reestablish dialogic relationships (37). The same condition can be
formulated differently by saying that when the unconscious ceases to act
as an autonomous (objective) force of compensation, to which the ego
reacts and responds adequately, changes brought about by the very
process and action of excluding (representing) change-contrary tendencies,
become irreversible.

Here, the most important element of reversibility should be mentioned.
When the contents of personal and of transpersonal experience have lost
their content-character in the process of structure change, when they
have ceased to be reachable even though depth analysis, the results of
this structure change are irreversible (p. 68). Hence, a *seventh law of reversibility* says that *reversibility depends on the extent to which the ego
succeeds (spontaneously or with the help of therapy) in discovering again
the contents of past experience, in bringing into consciousness, into the*

---

* Unlike the psychopath who experiences himself as the *subject* only of everything
non-ego (to be incorporated) and therefore never feels challenged to change from within.
But the extreme irreversibility of his condition (which often, though in our opinion not
rightly so, serves as the essential element of defining psychopathy) is certainly not the result of an overdose of staticness; on the contrary, an excessive tendency toward expansion no less than excessive staticness prevents reversal of structure change, the latter because the ego tends to identify too much with the state in which it finds itself at any
given moment, the former because it prevents objective evaluation (of both the ego and
the non-ego).

field of the ego, what has sunk into the unconscious (by way of repression), as well as on the spontaneous manifestations of the depth zones of the psyche.

Here we come back to what we have said above on this subject: to the extent that changes in the ego system can be defined as *structural* transformation, they indicate that the ego has become the aim and the object of the depth center rather than of the external non-ego. Structural transformation, we stated, "presupposes the intentional intervention of a reality experienced, in the very moment of its intervention, as transcendent ... though at the same time demanding from the ego readiness to cooperate in the ... realization of its intentions." Through this readiness, we repeat, the ego remains capable of *feeling* itself as intending rather than as intended, which fact can serve as a criterion of differentiation between ego-transcending transformation and ego-inherent developmental changes (p. 45). Not only repression but also the reverse process, that of reintegrating repressed contents in the ego system, goes on within that ego-system and does not indicate the activity of an ego-transcending agent of intention (p. 47). Genuine structure change, on the other hand, including also its reversal, proves the tendency of the total psyche to realize itself ever more completely, the ego being the reality organ of the total psyche and, at the same time, its aim and object (p. 48).

We have defined "knowing" as a function of the depth center by saying that its object is the ego structure in its changeability, and that it manifests itself in the very process of interference and change (p. 50). The function of the depth center was defined as system *change*, not as system *formation* (p. 51); that of the ego as the coordinating center of consciousness and as the—active and reactive—organ of realization of those depth zones (p. 54). Transpersonality was defined as the mode of expressing structural processes through the archetypal images of the psyche. As symbols, they become the vehicles of the ego's self-expression; as autonomous forces they become determinants of structure, factors of change, of development, of integration (p. 57). It is the autonomy of the transpersonal contents of experience, as against the dependence of personal contents on external realities and ontogenesis that accounts for the essentiality of the former and their possible effect on structurization and structure change (p. 58). In the process of structurization (we concluded our analysis), the contents of transpersonal experience cease to be experienced as such, become increasingly personalized, and thereby turn into forces of systematization. If so, the reversal of structurization, including structure change, requires a prior revival of the experiences of those transpersonal elements that have lost their experiential character in the very process of structurization (p. 59).

The question, then, arises, how a structurally damaged ego can be thought of taking the initiative for establishing that normative contact with the inner non-ego, the interruption of which is essentially responsible for the loss of intellectual or relational potentials, for the process of psychosomatic, neurotic, or character-neurotic pattern formation or even for the crystallization of psychotic or psychopathic conditions, that is, for all those processes in which we see examples of pseudo-structurization.* Is it not a *petitio principii* to say that the "damaged" ego must take responsibility for its own rehabilitation? Is not an ego that is capable of taking that responsibility already rehabilitated? Reversibility of structure changes, we claim, depends on the ego's self-direction to the contents of the personal and—particularly—the transpersonal experience, which becomes capable of being experienced in and through this very act of the ego's self-direction. Is not the latter a symptom rather than a condition of reversal?

Therapeutic experience proves that there are two phases in the act and process of reversal, a phase of conscious activity and a phase of receptivity *vis-à-vis* the autonomy of the psyche. The first phase does not lead automatically and necessarily to the second, as can be proved by those many cases in which the ego's self-direction to the experiential contents of the non-ego produces no more than purely intellectual manipulations that have no impact whatsoever on structure change.

What, then, determines whether or not the second phase will follow upon the first one? One of the decisive factors (though one that can not be controlled) is the support given by the environment to the ego, in its endeavor to understand the hidden meaning of the contents of personal and transpersonal experience. Although certain personality factors such as high intelligence or intuition will undoubtedly make the individual less dependent on that environmental support, guidance will never be entirely dispensable, and certainly not when it comes to reducing structure to the definable contents of transpersonal experience that may have gone into it.

There is yet another environmental condition for that active self-direction to the "reality of the soul" to lead to the second, the receptivity phase of the reversal process: the environment must make possible compensatory experiences in support of a general feeling (an atmosphere) of nonfinality, which, in turn, makes the individual ready for accepting occurrence as a basic condition of life.

We maintain that, in order to bring about reversal of negative structurizations, it is not sufficient to make possible reexperience of the traumatic

---

* Genuine structurization presupposes, as we have said, communication between the ego and the non-ego, normative interrelatedness between the two life tendencies, and organizational strength of the ego. None of these conditions is present in the above mentioned cases of negative structurization. This is why we use the term "pseudo-structurization."

personal past under "more favorable and protective" conditions (as psychoanalysts claim); modifications and attitude changes may be brought about in this way, but not radical structure changes or reversals; the latter require experiencing the reality of those transpersonal categories that had made experience (and structurization) possible in the first instance.

To give only one example: to the extent that the loss of congenitally given intellectual and relational abilities is due to earliest maternal deprivation, reversal of the damage thus caused will, if at all, be possible only through the experience of the maternal principle (and not through remembering the personal mother's defects and the own affective reactions to them). This, however, is a transpersonal experience which has many symbolic representations through which its autonomous *dynamis* channels itself into the "reality of the soul," into structurization and reversal.

But we should beware of treating the problem of reversibility, as if it were identical with that of making the ego receptive of the transpersonal contents of experience. No less decisive in the process of structure change is the degree of the organizational strength of the ego. Here *an eighth law of reversibility* may be formulated as follows: *Reversal of structural changes requires readiness on the part of the ego to recognize not only the absolute superiority of the depth zone, but also the fact that it is supposed to integrate into the system of its contents and functions those intentional and autonomous manifestations of the depth zone on which it depends.* To the extent that the ego has confidence in the compensatory functions of what we have suggested should be called the depth center, and is at the same time ready to act as its "realizer," to that extent only will it be strong enough to fulfill its functions of systematization in the reversal process.

It is unavoidable that even an organizationally strong ego will lose part of its strength in the very process of becoming receptive of the psyche (the second phase in preparation of the reversal of structure changes). On the other hand, this process or, for that matter, receptivity as such, and openness to the depth zone of the psyche are positive and normative only to the extent that they not only do not restrict the ego's organizational and integrational abilities but, on the contrary, help to restitute and strengthen them. It is relatively easy for an ego that resists communication with the inner non-ego to develop its organizational strength through the very mobilization of its energy and its functions in the defense of its positions and in the rejection of change. It is much more difficult for a normally functioning ego to preserve or even to regain its organizational abilities once it has opened up to the depth zone of the psyche, to the personal and the transpersonal unconscious. How, then, should we ex-

plain the return of the ego to that level of systematization that is necessary to make receptivity relevant for reversal processes?

We maintain that by experiencing the content character of structural
determinants, their non-ego character is, at least partly, being eliminated,
and that thereby the ego's feeling of autonomy (of relative independence)
is being strengthened. The experience of content provokes and necessitates evaluation, taking a stand, integration (as against passive subordination in reaction to the experience of the non-ego as determinant only).

In order to understand why restoration of organizational strength to the
ego in reversal processes implies reviving the content aspect of experience, we must take into account yet another factor, that of the essential
difference between personal and transpersonal experiences. In the direct
as well as in the remembered experience of personal contents these contents are *objects* of the ego as the coordinating center of consciousness,
but not *agents*. The transpersonal contents of experience, on the other
hand, appear not only as intentionally related to the ego in its actuality
but are also impregnated, as it were, with the dynamic character of the
depth center. As constituents of experience they have structure-changing
power (see p. 51); this is why, as contents of experience, they are capable of
strengthening the experiencing ego in its organizational functions.

Our first two laws of reversibility referred to certain developmental
conditions (the starting age of structure change and the length of the
period of traumatization and frustration), whereas all the others dealt
with structural and environmental conditions. We now return to the
role of developmental determinants. *The ninth* and *tenth laws* say that
reversibility depends on the results of structure change produced and
that the *ways and means of reversal depend on the developmental phase
through which the individual passes when reversal is being attempted.*

It is obvious that certain structure changes are more difficult to reverse
than others, not because they are more radical but by reason of their
inherent ego-syntonicity. Thus, structure changes that essentially, almost
by definition, are characterized by inner inconsistency and tension, such as
psychosomatic diseases, neuroses, and certain forms of character disorders
have better chances of reversal than psychoses, psychopathies, intellectual
devitalization, and character-neurotic tendencies toward (self-restrictive)
systematization. This is not the place to discuss these differences in detail.
We shall come back to a differential phenomenology of deviations in a
later volume where the question of reeducation and therapy will also be
raised. Only then shall we be able fully to understand the meaning of our
ninth law of reversibility.

Similarly, we cannot here discuss the meaning of the tenth law; to
understand it requires an analysis of the essentials of each phase of development, which we shall attempt in the Chapter 8. We shall then see

that in some phases reversal of preceding structure changes (or at least of certain varieties) is almost contraindicated, whereas others are what might be called "reversal prone." Moreover, whatever process of reversal takes place will be determined in part by the phase-specific elements of the structure change to be reversed.

5. SPONTANEOUS CHANGE, MATURATIONAL CHANGE, THERAPY

One of the most intriguing phenomena in an analysis of reversibility is that of *sudden and radical personality changes*. James (71) has included them in his discussion of religious experience under the heading of "conversion," and conversion indeed represents one of the most dramatic cases of personality change (certainly the one to which most "confessional" literature refers). But the development of modern depth psychology has made it difficult for us to accept the records quoted by James without discerning between clearly pathological distortions (of the hysterical, the schizophrenic, or the psychopathic variety) and genuine structure change.

The criterion of genuineness is, here, the emergence of a new identity as convincing and as structured as the former ("structured," as we have said above (p. 60), means having Gestalt character). But it is precisely this genuine change, this inner revolution giving birth to a new man, that makes the phenomenon so intriguing, whereas cases of "false," that is, of imaginary, loudly demonstrated, and unconvincing change—paradoxically—remain genetically explicable from within the individual's biography: such psychodynamic concepts as displacement, reaction formation, projection, are appropriate tools of interpreting them as expressions of hysteria, character-neurosis, or psychosis (not to speak of the psychopath who is capable of playing different roles with ever-equal power of conviction). And in most cases it will not be too difficult to discover in the life history of such an individual early indications of instability accounting for those later pseudo-revolutions.

Genuine changes, on the other hand, rare as they may be, transcend the individual's biography, can no longer be reduced, ontogenetically, to early phases in his identity development. They may have been prepared by a period of doubt, of inner conflict, of crisis, but such prodromal signs may as well be not demonstrable. The essential point is that such change comes from without, as it were, from a zone of psychic reality that transcends the individual's consciousness as well as his personal unconscious, the unlived and the repressed parts of his mind.

By including such cases of radical personality changes in a discussion of reversibility, we maintain that the ego system, whatever its roots and its genesis may have been, can be changed from without, not by being invaded and destroyed (as in psychoses) but by being reorganized and replaced, as if that new replacing ego system had been ready before. We suggest the hypothesis that *there are cases of ego development going on in two directions simultaneously, one supplementing the other, and leading either to the well known phenomenon of double personality* (if the ego is strongly entrenched in itself and does not yield), *or to fight and rejection* (if the ego feels threatened), *or to a sudden replacement by a parallel, mostly contrary, ego system* (see also p. 81).

These phenomena of two parallel, though contrary, ego developments are not as exceptional as we may feel inclined to think. In fact, all manifestations of lack of inner unity (of existential conflict and of behavioral duplicity) prove that ego development may take place on two levels simultaneously and without one relating to the other. The emergence of a "new man," that is, the radical transformation of an existing personality, will then be much more intelligible than one may think when suddenly confronted with its results.

From *reactive personality changes* (reactive to pressures from the unconscious, to inner threats and tensions) the revolutionary change differs not only in its suddenness but also in its all-including systemity. Reactive changes, though directly or indirectly produced by inner tensions, also produce additional tensions, inasmuch as they do not, as a rule, affect the total personality but certain functional areas only, and even those in part only. Reversal in these cases can generally be shown to be superficial only and therefore should not be included in a discussion of structure changes. It is the same personality that expresses itself both before and after the change has taken place, though in different, often enough unrecognizable symptoms of behavior and reaction. To discover the basic identity of seemingly changed behavior manifestations has undoubtedly been one of the most important achievements of psychoanalysis and individual psychology.

But essential as the deciphering of personality changes due to reaction formation or to sublimation or to any other method of transposition may be, particularly for the purposes of therapy-induced research, we should not forget that the problem of reversibility with which we are concerned here is not identical with that of therapy. The very *process of maturation** necessitates a number of changes, some positive, some negative, some conducive to growth, some restrictive. They should not and they need not be interpreted dynamically (in the psychoanalytic meaning of the term), nor as the expressions of a dialogue going on between two intentional agents of structurization, but rather as the results of certain definable sets of conditions: replacement of one attitude by another, elimination of behavior patterns through persistent lack of opportunity to make use of them, integration of an existent trait into another whole

* Meaning here: growth of maturity rather than functional differentiation independent of learning.

context, that is, into a different pattern of behavior, changes brought about by conditioning processes—these are some of the change processes that we have in mind when speaking of maturation, none of them requiring the use of finalistic categories of interpretation.

When man looks back from the vantage point of greater maturity to his past behavior patterns and value patterns and to the decisions and actions based on them, he may become aware of certain changes so fundamental that they sometimes obscure the identity binding together his past and his present. Autobiographical identity constructions often are more sophisticated then convincing (though they are meant to convince at least the writer of that autobiography). But even when the endeavor to find and define the connecting identity link is crowned with success, certain patterns of reaction and of behavior that we considered irreversibly "ours" when we were young, are liable to be experienced later as strange errors, as deviations from the line of identity, as pathologic distortions of our selfhood. Does this not prove reversibility as one of the essentials in the process of maturity-growth? And is not absence of self-alienation at least from part of our past identity indicative of immaturity, of extreme staticness, of *pseudo-identity?*

This is indeed our thesis: that true identity is not "sameness in change," as Erikson (25) believes, but rather *change in sameness;* that reversibility of patterns is an element of defining normalcy, health, maturity. Man must be capable of transcending himself in his present as well as in his past identity to reach maturity.

This principle finds an expression in Jung's conception of personality integration (76), that is, in his claim that, normally, attitudinal and functional specialization, the result of man's growth toward social effectiveness during the first half of his life, should be reversed during the second half of life. Resistance to this life-inherent law of integration (which demands ascendance of the hitherto neglected, unlived, hence unconscious, attitudes and functions, their active and conscious participation in man's choices and decisions) means danger to the personality, means crisis, defect, illness. But reversal, in this sense, does not mean elimination of the past (with the exception of those abovementioned cases of sudden and radical transformation (see p. 8o), in which we saw evidence of a latent development coming to the fore); it rather means supplementing a well established (a canalized) type of behavior (in orientation, reality-assimilation, adjustment, achievement) by different modes of operation.

Reversibility in this sense depends, of course, on those structural conditions we have tried to define previously: on the ego's readiness to be receptive of the outer and the inner non-ego, and its ability to fulfill its functions of organization; on the approximate equivalence and the interrelatedness of the two life tendencies. But to the extent that these conditions are fulfilled—that is, normally—crystallization of a type does not imply finality. This is one of the most important contributions of Jung's analytical psychology to the understanding of human behavior and development.

A few remarks only may be added here on reversal of attitudes, behavior patterns, or pathological structurizations through therapy.* Therapy means, of course, something different when the patient is a child, an adolescent, an adult, an old person. It means something different in regard to each personality problem that requires a solution. It means something different in each school of thought. But there is one recurring question that is of relevance in our present discussion of reversibility: when can the personality change produced by successful therapy be considered a genuine change of structure?

The skeptical evaluation of psychotherapy in general is based on this question (100): is there evidence that at least in the majority of so-called successful cases the change brought about has any chance of becoming a factor of essential determination in the patient's future life? In other words: is therapy-induced change (in those cases in which the aim of treatment was not defined from the start as "partial repair" only) capable of remodeling the patient's identity?

We believe that therapy has a chance of producing such radical changes, but on one condition only: it must succeed in reaching the transpersonal elements of experience behind those personal complexes whose clarification, reductive analysis, and dissolution should be considered a preparatory stage only. True enough, there exist many cases in which no more than such clarification and reduction will be needed. But it would be a mistake to expect in these cases radical changes to take place in the patient's personality structure. (We believe that the skeptical evaluation of the results of therapy is justified to the extent that it refers to those reductive analyses only; they, however, are in the majority, while nonpersonalistic methods of interpretation and treatment are to be found in very few schools of thought only.)

Thus, we see that genuine structure changes through therapy depend on the same conditions on which structurization and reversibility depend in general, on the establishment of dialogic relationships—in the course of the treatment—between the patient's ego and the transpersonal sources of the unconscious, the "reality of the soul."

* We have devoted to this subject a separate study (37).

6

Etiology

1. FUNCTIONS AND LAWS OF ETIOLOGY

We have so far analyzed a number of basic concepts which, we believe, will help us understand the main subject of our discussion, ego development under the impact of constitutional and environmental factors. To speak of development before having analyzed the meaning of these factors, which determine its course in the various phases, may be considered as questionable a procedure as it would be to start with an analysis of constitutional and environmental determinants before having analyzed the concept of development which determines the causal meaning of each of them differently in each phase.

We shall therefore divide our discussion of the concept of development into three parts: We shall first try to define it, within this chapter on etiology and its functions in the interpretation of ego development; we shall then return to the subject in Part 2 of this book, once in Chapter 8, with a view to defining the essentials of each phase (*before* analyzing the relevant partial factors of environment to which the bulk of the Part 2 will be devoted), and again at the end, after our analysis of environment, when we shall try to answer the question of how every phase specifically affects the causal significance of at least the most important of these factors, and of how some of the factors are liable to distort the structural function of this or that phase. Although some duplication will in this way be unavoidable, we believe that this is the only way to do justice to the intrinsic interdependence of the concepts required in a comprehensive theory of development.

But before starting with our analysis we should try to define the functions and laws of etiology in general, as a tool in any interpretation of human behavior.

Representatives of positivistic schools of thought tend to relegate to the realm of metaphysical speculations all varieties of psychological comment. In the very process of interpreting a specific phenomenon, they claim, elements that are not *in* (and *of*) that phenomenon are being added to it arbitrarily (the concepts and categories of interpretation) and are being used, "as if" they were in the nature of absolute realities.

This objection (that every *interpretation* of observable facts of behavior indulges in metaphysical speculation) cannot be countered simply by saying that the categories of interpretation are "nothing but *façons de parler*," because in the process of conceptual differentiation, which characterizes the history of every theory of behavior, we can see a tendency of these categories to live their own life, as it were, to become less rather than more dependent on the facts to which they relate.

Such is the case not only of dualistic theories which set out from the presumption that the area of observable behavior indicates the existence of antithetical forces and tendencies, but also of monistic theories which aim at reducing all phenomena to the level of manifestations of a one-and-only reality. Theorizing, the positivist maintains, has a proper place in science only to the extent that it helps classify observable data so that their present observation and the prediction of their future observability may become easier.

This claim, however, is based on the, at least, questionable premise that interpretation aims at finding out the objective truth about a certain phenomenon. Such absolutistic claim has indeed the absoluteness of facts as its counterpart. But we contend that interpretation has another purpose altogether: to make understandable the meaning of observable phenomena, which without such interpretation would not appear at all to be meaningful or understandable. *The criterion of validity of interpretational concepts and categories is the number of phenomena that can be explained through them in a more or less systematic and unifying manner.*

When we interpret a religious text or a difficult poem, an event of past history or a strange custom, or, for that matter, a human being's behavior and development, we set out from the presumption that there exists underneath the manifest surface an explicable depth zone of meaning, and that interpretation is called for to make the surface *reveal* its hidden meaning. *So defined, interpretation requires the placement of the phenomenon that is to be explained in some sort of comprehensive context which becomes evident (visible) through the very act of interpreting that phenomenon.**

---

* Adherents to various theories will, of course, disagree as to what constitutes a phenomenon to be interpreted and what is but a (more or less legitimate) tool of interpretation, a (more or less adequate) auxiliary concept.

Thus the Alderian and, even more radically so, the behaviorist, will deny the existence of the unconscious as an autonomously operating reality. The Freudian will claim that what Jung calls "transpersonal contents of the psyche" are but epiphenomena of personally explicable psychodynamics. The existence of telepathic or prophetic phenomena will be relegated by most theories into the realm of mystical speculation.

Theories tend toward a kind of chauvinistic exclusion of each other, an affective monism that often obliterates the scientific motivation behind them. Eclecticism, instead of being regarded as evidence of maturity and wisdom, is often considered a sign of mental inferiority.

This means, when applied to psychological interpretations, that an analysis of individual manifestations of behavior and development is justified only to the extent that it makes a total reality meaningful, that is, makes it reveal its hidden meaning. Its elements (forces, inner agencies, relations, processes, functions, defenses, etc.) should, of course, *not* be regarded as concrete realities but as conceptual means only for the purpose of elucidating that hidden meaning; but it is practically unavoidable to use them, *as if* they were concrete realities.

It is the ultimate aim of every theory of behavior to give adequate answers to such questions as: why a certain factor produces in an individual case a specific result, while seemingly similar facts have brought about different final results in other cases. We propose to base our answer on the principles of causal configuration which can be summarized in the statement that *every partial factor has a different causal meaning according to the other partial factors with which it combines into an inseparable causal unit.*

The definition of the functions and aims of etiology differ with its object, which may be a specific behavioral phenomenon, a definable behavioral picture, or an individual case.

Anxiety, aggressiveness, ambivalence, guilt feelings, shame, identification, sublimation, indolence are some of the numerous phenomena that can, and should, be analyzed both structurally and etiologically. The *elements* of causal explanation (constitutional propensities, endowments or deficiencies, positive or negative experiences and life conditions) are, of course, the same for all feelings, attitudes, and processes; but their *configurations* are specifically different for each phenomenon according to its essential characteristics. Hence, no purely empirical analysis of causes will ever be meaningful, unless it is preceded by a phenomenology, that is, by an attempt to describe in structural and dynamic terms the *essence* of the relevant phenomena, including a comparison of their essentials.* For, only on the basis of such a description (which can also be called a definition) can we try to distinguish between causal configurations *essential* to the emergence of a specific phenomenon and *accidental* factors which may be present in one individual case and absent in another one, without, however, being etiologically indispensable for the emergence and for the explanation of the specific phenomenon under analysis.

When we come to explaining the genesis of a *unit (picture) of normal or abnormal behavior,* the need for such a prior definition of its essence is still more evident. Here we can see that the causal and the clinical

---

* For an example see pp. 132 *ff.*, where anxiety and aggressiveness are analyzed in this way.

dimensions are so closely interlinked that we cannot even describe or define such a behavioral unit without including in its description (or definition) an analysis of its essential causes.*

Let us illustrate this point by one example only: The various forms of juvenile delinquency may be defined as separate clinical pictures, of neurotic delinquency, of primary behavior disorder, of waywardness, of "brain-stem-drivenness," of aggressive feeblemindedness, etc. (34). Each of these units should be identified and compared with all others according to their essential characteristics and their essential causes. It is not sufficient to compare the neurotic delinquent's compulsiveness and unconscious needs with the negative intentionality of primary behavior disorder, the occurrence character of waywardness, the inner discrepancies in the behavior of certain brain-injured children, and the unstructured automatism of the feebleminded delinquent. We must simultaneously bear in mind, on the causal level, that neurotic delinquency is brought about by a specific type of oedipal fixation and disappointment in a family atmosphere of intensive personal relationships, whereas in primary behavior disorders these oedipal disappointments occur in an atmosphere of economic stress, and waywardness is essentially the result of a continuous process of being conditioned by externalizing factors (while organic traumatization and structural deficiency are the essential causes of the two last-mentioned behavioral pictures).

This does not mean that any *individual case* belonging to this or that clinical unit† can be explained adequately by linking the individual's behavior to one of those essential causes. The category of causal essentiality applies to a psychic phenomenon or a clinical picture only, but becomes meaningless in the analysis of individual cases. *With regard to the former it is the function of etiology to participate, as it were, in their phenomenological analysis; with regard to the latter, to help elucidate the unique configuration of all partial factors. This configuration includes not only the partial factors themselves, but also their causal antecedents (the causes of each cause) as well as the partial results being continuously transformed into additional causes.*

The numerous monistic attempts to explain psychological and psychopathological phenomena by reduction to one causal factor belong, it is true, to the past; but their place has been taken by pluralistic attempts to formulate a *number* of causes, to determine their relative significance

---

* Although their analysis again presupposes knowledge of the essentials of the *unit* of analysis.

† No diagnostician who knows his job will be so naive as to label a patient with the name of a clinical picture. It would therefore be more appropriate to speak of "taking part in" than of "belonging to" a certain behavioral unit. (The same, incidentally, applies to such concepts as "type" or "developmental phase.") An individual case can be diagnosed only as showing *more* signs of a certain picture than of another.

statistically, and to isolate them from each other, *as if* each of them existed and operated as such.

In some areas, new partial factors have appeared (such as infantile frustration, repression and unconscious guilt feelings, inferiority feelings and overcompensation, etc.), each of them liable to claim universal validity and thus to turn again into the central concept of a monistic theory. In other areas, it is the low level of conceptual differentiation that accounts for the relative weakness of the configurational orientation. Even in the field of clinical analysis we often find a linear rather than a configurational approach,* though here the failure to explain individual differences may force the clinician into a configurational method.

True enough, the configurational approach to the problem of cause necessitates the use of abstractions. How else could the psychologist describe, or even hint at, integration of partial factors in an individual equation? Abstraction of partial factors is therefore a methodological necessity; it becomes a scientific fallacy only when we "absolutize" them and thereby endow them with the character of measurable realities.

By comparing individual cases showing *similar* causal equations (and similar or dissimilar behavioral outcomes) with cases *differing* in as many parts of the causal equation as possible from the former group (and showing essentially different or essentially similar symptoms), we may arrive at the following conclusions:

(a) that only a few partial factors invariably, and irrespectively of whatever other partial factors appear together with them in the causal equation of the individual case, tend to lead to certain symptom manifestations or even to certain clinical entities;

(b) that most partial factors are not significantly correlated with any specific behavior symptoms or clinical pictures but receive their determining significance only through their configuration with other partial factors;

(c) that a few of these factorial configurations are of a purely quantitative nature (one partial factor being reinforced and brought to the level of causative function through the addition of other partial factors only), while most configurations are of a basically qualitative nature (one specific partial factor receiving its specific causative function through interaction with one or more other specific factors only).

But even if we were able to arrive at the formulation of such abstract laws of causation by isolated, reinforced, or configurated partial factors, it would still be doubtful whether we could call them "laws" in the

* The partial causes following each other or, at best, intensifying each the pathological outcome of the other, but not receiving each its specific meaning through its multidimensional connections with all others.

scientific sense of the term—because of their rather doubtful prediction value. Even if we could say that certain isolated or quantitatively re-inforced factors tend to produce certain symptoms or clinical pictures, could we be sure that these partial factors had been sufficiently well isolated in our original analysis to make possible their reidentification in any other case? Or does not the very infinity of possible combinations and constellations of reality factors make such an undertaking illusory? And could we ever hope to be able to rediscover exactly identical con-figurations of *specific* partial factors, interacting to produce a certain re-sult?

Moreover, whenever we try to explain human behavior by connect-ing a certain manifestation with its causal antecedents, its structural concomitants, and its intentional vectors into the future, we are faced with the problem of constant change taking place in the structure and contents of each causal factor. The law of configuration operates not only horizontally, in the interaction and interpenetration of coexistent partial factors, but also vertically, in the dynamic growth of each factor and of each causal configuration; not only does each result tend to become an additional cause, but each factor incorporates in itself its effects, as it were, thus growing in functional intensity and often alter-ing its direction and its meaning. (This is particularly evident in the case of repression or in that of reintegration in the ego of repressed contents.)

Even if it were possible fully to understand and explain the causal function of, say, a specific traumatic experience, by reconstructing the path leading from the occurrence of that experience through the devel-opmental phases and the sequence of reactions and partial character formations to the final behavioral result, such a reconstruction would necessarily remain fragmentary and hypothetical, because no amount of etiological analysis will ever suffice to rediscover and redesign every de-tail of the actual life path. We must content ourselves with ascribing functional autonomy (in Allport's (6) sense of the term) to certain causal factors of an interactive process of crystallization (of partial factors with their partial results), without ever being able to rediscover all the genetic elements of this process of growth.

While formulating the laws of causal configuration, we have em-phasized the interdependence of all partial factors, the determination of the meaning of each partial factor by its own causes and the causal role of every—partial—result. We have proposed to distinguish between quantitative and qualitative configurations. We have mentioned the fact that some developmental outcomes can be called functionally auton-omous. We could perhaps sum up what we have said so far by recalling that every development is the outcome of a homeostatic process of differentiation and integration, of expansion and systematization. The structural tendency toward systematization finds its expression in the tendency of partial factors to relate to each other in configurational relationships; the tendency toward expansion, in the interconnection of each cause with its antecedents and its results.

We have mentioned that the concepts of causal configuration have different meanings according to its object, which may be an individual case or a behavioral unit. Only to the first should we apply the term, *causal equation,* whereas in the discussion of a behavioral unit (a specific phenomenon or a clinical picture) the configurational approach aims at clarifying the essential causes, irrespective of individual variations.

2. The Causal Equation

In a configurational theory of behavior the term causal equation is obviously not meant as an additive concept. A statistically oriented pluralism may define it as a mathematical formula symbolizing a quantitative reinforcement of a given factor by simultaneously and/or consecutively operating factors. Configurationally, the term should be understood as an attempt to describe a certain factor dynamically, that is, in its dependence on, and its interrelatedness with, a number of other—coexistent, preceding, or consecutive—factors. Theoretically, reinforcement of a certain causal factor by others could, of course, be shown as the sum total of a large number of equivalent or even identically repeated factors, each of them defined configurationally. The elements of which each of these factors is composed are easily enumerated: heredity, fetal experience, birth experience, parents' personalities, social conditions, patterns of culture, primary mother experience, environmental reactions to the child's behavior, somatic and mental endowments and handicaps, type, reaction patterns, thresholds of perception and of frustration-bearance, organizational strength of the ego, its openness to the outer and to the inner non-ego, relative equivalence of the two basic life tendencies or prevalence of one, educational climate, historical conditions, later satisfying or frustrating life events, the intrapsychic tensions, solutions and processes of personality formation set in motion by them. But not only is each of these partial factors a composite of numerous subfactors, *each subfactor is determined in its causal significance by the way in which it is configurated with all other factors and subfactors in a given moment.*

Now, a factor analyst could, of course, claim that such configurational refinement does not preclude statistical methods, since there is no difference in principle between one hundred and one hundred trillions of definable units of calculation (though "one hundred trillions" is, of course, an understatement). We must, however, ask what purpose the statistical method could serve in this case. The larger the number of defined factors, the smaller is the measurable difference between them bound to be. And yet, the causal effect of each of two such similar factors, factors of almost equal relative frequency, may be extremely different. Thus, measurement does not contribute much to the understanding of human behavior and development; on the contrary, it is liable to obliterate the differential meaning of its manifestations.

What, then, is the function of the causal equation? In one form it shows the *universal* genesis of a certain factor out of the interaction of other factors in a developmental sequence. In another form it shows how a certain *individual* pattern, personality, achievement, or failure emerges from the continuous and unique interaction of a large number of qualities, attitudes, events, processes. And again another form of the causal equation relates to the different outcome of a certain factor according to its different antecedents. Each typological model based on multidimensionality of factors can be interpreted as a causal equation. In all these forms the causal equation allows for a clear distinction between "cause" and "cause of cause."

As an example for *the first-mentioned function of the causal equation,* that of showing the genesis of a certain factor of determination, we shall analyze the concept of *constitution.* The term designates the totality of those structural factors that determine the individual's selection of experience, that is, his reaction patterns, his degree of activity and vulnerability, his somatic, mental, and relational endowments and deficiences.

Although the constitution may be alterable as the result of paranatal and at least earliest postnatal traumatizations, and although the functional preferences (which form a central part in it) are, according to Jung, subject to radical changes during the second half of each individual's life, we are still justified in defining constitution as *determinant.* Neural sensitivity and activity, the intensity and efficiency of the sensory screening system, love-needs and frustration-bearance, and many other elements of constitution may be extant at birth (congenital) and partly even at conception (hereditary), but they are also the outcome of later life occurrences. (Structure is the result of structure and experience; so is experience.) And yet, even in the very process of structurization (see Chapter 5) the crystallizing constitution determines its own crystallization process. (Structure directs, and results from, structurization.)

The following is an attempt to express these statements through symbols.

The hereditary part of the constitution (a), as determined by parental genes (x), grows within, and acts on, the mother's psychosomatic structure (b) which, in turn, is the result of her own constitution (I), life experiences (2), and psychodynamic elaborations of those experiences (3), and operates within a universe (c) of objective natural (1), social (2), and cultural (3) conditions, while at the same time, reacting to the growing fetus. The result of this interaction process is the psychosomatic structure (d) immediately preceding the birth process (e), the latter, in turn, being determined by, and modifying, often even radically changing, this pre-birth constitution as well as the mother's psychosomatic structure at the time of birth, but also depending on the objective birth conditions, as expressed in cultural patterns.

We can symbolize the process so far described by the following symbols:

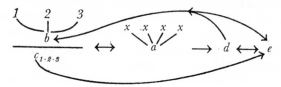

The result of this birth process, then, is the psychosomatic structure of the neonate (f), including his congenital physical and mental abilities and deficiencies, his thresholds, reaction patterns and needs, etc. It is evident that in many cases the postnatal and the prenatal constitution radically differ from each other, owing to the hazards of the birth process (although we cannot make any clear statement about that prenatal condition). But the neonate's constitution is immediately exposed to a variety of acting and reacting environmental figures, upon which he acts and reacts. All of these figures (Σg) are again determined by their constitution (1), life experiences (2), and psychodynamic elaboration of these experiences (3), and operate within a universe of natural, social and cultural conditions (Σh), which, to some extent, operate also independently on the neonate's developing constitution (although they become causally meaningful for the individual only through representative personal figures). Through the interaction of these factors the congenitally present constitutional nucleus (f) is being modified or reinforced, until the empirically relevant constitution (i) crystallizes. The symbol, thus, is:

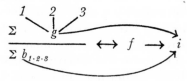

The infant's behavior as determined by his structure (i) and his maternal (k) and nonmaternal (l) environment (which are, of course, causally interlinked as well), elicits again reactions on the part of that environment. The interaction of both constituting what we have analyzed, in Chapter 2, as the infant's primary experience, sets in motion successful or unsuccessful adaptation processes (m), which are, however, determined not only by the outer but also by the inner non-ego, not only by the maternal (k) and the nonmaternal (l) environment but also by the personal (n) and the transpersonal (o) unconscious, and which gradually lead to the formation of the personality type (p) with its individual degree of normalcy and abnormality, the process being subject to the laws of maturation, that is, to the impact of the structurally defined functions of developmental phases ($I, II, III \ldots$).

The relevant symbol, therefore, will be:

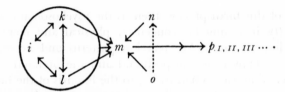

Whereas $a, d, f,$ and i symbolize the constitution at a certain moment, at conception, immediately before and immediately after birth, and at the end of the primary structurization period, p symbolizes the constitution in its phase-conditioned variations, that is, the structural determinant of the individual's reactions and behavior in each phase of his maturation. Not only such variables as environmental influences and reactions and not only the inner non-ego (see pp. $$ ff.) determine this (constitutional) determinant but also the maturation phases, that is, their essential functions, as we shall try to define them in the Chapter 8, on maturation and development.

Retrospective studies of behavior disorders tend to emphasize the causal responsibility of a specific partial factor, for instance: "maternal deprivation" (4, 12) for the extreme weakness of relational abilities and intellectual apathy, parental "frigidity" for infantile autism (80), certain forms of oedipal disappointment for behavior disorders (101), others for neurotic deviations (104), etc. But none of these causal generalizations is tenable, according to the principles of configurational interpretation of behavior and development.

We propose first to analyze one of those factors, that of maternal insufficiency. It is self-evident that there exist many forms in which this insufficiency may manifest itself, forms differing so radically from each other in causal impact that the comprehensive concept becomes almost meaningless. The following is an (incomplete) list of these forms of maternal defects:

(a) Early and continuous experience of the impersonal atmosphere of an institution
(b) Early and noncontinuous experience of the impersonal atmosphere of an institution
(c) Early and continuous experience of personal diffuseness under conditions of poverty and neglect
(d) Prolonged removal of the child from the parents' home at a later stage
(e) Impersonal family atmosphere under conditions of plenty
(f) Relative insecurity and later loss of maternal attention owing to economic stress
(g) Maternal rejection of the child
(h) Maternal indolence toward the child
(i) Maternal insecurity and inconsistency
(j) Maternal overindulgence
(k) Maternal overprotection
(l) Maternal withdrawal in general, and therefore also from the child

Here is not the place to explain the causal significance of each of these forms of maternal insufficiency according to its own causal roots, or to compare their results with each other, that is, to show in which ways they are liable to affect the child's development specifically when all other objective and subjective conditions are being kept constant. We shall come back to these and similar questions in Part 2, "Environment and Development." In our discussion here of the causal equation and its functions in the interpretation of human behavior, we must limit ourselves to asking two questions: What are the relevant qualifications of each of the above mentioned subfactors? And what are the most important structural factors in the affected child's personality that determine the causal effect of each of these, so qualified, factors?

Impersonal educational atmosphere (cf. 33),* for instance, may appear in different degrees of intensity, depending on the operation or non-operation, in the child and in the environment, of compensatory factors. (It should be obvious, here as in any similar case, that intensity depends on the subject no less than on so-called objective conditions.) When speaking of relative insecurity in the child as a factor paving the way for violent reactions to later (reinforcing) disappointments by real or imagined loss of maternal attention (under conditions of poverty or otherwise), the relevant qualification is the time factor rather than intensity (the

* We shall dicuss this in greater detail in our analysis of externalization, in a subsequent volume.

earlier the disappointment occurs, the more radical and the less reversible the results are liable to be). As regards the various forms of negative maternal attitudes toward the child (rejection, indolence, inconsistency, overindulgence, overprotection, withdrawal, etc.), the most important modifying and qualifying factor is the presence or absence of a compensatory relationship to another meaningful person in the child's immediate environment, particularly to the father (*cf.* pp. 258 *ff.*).

The decisive determinants of the outcome of maternal deficiencies, however, are those *structural* factors that we have analyzed or at least mentioned in Chapter 5: the relative prevalence of one life tendency over the other (that toward staticness over that toward expansion, or *vice versa*); the organizational and integrational abilities of the ego and its openness toward the outer and toward the inner non-ego (the environment, the personal unconscious and the transpersonal contents of the depth zone of the psyche); the attitudinal type and, to some extent, also the functional type, not to speak of the congenital level of sensory acuity and of intelligence, of vulnerability, of somatic vitality.

Out of the almost infinite number of possible configurations of these structural factors we propose to define four composite conditions that determine the outcome of maternal deficiency differentially: normality, rigid defensiveness, high vulnerability, apathy.

(a) We speak of *normality* when the tendency toward staticness is related to that toward expansion and both are approximately equal; when the paternal principle of differentiation and internalization (see pp. 22 *ff.*) is strong enough to support the infant's growing time-consciousness and feeling for regularity even where the primary mother experience did not altogether facilitate the experience of nearness; when the organizational, the synthetic, function of the ego is neither being overtaxed by an excessive degree of openness toward the external world (which is identical with saying that the ego adequately fulfills its functions as a screening system), nor starved by an insufficient supply of stimuli (owing to insufficient receptivity); when the ego is in communication with the inner non-ego, that is, maintains dialogic relationships with the depth zone of the psyche and its autonomous contents, the symbol manifestations of the categories of experience.

This normal individual may be an extravert or an introvert of high or at least average intelligence, though excessive extraversion or excessive introversion is incompatible with normality (as Horney (64) has rightly pointed out in her discussion of Jung's typology). It is obvious that a normal individual cannot be of low (subnormal) intelligence, though we should add that the latter is *not* incompatible with certain characteristics of normality, such as an approximate equivalence of the two basic life tendencies.

(b) We speak of *rigid defensiveness* when the life tendency towards staticness is so strong that the normal interrelatedness with the opposite tendency is liable to be weakened, and system formation then becomes an aim in itself, preventing, rather than preparing for, growth. One of the almost unavoidable consequences of such a constellation is: insufficient differentiation between ego and non-ego and between different manifestations within the non-ego or within the ego. Reality testing is bound to be inadequate; and internalization, to the extent that it takes place, is likely to be repressive and unrealistic, that is, unrelated to its corollaries in reality. It is obvious that, the paternal principle of differentiation being defective, the consciousness of rule and regularity will be slow to develop, the experience of nearness and trust and the "courage to be"—to use Tillich's expression (121)—will always remain precarious. Although the ego's organizational abilities may be sufficient to cope with the limited influx from the non-ego (limited because of the relative lack of openness to the non-ego which, by definition, goes with rigidity), the ego nevertheless will always be on the defense; since rigidity obviates the emergence of a sense of regularity, fear of unforseeable change and otherness is bound to persist, and ego strength tends to be invested in defensive organization rather than in growth. It is this very defensiveness that restricts or prevents contact and communication with the inner non-ego as well.

As a rule, the rigid person is not an extravert, and his intelligence is liable to sink to a lower than congenitally given level of functioning because of fear of otherness and differentiation (although an exceptionally high level of intelligence may compensate for, may even help to overcome, rigidity).

(c) The *highly vulnerable child*, as a rule, suffers from an excessive openness to the outer and/or the inner non-ego and an inability to cope with the stimulus influx through adaptation and systematization (synthesis). It is the second more than the first factor that accounts for the objective danger of being overwhelmed by forces beyond the ego's control, and it happens not infrequently that even where openness is objectively far from being excessive, the *feeling* of being threatened is all-pervading only because of the ego's organizational insufficiency. In terms of the relationship between the life tendencies, the two varieties of vulnerability—the one due to excessive openness, the other due to extreme ego weakness—could be defined by saying that in the first the life tendency toward expansion is not supported by the opposite one (for which reason openness is being experienced as dangerous), whereas in the second the life tendency toward staticness is so weak that every change, every growth, every expansion is traumatizing *per se*. The difference between the extravert and the introvert varieties of vulnerability is determined by the *source* from which dangers to the ego threatens, from the outer reality in the extravert, from the inner non-ego, the "reality of the soul," in the introvert variety.

In all these cases, however, it is unlikely that intelligence, even if it had been functioning on a high level (congenitally), can be saved from deterioration, although (paranoid) ego concentration on the sources and reasons of threat, that is, on the structural and experiential basis of vulnerability, often serves as a secondary, unrealistic, and yet effective tool of restitution, as it were.

(d) In the last of the four abovementioned structural constellations, the one we suggested should be called *apathy*, the ego is neither open to the non-ego nor organizationally strong. Here, we can—paradoxically—speak of a relative equality of the two life tendencies, though on an extremely low level of intensity; so low, in fact, that practically no elaboration, no internalization, no structurization of experience can take place. Neither the paternal principle of differentiation and internalization nor the experience of nearness and trust—resulting normally from an approximate equivalence of the two basic mother experiences—are here at the disposal of the child's development, the outcome being general retardation and passiveness.

Here, the causal equation is best represented with the aid of a correlation table in which the various forms of maternal deficiency, with their relevant qualifiers, are being shown on the one axis, the various structural constellations (including intelligence, type, life tendencies, etc.) on the other axis; and a comparative synopsis of outcomes of the various configurations makes the concept of "maternal deficiency" meaningful.

(The question, then, arises, whether a certain element in the environment or in the structure (which "meet" in configuration) can be held responsible for actually producing a specific *variety* of behavior, so that in the end each result would again be shown to be the result of a partial cause. Is, for instance, we should ask, the type factor of introversion in the genesis of psychopathy causally responsible for the emergence of the "queer saint" variety of psychopathic behavior, whereas extraversion accounts *ceteris paribus* for the "impostor" variety (*cf.* 34)? Does paternal adequacy produce integrational abilities, which, in turn, enable the child to cope with maternal inadequacy? Such questions, however, are rather academic, since, in the reality of the causative processes, a partial factor can never be isolated: introversion in the genesis of psychopathic varieties is not identical with introversion in the causal equation, let us say, of choosing a neurotic solution or of creative sublimation; its symptom manifestations, not only its causal effects, are different in each case. Hence, there is no way back from the configurational to the additive approach.)

Another way of representing the causal equation of earliest traumatization is that of comparing the possible outcomes of *specific* maternal failures in cases of excessive expansion or excessive staticness, when the affected individual is either an extravert or an introvert (while excluding all other determinants, such as the congenital level of intelligence, the organizational and integrational strength of the ego, the thresholds of frustration-bearance, of perception, etc.). We should, of course, remain aware of the fact that such an abbreviated version of the causal equation is but an abstraction and is bound to suffer from all the shortcomings of abstraction. The following are examples of the method suggested here.

(a) *Maternal rejection* of the infant in the earliest, pre-ego, stages of development, is liable to produce aggressive denial of staticness, where the life tendency toward expansion structurally predominates, while it may lead to fearful denial of expansion in the opposite case. Aggressive denial of staticness, however, may lead to open destructiveness in extraverts and to an accumulation of nonexpressed affects in introverts, while fearful denial of expansion may produce infantile demandingness in extraverts and apathy in introverts.

(b) *Maternal indolence* may cause a pathological evanescence of anxiety, where the life tendency toward expansion structurally prevails, and a serious delay in the crystallization of the ego where the opposite tendency is dominant. We have suggested in another study (34) that in the first case two varieties of psychopathy are liable to emerge, the oscillating type, where the affected individual is an extravert; the drifting type, where he is an introvert. We now add that when the opposite life tendency, that toward staticness, prevails, passive intake of reality may be the reaction of an extravert, withdrawal from reality that of an introvert individual, both reactions indicating a basic defect in the process of ego formation.

(c) When the life tendency toward expansion is dominant, *maternal overindulgence* supports the emergence of an ego neither understanding nor recognizing objective limits. Where the tendency towards staticness is excessive, maternal overindulgence is liable to act as a factor reinforcing the structurally given reluctance to change and to develop. In the first case certain psychopathic types are again liable to emerge, the imposter type in an extravert, the eccentric and queer personality in an introvert. Reinforced staticness, on the other hand, may produce a tendency towards overdependence in an extravert, toward obsession-like self-limitation in an introvert individual.

(d) *Death of the mother* is—absurd as it may sound—the most severe maternal defect, if it occurs before the experience of nearness is strongly enough established in the child's structure to allow for transfer to a mother substitute. If the life tendency toward expansion is overemphasized, at the expense of the opposite tendency, and therefore obviates structurization, the mother's early and sudden disappearance means the elimination of the only control agent that has reality value in the life of such a child, and *expansion* will then be replaced by *being expanded*. For the extravert this means identity-definition through "devouring the non-ego as it occurs; for the introvert, identity-definition as being negated by the non-ego. When the life tendency toward staticness is overstrong, early loss of the mother may cause withdrawal from contact with the environment; such life without contact may then manifest itself in the extravert as demonstrated aloofness, in the introvert as general ineffectuality.

(e) *Absence of maternal care from the beginning,* in hospitalized or institutionalized infants, has not yet been studied as correlated with various structural determinants. We suggest here the thesis that, where the life tendency towards expansion is dominating, early institutionalization accounts for primary repression of anxiety (this central characteristic of noncongenital psychopathy); the latter then is liable to produce the shallow attachment type of psychopathy in extraverts and the unstable, mirroring type of psychopathy in the introvert (34). Where the life tendency toward staticness prevails, early institutionalization prevents, as a rule, the development of the child's ability to differentiate. In the extravert, the outcome is liable to be infantility; in the introvert, a certain form of feeblemindedness.*

We need not go on analyzing additional forms of maternal deficiency to illustrate this form of the causal equation, which is of particular importance in any differential analysis of pathological phenomena. The concept of causal equation has, however, yet another function, that of explaining progressive and regressive individual developments and showing the different outcomes of a causal factor according to its own causal roots or the different ways in which an effect may become a new cause. It will be one of our main tasks in the analysis of environmental factors (Part 2) to illustrate this law of vertical configuration. Here we shall confine ourselves to showing how this law finds its expression in the concept of causal equation.

We suggest an example from the area of "normal" development:

A father may have high intellectual expectations from his son *either* because his life is based on internalized values (and he therefore keenly feels himself to be responsible for their realization, through himself and others, hence also for the learning tasks implied), *or* because he needs some kind of compensation for his own failure. In the first case the

---

* This will be elaborated on in a subsequent volume dealing with individual varieties of externalization.

father's expectations from his son are based not only on his primary respect for objective values but also on a recognition of the child's objective abilities (since the learning process is part of a value-related, not a person-related, orientation). In the second case, on the other hand, neither the learnable contents nor the child's objective inclinations and abilities are important *per se* but only as instruments for the (irrational) fulfillment of (mostly imaginary but in any case only subjective) needs.

The results in the child are bound to be radically different. While in the first case the child is likely to identify, in due course of time, with his father and his intentions, will take part in learning and "feel well" with his learning tasks, the father's tension and basic dissatisfaction, in the second case, is bound to communicate itself to the child. While the first will come to experience security, nearness, and trust not only in the emotional and the relational areas of his existence (which, as a rule, is a precondition for objective learning in any case) but also when faced with tasks of thinking and learning, the second will either take over, as it were, his father's irrational ambitions and therefore live in constant fear of failure, or will "succeed in failing" in order not to advance beyond his father.

The intellectual security and objectivity resulting from living up to the father's expectations in the first case will turn into an energy-producing causal factor in the child's intellectual development; he will have learned to develop initiative, that is, will be capable of handling his thinking and learning tasks autonomously. In the second case, on the other hand, even considerable achievement will not provide the learner with that feeling of security that makes possible and guarantees objectivity. Moreover—and this is perhaps an even more important criterion of differentiation—the positive effects of value-oriented paternal expectations are primarily intellectual, and to the extent that they influence other functional areas, particularly those of interpersonal relationships and of feelings, they make themselves felt as objectivating factors; the negative effects of tension-producing, because person-oriented paternal expectations are multilinear, branch out, as it were, into nonintellectual areas from the start and emotionalize the thinking and learning processes.

It is self-evident that the two lines of causation drawn here schematically should be understood as "ideal type" constructions only; the real causes are lying between these two extremes, approximating one or the other in different degrees. The following model may serve to illustrate what we have said.

$$
\begin{array}{ccc}
x & & y\leftarrow c- \\
\downarrow & & \downarrow \\
a+ & & a- \\
\downarrow & & \swarrow\ \searrow \\
c_b\leftarrow\!\!-b+ & & b+\quad b- \\
\downarrow & & \downarrow\quad\ \downarrow \\
b++ & & b+_{c-}\ b-_{c-}
\end{array}
$$

Where x = internalized value-orientation of the father

     y = emotionally conditioned person-orientation of the father

    $a+$ = objective expectations from the child, seen as instrument of value-realization

    $a-$ = affective, nonobjective expectations, usually based on projection of own failure

    $b+$ = child's high intellectual achievement according to father's expectations

    $b-$ = child's failure to live up to father's expectations, either because of objective inability or because of fear of, or protest against, the father

   $b++$ = autonomous use and continuation of intellectual achievement primarily made possible through identification with the father and his intentions

   $b+_{c-}$ = intellectual achievement, even when apparently positive, becoming tinged by, and dependent on the negative, tension-creating emotionality (which the child "takes over" from the father)

   $b-_{c-}$ = intellectual failure based on negative identification with father's expectations, tinged by, and dependent on, affective factors interfering with the thinking and learning processes

    c_b = feelings objectivated by thinking

    $c-$ = father's affectively distorted feelings responsible for his person-orientation

3. The Developmental Process as a Factor in the Causal Equation

To define development as "progressive change in an organism, continuously directed towards a certain end-condition" (20) or as "gradual unfolding" (102) implies the presumption that every development is predetermined by an inner "plan," an inherent "form" (in the meaning of Goethe's concept of *geprägte Form*); the definition does justice neither to the impact of the multitude of unforseeable life occurrences on the process and its direction nor to the determination of its course by phase-specific qualities.

Development is *not* "continuously directed towards a certain end-condition," but may be progressive *and* regressive, in fact, is always both, precisely because each operating personality structure at any given moment contains all preceding structures, just as each phase-specific determinant is present in each preceding and subsequent phase.

True enough, *directedness* (a concept closely connected with that of *intentionality,* since both postulate the existence of an *agent* of direction or of intention) is an element of defining the life process *per se,* particularly the normal process ("normal" meaning, as we have previously explained, interrelatednesss of the two basic life tendencies, meaning, *inter alia,* that every change aims at systematization, every systematization prepares for change); but it does *not* apply to development as such, particularly not to *human* development in its dependence on the infiniteness of the non-ego, and in its bivectoriality, that is, the simultaneity of progressive and regressive direction.

We have defined structurization as the result of a polar (dialogic) relationship between two agents of change and synthesis (the ego and what we suggested should be termed the depth center), as the result of an activity requiring a normative relationship between the two life tendencies (p. 64). We have mentioned transformation of experience into structure as the essential element of structurization (pp. 60 *ff.*). Are not, we must ask now, these two elements equally essential elements in a definition of *development?* Transformation of environmental and organic events and processes into experience leads to ever-repeated (though by no means continuous and certainly not unidirectional) structure changes; these may then be described as a gradual unfolding of pre-existent dispositions, or as a genuine enlargement of the personality (through the addition of hitherto absent qualities), or as a series of defenses, giving rise, in turn, to regressive or progressive system formation; in other words, as development. *Development, thus, could be defined as continuity of structurizations related to each other.* What does this concept of *continuity* mean?

When psychoanalysis claims that every child (some orthodox representatives of the theory will add: irrespectively of culture and social environment) goes through a certain temporal sequence of forms of libidinal satisfaction, development means "following a biological pattern." This process can be disturbed by the environment, which, through its traumatizing interferences, may cause points of fixation and regression, thus interrupting and even preventing development.* What then follows, the pathological development, is characterized by the growing individual's inability to relate to his experiences in changing, phase-specific ways (see pp. 146 *ff.*). He grows, of course, and matures functionally; but his dominant modes of reaction and assimilation will always bear the stamp of the phase to which he is fixated. Normally, a phase-specific pattern, once is has fulfilled its structural function, will merge into the following pattern and subsist in it as a modifying element, translated, as it were. It is this modification of the ever-following phase pattern that guarantees progressive development, while fixation accounts for regressive tendencies, precisely *because* the pattern of the fixation phase persists in all following phases.

But the Freudian concept of "phases of development" is inadequate as

---

* The structural factor of abnormal erogeneity of certain body zones is accepted as an element of differential interpretation of development, but as a *refugium ignorantiae* rather than as a legitimate element of causal interpretation.

a tool of interpretation from yet another point of view. Orality, anality, oedipality, etc., refer to the modes of libidinal satisfaction only which, in turn, are believed to exercise a decisive influence on the individual's total behavior, including his reactions to the educationally and emotionally relevant environment and his relationship patterns. But they do not primarily refer to ego functions such as verbal communication, imagination, phantasy, thinking, moral judgment, etc.; the latter are regarded as lying outside the area of competence of psychoanalytic libido theory, although efforts are made to show their so-called psychodynamic dependence on the phasal patterns (cf., for instance, Isaacs' studies (69, 70) of intellectual and moral development).

Erikson's modification (23) of the Freudian phase theory comes near to what we would call a structural interpretation. Not only does he use ego psychological terms such as "trust," "autonomy," "initiative," "identity," "doubt," "guilt," "inferiority," etc., not only does he show the peculiarity of each phase in its positive *and* negative meaning, he emphasizes the principle of integration of each phasal "achievement" in each preceding and following phase, a principle which would seem to make sense only when we transcend the purely personalistic approach to explaining development as the result of reactions to life events* and understand it as the gradual realization, in each phase, of all phasal qualities and attitudes, that is, of psychic structure.

We have emphasized in various contexts that constitutionally and experientially determined reactions to life events determine, in turn, the individual quality of development but not the *possibility* of experiencing reality within and without. The *structural* conditions of this possibility are, we have said, differentiation between the ego and the non-ego and interrelatedness of the two life tendencies, on the one hand, and the categories of experience, on the other hand, which are represented, reflected, and elicited—but not "created"—by personal experience (see, for instance, pp. 11 *ff.*). The primary mother experiences of the infant, we said, elicit the categories of whole and part, of full and empty, of present and absent, of near and distant, of approach and retreat, of giving and taking, of intrusion and expulsion, of protection and threat, of sameness and otherness. These categories are represented in the human mind by transpersonal images which, in each phase, change, irrespectively of the quality of personal experience, but, at the same time, merge with that experience, until their structural meaning becomes less and less recognizable.

It is this last aspect of the problem with which we are concerned here: "Phase" could actually be circumscribed, in terms of structural psychology, as a "station" in the temporal sequence of images representing the cate-

---

* Although Erikson himself tends to remain faithful to the principles of personalistic interpretation.

gories of experience. Although the latter are independent of individual or collective determinants of behavior, their meaning and their manifestations differ from phase to phase, according to the structural functions of these phases (nondifferentiatedness and gradual transition to the experience of a separate non-ego; emergence of ego-consciousness based on the autonomy of both, ego and non-ego; progressive differentiation within the ego and within the non-ego, as the result of conscious initiative; internalization; structurization after a "life in principles," etc.).

In Part 2, we shall analyze these structural functions of the various developmental phases and show what differential meanings they convey to various environmental causes of development and behavior, which will be considered in detail. Here it may be sufficient to give two examples only to show the meaning of "phasal structures":

Wholeness appears in the beginning as a challenge to the differentiating activity of the ego nucleus, that is, as *separandum;* later as something to be created in a process of give and take, that is, as *faciendum;* then as possible object of understanding and domination; still later, as the object of learning, until it may become an ego-transcending principle of regulation. As another example may serve the category of *threat*, which we encounter with a feeling of particular immediacy in anxiety dreams, though in each phase differently symbolized. It appears as threat and danger of being devoured or dominated or destroyed or confused or alienated. It should by now be evident why we regard the factor called "phase of development" or, better, its specific structural function, a decisive factor in the differential meaning of the causal equation.

We now refer again to the definition of development suggested above (see p. 101): *Continuity of structurizations related to each other.* It is the universality of the categories (the constituents) of experience that accounts for this continuity, the interconnectedness of structurizations and structure changes taking place in the different phases of development. Another implication of this definition is that not every change is relevant for the understanding of development, but only a change affecting the structure, the Gestalt of the thus-developing ego. (Other changes bear the character of accidentality, and accidentality precludes continuity.)

Here, then, arises the question: In what way can we speak of a *pathological* development? It is obvious that in the absence of normative interrelatedness between the two basic life tendencies (that toward expansion manifesting itself in change, that toward staticness in assimilation of change, that is, in system formation), pathological processes are bound to take place, whatever the cause of the interruption of that normative interrelatedness of the life tendencies may be, whether constitutional defects, traumatic events, or factors inherent in the very process of development.

The last-mentioned of these factors, accounting for the disruption of this normal condition of development in every individual, poses an interesting question: How do we explain the strange fact that development counteracts itself? There are phases in which systematization cannot keep pace with the rapidity of change taking place in the organism, while others are *per se* periods of relative emphasis on organization and systematization. We then speak of maturational or phasal susceptibility to disorganizing factors. Behavior disorders or other disturbances will, of course, not result from such apparently biologically caused disruptions of normal balance, unless the process is reinforced by sociocultural factors. (Where the environment provides behavioral outlets for such biological tension factors, phasal conditions alone will not be pathogenic, whereas a rigidly average-oriented environment will make individual crises in these phases unavoidable although they may be culturally sanctioned.) But the fact remains that the phasal sequence as such contradicts the very principle of equivalence of the two life tendencies, this primary condition of normal development. (We are *not* referring here to cases in which structural defects produce developmental anomalies including acceleration or protraction of the process at a certain point of transition or permanent prevalence of one of the two life tendencies.)

We are accustomed to regarding childhood as the life period of development *par excellence,* a view clearly reflected in the fact that almost every theory of human behavior and development stops at the end of adolescence and, in any case, devotes to adulthood and senescence considerably less attention. On the other hand, we know that childhood as such is characterized by resistance to change or, at least, by increased susceptibility of traumatization through change.* Does this mean that childhood as such is characterized by a disruption of the normative interrelatedness of the two life tendencies, resulting from a maturationally conditioned increase in the tendency toward staticness and causing anxiety and resistance to change? Or, to put it even more paradoxically, does this mean that the life period of development *par excellence* is a period of staticness *par excellence*? Such a statement would certainly not seem to make sense, no more than if we were to maintain that childhood, being a period preceding adult maturity, is pathologic.

* Transition from one environment to another, from one school to another, from one economic status to another, from one family constellation to another, all these and many other experiences of change are liable to operate as precipitating traumatic factors in the life of a child and to set in motion other disrupting factors. Adults often overlook the significance of such precipitators, either because they naively identify their own reactions to such occurrences with those of the child (which Loosli-Usteri (92) has aptly described as symptoms of *Werdeangst*, of anxiety to grow), or because they tend, prematurely, to look for deeper-lying causes, when suddenly some disorder manifests itself in the child's behavior. But without taking into account the child's developmentally conditioned resistance to change we shall never be able adequately to understand, or to deal with, a behavior problem in childhood.

But on closer view, this seeming paradox reveals its deeper truth and adds an important element of definition to those already mentioned: It is no doubt correct to say that, normally, with increasing age, that is, with growing opportunity to deal with different and ever-changing life situations and tasks, the ego's organizational ability grows stronger, the need to fear ego loss in the face of unavoidable interruptions of staticness by intervening events grows weaker, and receptiveness of the intimations emanating from the inner or the outer non-ego ceases to be dangerous.

It follows that childhood anxiety of, and resistance to, change *supports* ego development against the autonomy of the non-ego. In other words, *in childhood it is precisely resistance to change that makes structurization of change possible, since being thrust by biological and social factors of development into the danger of losing a precarious ego position is indeed a real danger.* Resistance to change therefore fulfills an important developmental function, that of screening experience (though the term should not be understood to indicate *conscious* intention). It is true that in such normative resistance to change the life tendency toward staticness finds its expression. But this very normativeness, that is, the structural necessity and purposefulness of developmental change-resistance allows us to conclude that, far from indicating disruption, it *proves* the *interrelatedness* between the two life tendencies. In other words: *normally, resistance to change in certain childhood periods is future-related, is progressive and not regressive, dynamic and not fixational.* This additional element in the definition of development also offers an answer to the question from which we set out: What is the meaning of the term when we speak of *pathological* development?

The psychopath "develops," so does the psychotic, not to speak of the representatives of less extreme disorders, in all of whom the conditions of normality are not absent but not fully present either. In fact, interrelatedness of the two life tendencies is *not* an all-or-nothing quality: no life course is ever immune against the dangers of unbalance, none is ever entirely unbalanced, based on an isolated tendency toward staticness only or on an isolated tendency toward expansion only, not even those of the psychotic or the psychopath.*

To the extent that the life tendency toward staticness predominates, either structurally or as the result of certain psychogenetic configurations, every development will risk the danger of being determined by regressive tendencies or, to be more correct, every structurization is liable to be of the fixation type (conducive to regression).† When the

---

* It would be more correct to say that what we call the psychotic or psychopath does not exist in reality; these are ideal type constructions only that help us in the diagnosis of individual cases (of "more or less").

† In another study (34, p. 51) we have maintained that fixation presupposes inter-

opposite life tendency, that toward expansion, is so prevalent that every form of systematization is liable to be slow and incomplete and inadequate, structurization of developmental changes is bound to be equally weak, so that development will bear the stamp of accidentality, of lack of identity, and externality of change. In neither one of these pathological conditions will the past be present in any phase of development as a structured point of reference, as part of a felt continuity. Nor is the future present as vector of relatedness.

We have mentioned the bivectoriality of structure change, the simultaneity of progressive and regressive direction of development (the extent of progressivity and regressivity being determined by structural and experiential conditions). Regressive tendencies normally supply relevant memory material and help maintain the individual's identity; progressive tendencies manifest themselves primarily as vectors into the future, characteristic, we said (p. 105), of normal development *per se*. Both qualifications are absent in every form of pathological development: memory material becomes irrelevant (for the inflated ego of the psychopath with his excessive tendency toward expansion, for instance) or distorted (through repression and defense, for instance). The dimension of the future does not enter the causal equation of psychopathy, psychosis, or, for that matter, of any abnormal development, not as a definable end condition (in the terms of the above-quoted definition of development), or as the unknown and unknowable infiniteness of possible occurrences and of possible changes.

But whether we speak of fixation, defense, rigidity, reality distortion (in neuroses, character-neuroses, psychosomatic pattern formation, or psychotic systematizations), or of the individual's weakness in structuring his experience (in the varieties of externalized behavior, in acting out, in psychopathy)—we should always remain aware of the fact that no individual can be *defined* by his pathology. The neurotic and the externalized, the psychotic and the psychopath, develop in their somatic, their intellectual, even their emotional and social functions at the same

---

relatedness of the two basic life tendencies. Normally, we said, development and growth are being felt not only as a structural necesity but also as a threat. To the extent that fixation, that is, the tendency to remain statically bound to a specific stage of development, is the individual's reaction to his growth anxiety (92), it is the tendency toward expansion that supplies the anxiety incentive. Where the latter life tendency is abnormally weak (as, for instance, in the psychotic), growth will not be felt intensely enough as a threat to provoke fixation as a defense, irrespective of the relative strength of the tendency toward staticness. Where, on the other hand, the life tendency toward expansion is abnormally strong (as in the psychopath) a strong need "to avoid constancy" will counteract fixation. But when we exclude these cases of extreme pathology, the above statement about the connection between predominance of staticness and fixation remains valid. In other words: fixation *does* presuppose a certain measure of interrelatedness of the two life tendencies, but within this interrelatedness it is the relative predominance of the life tendency toward staticness that accounts for fixation.

time that their abnormality patterns take shape, following certain inherent laws. True enough, the abnormal individual's development will inevitably be affected by the development of his abnormality, and the latter will, of course, develop differently in every individual. But changes do take place in him also independently of his disorders, though they will differ qualitatively from those taking place in the normal person, phase by phase.

Normal development, we said, is characterized by the simultaneity of the vector into the past and the vector into the future. Abnormal development, whatever its type and clinical definition may be, is always characterized by its *high degree of repetitiousness*. Whereas *normal* development is a unifying process, in which every *functional* change is, or becomes, part of a *structure* change, related to the total personality, and every process of conditioning or reinforcement somehow relates to functions rather than to the essence of the individual, in *abnormal* development these relationships are fundamentally different: functional changes relate to a function in its isolatedness rather than to the Gestalt of the total personality, whereas processes of conditioning and reinforcement have as their object the pathology rather than a function; functions tend to become auxiliary, as it were, to the pathology.

This explains, *inter alia,* why abnormal behavior is either full of inner contradictions, lacking in consistency and inner logic, unreliable and unpredictable, or lifelessly rigid and patterned. Both basic qualities of abnormal behavior—which, incidentally, often coexist—are expressions of that repetitiousness which we have mentioned as its essential characteristic. It may be an ever-recurring reaction pattern, peculiar to the phase of primary fixation, that determines development from childhood to adult age, for instance in neurotics; it may be a kind of circular causation process that leads to the emergence of patterns of externalization or of acting out fairly early in life. True enough, functional development *does* take place, and the phases through which the individual passes leave their impact on the development of the abnormal as well as on that of the normal individual. But all these differences and all these changes serve the development of the pathology more than that of the personality. Repetitiousness, we can say at the end of our discussion, precludes genuine ego development.

PART 2

Environment and Development

7

Varieties of Human Behavior

1. Introduction

The second part of this study will be devoted to an analysis of the environmental elements in the causal equations that account for the individual varieties of ego development. We have already pointed out that an analysis of phasal peculiarities must both precede and follow that of environmental factors. Even though it is obvious that not all factors will be found to be of equal causal relevance in each developmental phase, we cannot prove the differences without analyzing them in the changing contexts of those phases.

But the issue becomes still more complicated when we consider the meaning of the *terminal concept of individual varieties of ego development*. Any analysis of behavior and development actually requires a prior analysis of those many possible behavioral outcomes that serve as points of reference in differential etiology. In other words, if we want to know why a specific configuration of partial causes in the environment and the personality produces a specific behavior (a more or less definable unit or picture of behavior), we must start with a phenomenological analysis of the essentials of that form of behavior, including a comparison of its essentials with those of other units. How else could we make meaningful statements about a certain factor or cluster of factors being responsible in one configuration for, let us say, a normal development toward autonomous and flexible conscientiousness, while in another configuration it accounts for neurotic compulsiveness, and yet in a third for neurotic delinquency.

Just as the concept of causal configuration becomes meaningful and applicable only after an abstract (nonconfigurational) analysis of the many partial factors constituting the configuration, so the concept of *causal effect* becomes meaningful only if preceded by an abstract comparison between the essentials of various units of behavior. We suggest, therefore, starting with such a phenomenology of at least the most important varieties of human behavior. But how do we determine what these most

111

important varieties are? Is the criterion a quantitative one only, that is, the relative frequency of occurrence? And how do we define the units of behavior? What categories of classification should determine the organization of the multitude of observable behavior patterns? It is obvious that we cannot hope to be able here to answer these questions, because a detailed discussion of the principles of classifying human behavior would far transcend the limits of the present analysis; it would also seem that the question of the suitability of such principles cannot be answered inductively at all, but only within the framework of a total theory of behavior of which it is a function and an expression.

It will be remembered that we have suggested the following three dimensions in our analysis of the basic concepts of ego development: (a) the relationship between the two life tendencies, that toward staticness and that toward expansion, their relative intensity, the degree of their interrelatedness; (b) the relationship between the ego's organizational strength and its openness toward the inner and the outer non-ego, the unconscious, the depth zone of the psyche, the environment; (c) the degree of introversion and extraversion. It is the interrelation of these dimensions that makes the differential outcome of causal configurations (of environmental and constitutional factors) intelligible.

We shall describe in the following only three types of behavior—the externalized, the neurotic, and the aggressive—well knowing that each of these general concepts covers a large variety of behavioral subunits. We have chosen them because they lend themselves better than more specific types to demonstration of the range from near normality to extreme pathology, and because the vast majority of all behavior forms can be classified within this trichotomy.*

2. EXTERNALIZATION

We have already pointed out that internalization is not identical with autonomy, although the latter will never emerge without the former. In neurotic patterns, we shall see, it is precisely the process of (excessive) internalization that produces heteronomy, that is, dependence on those very complexes of the unconscious that take the place of external realities and are no less autonomous toward the (neurotic) ego than manifestations of the physical or social non-ego.

In this way, internalization may lead to heteronomy. Where, on the other hand, it *does* produce relative autonomy, that is, independence *vis-à-vis* the internal and external non-ego, this autonomy is accompanied

---

* Since subsequent volumes will be devoted to an analysis of the cultural varieties of externalization and to a study of individual pathologies, including certain aspects of neurosis and aggressiveness, we shall confine ourselves here to a summary of ideas which have been elaborated on in other published work (33, 37), from which parts of this chapter are translated.

and characterized by a self-evident feeling of freedom and productiveness, by the ability to enlarge the frontiers of internalization (of concepts, values, ideas and ideals, directives and inner agents).

On the other side, we can distinguish between *internalized and externalized heteronomy*, which shows that heteronomy and externalization are not synonymous either. The difference between internalized and externalized heteronomy can be made clear through the example of what Riesman (112) calls "tradition-directed *versus* outer-directed" behavior.

Internalization in a tradition-directed society (and individual) means: conscious identification with the basic ideas and ideals of the tradition and ego involvement in their realization. Although the individual is not free to decide on his own or even to develop initiative in order to bring about changes, although he feels bound to the directions implied in the tradition which, to him, is an outside reality, a non-ego, he is able to relate himself to this non-ego in a polar relationship. In other words: *internalized* heteronomy presupposes the discovery of the ego as partner of the tradition. On the other hand, we speak of *externalized* heteronomy, when the individual is "contained" in the tradition as part and not as partner of a system of rules and directives, a situation which essentially precludes internalization of values. Absolute subjugation under the rule of authoritarian forces is another example of externalized heteronomy.

Externalization is the process which leads to externality of experience and behavior, that is, to a situation where reality is not organized on the basis of polarity, where ego and non-ego are not related to each other (each being the subject *and* the object of the other), but every occurrence, every process, every action, every object is a manifestation of external factors only. What we call, in the case of normal ego development, the internal realm of the psyche, exists here as expression or manifestation only of the external non-ego. Accidental appearance is the binding reality; there is no meaning hidden behind it; whatever appears is "meant." This applies to thinking and judging as well as to feeling and action. *The ego becomes part of the non-ego.*

(It would therefore be more appropriate to speak, in the case of externalization, of "occurrences"—rather than of the ego—being determined by external factors; the ego does not exist as a definable object, but as a result only of an ever-changing and ever-accidental "outside.")

This, then, raises a number of questions: What kind of externality of behavior, thinking, and feeling emerges under which individual or cultural conditions? What does it mean when it characterizes a phase of normal development, or a cultural pattern, when it is an essential element of certain mental phenomena, when it is symptomatic of certain forms of abnormal behavior? We regard the form of externalization which we find frequently—though of course in different degrees from individual to individual—under conditions of extreme poverty, as the "ideal type" of externalization.* It is this ideal type that serves as a criterion of comparison with all other forms in which externalization can be observed, in the fields of developmental psychology, of social and anthropological psychology, of phenomenology of feelings, of psychopathology.

The following is a brief summary of the essentials of externalization in the so-called ideal type, this existential counterpart of what our society still continues to consider the aim of education—internalization of concepts, values, feelings, relationships. This summary will prepare the ground for a differential analysis of the environmental factors of causation in the various phases of the growing child's development, since all cultural and individual varieties of human behavior can be shown to lie between the two extremes of ideal internalization and ideal externalization.

Feelings of the externalized variety depend on the precipitating situation; they are regulated and modified through reactions of the environment rather than through the ego as the organizing center of consciousness. To the extent that the individual is at all capable of making a reflective statement about his own feelings or those of others whom he observes, he will identify them with their expressions rather than see their relatedness to the ego-identity behind them. (The same holds good for *values*, which are identical with their external representations, or for moral feelings, which are represented in the individual's consciousness through the eliciting demands only.)

There is *no second dimension of meaning:* whatever appears is, in its accidentality, the only and the total reality. This explains not only the passiveness, the suggestibility, of the externalized individual, but also the tendency in his life, of events and actions to spread automatically (inductively). His ego lacks all selectivity.

There is little transfer of experience, since his ability to abstract from the areas of personal relevance is weakly developed. But it would be incorrect to interpret this rigid dependence on personal experience as evidence for a strongly developed ego-consciousness. The opposite is true: latter manifests itself precisely in mental and practical mobility, in the ability of the ego to distantiate itself from its positions, in conscious and volitional separation of the experiencing ego from its experienced content.

Weakness of this ability is, according to Goldstein and Scheerer (57),

---

* We shall analyze in a subsequent volume the so-called "ideal type" of externalized behavior, as it emerges under conditions of extreme poverty and educational neglect, in order to compare its manifestations with those of other forms of externalization as they appear, for instance, under conditions of parental failure in the middle-class family of our time, or under conditions of plenty, or in the affluent society *per se*, or under conditions of primitiveness, of cultural transition, in the rural society, etc.

proof of *defective abstractiveness.* Abstraction requires basic security and courage, he says. They, in turn, require, in addition to certain constitutional dispositions and qualities, an early experience of protectedness by the mother, of rhythm and regularity in the sequence of tension and satisfaction—which, under conditions of externalization, is so weak that abstractive abilities are bound to remain weak and underdeveloped. We shall later see that this attribute of externalization is absent in certain of the varieties and shall discuss the reasons; but in the ideal type at least, defective abstractiveness is one of the central characteristics.

It manifests itself *not only in the intellectual but also in the relational areas of functioning:* we speak of rigidity, of *being tied to the known* or to what the individual considers known to him. Only in his immediate environment does he feel secure (in spite of the many negative forces that are active in it, painfully, frustratingly negative). Only here does he feel protected against surprises and social demands that he is unable to fulfill. The immediate environment is a kind of moratory area (paraphrasing Erikson's concept in his analysis of adolescence). Needless to add, this feeling of protectedness is an illusion reflecting that inability to establish, to maintain, and to modify meaningful relationships that originates in the infant's basic insecurity with his mother.

It is this factor, the quality of the primary relationship between the child and his mother, that explains the varieties of externalization emerging under similar or equal conditions of structure. We have called the relative equivalence of the two basic mother experiences—that of the "absent mother" (AM) and that of the "mother as part" (MaP)—the precondition of normal development, which we have defined as readiness to expect the mother's regular return, "the mother as the near one" (NM) (see pp. 15 ff.). And we have mentioned some of the behavior disorders which may result when one of the two basic experiences is significantly stronger or weaker than the other so that the basic sense of security or the experience of nearness does not emerge (see pp. 18 ff.).

But to the extent that externalization processes are set in motion through these earliest deficiencies in the child-mother relationships, whatever their nature and their causes may be, one essential symptom will be found in each of the behavioral outcomes: *weakness of ambivalence tensions and inner conflicts,* which, as a rule, require a much stronger personal relationship between parents and children than the life conditions here under consideration allow for. Weakness of ambivalence, however, is responsible for the relative weakness of relational abilities in the externalized individual, and particularly in that variety of externalization that emerges under conditions of extreme poverty and educational neglect; the weaker the ambivalence tensions are, the weaker will be the need to get rid of certain strivings through repression, and the more unambiguous will be the tendency toward direct need-satisfaction. This accounts, in turn, for the weakness of internalization and polarization. The results will be univalence of feelings (hatred *or* love, displeasure *or* joy) and replacement of ambiguous, polyvalent feelings and intrapsychic tensions by external conflicts.

Projective transformation, and distortion of reality, and the resulting neurotic patterns of reaction and behavior which are preceded by repression and internalization, are, therefore, almost unknown in the life of the externalized individual. His inclination to make other persons or external happenings and circumstances responsible for his suffering or his failures has nothing to do with projection but is simply an expression of his naive heteronomy. What we call the "inner life" of the person is, for him, nothing but an uncoordinated mass of changing responses to changing situations.

This heteronomy does not preclude the seemingly contradictory attitude and belief that he can manipulate reality "magically," although chance, this all-pervading life principle, requires *fatalistic capitulation.* The coexistence of these contradictory attitudes not only proves the lack of structurality (see pp. 60 *ff.*) in the externalized individual but also proves his relative inability to use abstract thinking for the purposes of his orientation and adjustment, to think in terms of inherent cause and necessary effect: nothing is inherent and nothing is necessary, everything "is" as it happens to be.

It is needless to add, then, *that we shall not find many signs of intentionality and rational planning under conditions of externalization.* "Solutions" are being expected to come from without, almost mechanically, and neither instrumentalistic nor manipulative tendencies are capable of bringing about changes. Thus, the pattern perpetuates itself automatically—since there is no ego to plan, attempt, control, and coordinate change.

This, then, is an existence without that experience of staticness that normally supplies both a feeling for rule and regularity and the confidence that the "known" will remain "there," will remain available, even when the ego leaves it for a while in order to imagine another reality, something unknown, or to form a universally valid concept, or to find and formulate a law.

We shall see later that all these symptoms of externalization (identification of feelings with their manifestations and their eliciting causes, or of values with their representatives, relative absence of meaning as a "second dimension hiding behind the facts," weakness of transfer, of abstraction, of ambivalence, of internalization, of intentionality, of relational ability, fixatedness to the area of the known, heteronomy and belief in chance) do not mean the same in all varieties of externalization, and that each variety has its specific attitudes, essentially connected with those causal configurations that are responsible for its emergence (the life patterns of poverty, of plenty, of primitiveness, of cultural transition, of waywardness, of feeblemindedness, of apathy, etc.).

A few examples should be sufficient, at this stage of our analysis, to make our point clear: "Fixatedness to the known" is, under conditions of want, closely linked with the illusion of "haveability"; thus, a distorted perception of all objects as "wanting and haveable" or as "wanting and unreachable" is being produced. This distortion, in turn, reinforces the illusion of knownness, and although seriously handicapping man's ability to orientate and adjust himself effectively, fulfills the important function of protecting him against the danger of despair. Similarly, the externalized individual's tendency to live in a variety of noncommittal chance groups, without personal involvement or relatedness, fulfills that function of protecting him against the dangers of feeling helplessly alone.

But *fixatedness to the known* is liable to emerge also under opposite socioeducational conditions, those of a life in plenty, though it has, then, a different meaning altogether and produces different patterns of behavior, since it is not linked to that illusion of "haveability" that is so characteristic of externalization under conditions of want; rather, we see here how its essential link with the experience (and the illusion) of limitless availability produces another attitude, that of naive egocentricity (though the latter reinforces the illusion of knownness no less than the former, and both are equally conducive to dedifferentiation). In cultural transition it is the link between the illusion of knownness and fixatedness to the cultural past which accounts for that same dedifferentiation (or lack of differentiation). In the feebleminded it is perseveration, in the wayward child, the frequently recurring enjoyment of discharge of tension, that account for the illusion of knownness and its negative impact on the process and the capability of differentiation.

That the meaning of externalization depends on its main causes can be shown in every symptom area. Let us briefly consider one in which the differences *prima facie* outweigh the similarities, that of *abstract thinking*. While it is self-evident that conceptual disorientation and value disorientation in periods of cultural transition, or the perceptive distortion of reality under the impact of the illusion of "haveability" in the poverty variety of externalization, or passivity and lack of structurality in the life of the wayward child, must have an obnoxious influence on the development of abstractive abilities, the form of externalized behavior as it is liable to emerge under conditions of plenty is *not* essentially characterized by factors damaging or limiting mental mobility. But as a result of the egocentric illusions of "all-availability," the need for polar relationships within the universe of possible objects of cognition is bound to be

felt less and less until its deficiency may again affect the ability to differentiate and to evaluate reality objectively.

Weakness of ambivalence may serve as a third example. The impersonality of the parents which lies at the root of externalization *per se*
may result from their overconcern with the use of ever-available material
resources or with their own personal problems, or with social status resentments, or with the "haveability" of what they have not, or with the patterns and traditions of a cultural or a social group. In each of these cases
the relative weakness of ambivalence will have a different meaning and
different expressions. Here, it may mean absence of tension toward
achievement and growth; there, absence of emotional involvement. Here,
it may mean self-identification with external achievement; there, general
lack of differentiation. Or it may be an expression of feelings and values
being determined by culture-conditioned expectations.

3. Neurotic Behavior

Every neurosis manifests itself in more or less extreme reality distortions
which hinder, on the one hand, the development of genuine autonomy,
and, on the other, the development of naive enjoyment of whatever happens in an unstructured environment, so typical of the externalized individual (and particularly the wayward child). In every neurosis, projection of repressed feelings and strivings is at the root of the abnormal
behavior patterns, and it is precisely this projective distortion of the non-
ego through which the ego loses its subject character. Here, however, the
inherent paradox of neurosis becomes evident: the more it restricts the
individual's functional efficiency, the deeper is his conviction that everything depends on him and is related to him.

This holds good not only for the *compulsion neurotic* with his protective self-restrictions or for the various forms of what psychoanalysis calls
"anal" character disorders, but also for the *anxiety neuroses*. Thus, acute
anxiety states with their somatic symptoms cause at least a partial reality
loss; in the course of this development the ego, delivered to the mercy of
complexes threatening from within, increasingly assumes defense functions, although its sole instrument of defense is anxiety. To give up
anxiety would mean still more endangering existence, so uncertain and
questionable in any case.

The same coexistence of projective transformation of reality into an
area of threat and danger, not only with a strong feeling of helplessness,
but also with the opposite feeling (of the ego standing in the center of
the universe, forced to guarantee its continued existence), this same contradictoriness characterizes chronic anxiety states as well, although their
somatic and emotional symptoms are not explained as expressions of
defense mechanisms but rather as direct results of traumatic experiences

and structural ego weakness. Here, too, neurosis is an expression of the ego's inability freely to communicate with the non-ego, with the environment as well as the unconscious. (Pavor nocturnus is one of the most unequivocal expressions of this inability.)

In phobias we see the coexistence of reality distortion with ego emphasis no less than in compulsion neuroses; but whereas in both the ego is strong enough to systematize its anxiety and to limit it to certain areas of existence only, phobia differs from compulsion neurosis in that the autonomy of the unconscious constantly threatens this systematization. In this respect phobia resembles acute anxiety states: in both the illusion that protection of life depends on the intensity of ego emphasis is equally evident.

Different are conversion hysterias, tics, stuttering, and psychosomatic illnesses. Hysteria, for instance, is based on the neurotic's failure to take cognizance of the danger, a kind of "playing with reality." This is why Kretzschmer (87) calls hysteria the "neurosis of falsity." The pains and the somatic anomalies of the hysteric lack genuineness, not (or at least not only), as Adler (2) maintains, as means used by the socially immature individual to arouse attention and to dominate the environment, but also (and perhaps even primarily) as means to cheat fate and environment.

The hysteric masturbates, as it were, with his pains and exhibits his sexual strivings in organic translation. Rather than distorting reality (projectively) he falsifies his *perception* of reality, while remaining basically aware of its true meaning. But this distortion requires a permanent ego investment, which ultimately is meant to maintain suffering as punishment and as protection. We could speak in this case of a perverted feeling of responsibility: the hysteric feels responsible for his "playings," for maintaining the illusion of being restricted.*

What Fenichel (27) calls "pregenital hysterias" (tics, stuttering, etc.) differs from oedipal conversion hysteria in two respects: on the one hand, the intensity of unlived aggressiveness is much stronger than in conversion hysteria; on the other hand, the symptoms are much less ambiguous and, therefore, much less exchangeable. The *lack* of genuineness, to put it paradoxically, is here much more genuine, much deeper, much more human (central nervous system dispositions are probably more strongly represented in the causal equation).

In psychosomatic illnesses the difference is still more clearly in evidence than in the varieties of pregenital hysteria: here, the organism is still more independent and split off from the ego's synthetic function, and, as a re-

---

* Not only the time factor in the history of traumatization and its passive character account for the emergence of hysteric syndromes, but also a certain constitutional disposition for organic demonstrativeness.

sult, the individual in his suffering "convinces" much more than the hysteric. In many cases it will even be difficult to discover the neurotic elements of reality distortion and ego-relatedness. Such cases are, as a rule, characterized by a relatively normal ability of the patient to adjust himself to his social environment and by his strong tendency to integrate his experience into a personal whole context, sometimes to such an extent that we hesitate to classify him as a neurotic. (Etiologically, the difference between psychosomatic illnesses and hysteria becomes understandable when we consider the fact that the underlying tensions remain in the first case, at least partially, the object of conscious confrontation.)

A few remarks should be added here about the symptoms of introversive character neuroses. Here we find, on the one hand, extreme shyness, oversensitivity, withdrawal, inability to make decisions, lack of initiative, ineffectiveness in thought and action, and, on the other hand, some of the so-called anal symptoms of compulsiveness. Overt anxiety and hidden aggressiveness are typical of the first group, hidden anxiety and overt aggressiveness of the second. Here, too, the neurotic character of the disorder finds its expression in a relative inability to establish polar relationships. The non-ego loses its subject functions in the process of character neurotic systematizations; it coagulates, as it were, into such functions as the ego determines and attributes to the world around. And again, the neurotic indulges in the illusion that everything depends on the ego, though on an ego, we must add, whose organizational ability has remained intact much more than in the aforementioned psychoneuroses.

To sum up: The neurotic is characterized by his inability to relate to the non-ego as to a partner and so to see himself as independent pole of relationship, by his tendency to avoid the danger of autonomous existence through escape into dependence on a projectively distorted and elevated, pathologically autonomized, non-ego. On the other hand, the neurotic indulges in the illusion that everything depends on this impotent and helplessly dependent ego. How can we explain this inner contradiction?

We have pointed out (p. 34) that genuine autonomy manifests itself in the ability to experience that "what determines the ego at any given moment is, in this very moment, *being* determined both by outside factors and by the ego itself; and whenever the ego tries to determine . . . the non-ego, it should not lose awareness of its own dependence . . . on inner and outer factors of determination, including the presently determined non-ego itself." If so, however, the neurotic's illusion that everything depends on his distorting ego precisely proves autonomy defects. Primarily, he feels his traumatizing non-ego as omnipotent and any form of mutuality as dangerous; absolute dependence is his safeguard against destruction, and the neurotic symptoms are the instruments through which he builds that (distorted) non-ego on which he can depend. It is evident that the dependence on his neurotic creation is as illusory as the creation itself (and the therapeutic conclusion to be drawn from these interpretations is that he must learn how to live in partial dependence and partial responsibility).*

4. Digression: Projection and Externalization

Psychoanalysts and psychoanalytically oriented psychologists tend to use the terms "projection" and "externalization" as synonyms. Thus Fenichel (27) interprets the symptoms of projection as externalizations of guilt feelings, of anxiety, of homosexual tendencies, of superego demands. He reduces the various manifestations of projection to the tendency in a structurally weak or injured ego to defend itself by eliminating everything unpleasant so that it may be experienced as part of a non-ego. Isaacs (69) says that the child externalizes inner conflicts in his plays. Heiss (61) defines projection as "externalization of inner processes" which thereby become "objectified," and "happening from without" (though in essentially different forms when they appear in plays, in dreams, in phantasies, in test reactions, in neurotic or in psychotic symptoms). Horney (64), although calling externalization a wider concept than projection, because it includes experiencing in others "not only one's faults ... but ... all feelings," nevertheless gives only examples of what psychoanalysis in general calls projection.

Projection is defined as unconscious transfer of unconscious or of partially conscious strivings and contents onto suitable environmental figures, a transfer which aims at liberating the ego from the pressure of unbearable feelings and affects. What has been projected, then returns to the ego as non-ego contents (though only after being distorted in the very process of projection).

It follows that projection presupposes prior internalization and the existence of a strong inner life of feelings, of strivings, of tensions. In projection, the ego's tendency toward systematization is strongly developed, while the opposite tendency, that toward expansion, is structurally weak. Hence the rigidity that is characteristic of every projection.

We now understand that projection, far from being identical with externalization (as we have defined it), is rather its exact opposite, and this in spite of the fact that in both the non-ego "occurs" to the ego. This occurrence character has an essentially different meaning in both: in pro-

---

* When we compare the neurotic with the aggressively acting-out individual, we discover that the neurotic's relational ability is structurally intact although he is unable to make use of it as long as he is enmeshed in his pathology. This can be proved by the very tendency in the neurotic to escape into *dependence* on a non-ego, or by his ability to establish transference relationships in reaction to therapeutic endeavors and thus to regain his potentially normal relationship ability. It is only his fixedness to the phases of early traumatization that make him unable to *use* his relational ability realistically.

jection, the ego reacts to what returns from the non-ego as being intentionally directed toward the ego. The latter, though remaining unaware of the actual meaning of the external occurrence, reacts to it consistently, in contrast to reactions under conditions of externalization, which are characterized by their irregularity and their unpredictability. What elicits in one case of externalization aggressive reactions may, in another, produce a feeling of helplessness, or it may pass unnoticed, that is, remain insignificant.

Absence of the experience of an unambiguous intentionality in the manifestations of the non-ego and absence of a system of consistent ego reactions characterize, so we have said, the occurrence character of the non-ego in externalization, in contrast to projection, where the experience of the non-ego as intentional is matched by the logic (and the logistics) of ego defense. In the former, both the non-ego manifestations and the ego reactions constitute a more or less undifferentiated field of outside forces; in projection, ego experience and ego reactions are the filter through which the "outside" must pass. Whoever uses the two terms as synonyms should bear in mind that what is externalized by way of projection, remains ego-related (or can at least always be related to the ego). Hence, when we speak of externalization in this case, it should be regarded as unsuccessful, as fictitious. That the ego is unaware of this failure or this fictitiousness does not alter the fact that it continues to function as ego, although the spell of its projections may be cast upon it, and part of it may even be transplanted to the outside.

Projection is always connected with regression, hence, with an at least partial abolishment of prior internalization. This explains the essential difference between neurosis and externalization, between neurotic and reactive delinquency, between psychosis and psychopathy. *Regressive deinternalization is not identical with externalization.**

A clear distinction between these two concepts is of particular importance in consideration of the essence of the various forms of aggressive behavior, which we are now going to define.

5. Aggressiveness—A Structural Analysis

The forms of aggressive behavior are as different as are the clinical pictures of which they are symptomatic. Loss of cortical control or "brain

---

* Let it be mentioned here, though only in passing, that the identification of projection and externalization in psychoanalytic theories of neuroses is strangely contrasted by the distinction between the neurotic, who is said to internalize his conflicts and to act them out by way of projections only, and the delinquent, who is said to act out his conflicts openly and directly, to externalize them, and thus to avoid neurotic involvement (22). Although we do not accept the identification of "acting out" with externalization either (as we shall try to show in the section on forms of delinquency), it would seem to us that the latter identification (of acting out and externalization) *precludes* the first one (of projection and externalization). "Projection" should certainly not be equated with "acting out."

stem drivenness" (114) following cerebral traumatization, certain forms of constitutional psychopathy or of feeblemindedness, certain perversions or manias, neurotic character or behavior disorders, but also maturational negativism, cultural patterns, identification with aggressive standards or images—all these produce aggressiveness as an essential manifestation, though it obviously means something different in each unit of behavior.

But we speak of aggressiveness not only in the context of abnormal behavior—in every individual a certain amount of aggressiveness belongs to his "normality," though type conditions and integrational strength account for differences in degree and in quality. The question, then, arises how to define aggressiveness as such, and how to define the criteria of distinction between its negative and its normative manifestations.

The answer to both parts of the question should take into account the well known, yet not always well understood, fact that at least in Western civilization we witness a strange discrepancy between antiaggressive Christian ethics and the ideal of aggressive efficiency. Here we identify aggressiveness with destruction and reject forceful alteration of existing conditions; there we educate our children to become adults capable of "conquering" positions and status and to rely on calculation rather than on empathy, on impersonality rather than on feeling, on rationality rather than on intuition. We want them to be ready and willing to surpass others, and to enforce solutions. *In this discrepancy, the life-inherent contradiction between the tendency toward expansion and that toward staticness finds its value expression,* expansion being represented by the extravert ideals of forceful determination, and staticness by the ideals of obedience (to elders, to society, to conventions) and of goodness.

This is the specific form in which *structural* ambivalence manifests itself in our culture (whereas it finds other specific expressions in other cultures, even in those with seemingly less contradictory value orientations). Independent of it, and yet reinforced by it, is the *dynamic* ambivalence of environmental interventions being experienced as frustrating interruptions of staticness and being expected as means of rescue and restitution; aggressive elimination of the frustrating figures and forces is being wished for and feared (since it would entail isolation or counterattack).

This is why repressing aggressiveness serves as a means of protecting the weak ego against the dangers of environmental counteraggressiveness. But repressed aggressiveness returns in different forms: as seemingly unaggressive, "good" behavior of a strongly defensive character; as compulsive moralism; as partial sublimation; as vitality loss with its various symptoms (from fatigue and apathy over lack of intellectual and relational initiative to psychosomatic and clearly neurotic syndromes).

The question of why and how repressed aggressiveness returns has been studied and described by psychoanalysts. But what aggressiveness essentially is, how its normative function differs from its pathogenic form and how both differ essentially from anxiety—these and similar questions are *not* being dealt with by psychoanalysis.

We quote from another study (31):

"Leaving and transcending an extant life constellation is, normally, a preparatory stage only, related to the goal of higher integration. It presupposes a process of loosening the relatively stable context of interrelated parts in preparation of their restructurization on a higher level of functional significance. In pathological processes, however, which are characterized by a relative disruption of the normative interrelatedness of the two life tendencies and by their relative isolation from each other, their destructive aspects become visible: the tendency toward expansion is then liable to manifest itself as an aggressive tendency toward destroying meaningful wholes into meaningless parts (a tendency which may cause those isolated parts to 'grow wild'), and the tendency toward staticness is liable to manifest itself as a tendency toward compulsive clinging to an actually extant state, usually resulting in devitalization and structural shrinkage. Dissolution of wholes into unrelated and pseudo-autonomous parts, morbid refusal to change, shrinkage of vitality, of structure and of function—these are the essential elements of negative, destructive aggressiveness in its allotropic and its autotropic forms.

"However, if we want to understand the essence of aggressiveness, we must include in our analysis its positive and constructive aspect as well. To discover it we should ask ourselves which elements of aggressiveness are contained in the normative interrelatedness of the two basic life-tendencies.*

"Every organic expansion, every developmental change, is preceded by the break-up of a whole, every restructurization of elements presupposes a prior destruction of the unit in which these elements are tied together 'systematically.' Though it is true that in a normal process of development and growth these elements remain, to some extent, related to each other also when taken out of their systematic whole context, they must be free to combine with new elements. This, however, means that the break-up preceding the formation of more complex and more comprehensive units of organization must be forcible enough to extricate parts out of their whole cathexis and so transform them into 'freely usable' elements. The source of the energy needed for this process is the life-inherent tendency toward expansion, whereas the tension potential generated in

---

* The following footnote is also given as a part of the material here quoted:

"We would, of course, be utterly wrong if we would try to discover the positive aspects of aggressiveness by analyzing the aggressive elements in our moral and cultural orientation. For, the latter may be but an epiphenomenon of that very pathology which we have tried to describe in short and which, we add, may be responsible for our conscious rejection of aggressiveness."

the course of the break-up of the extant whole is normally being used for the subsequent resystematization. Here, the positive aspect of aggressiveness becomes visible: it is that of the forceful dissolution of an organic whole into independent elements capable of combining with other independent elements to form new wholes, on a relatively higher level of integration.

"Thus, the first common element of negative and positive aggressiveness is the dissolution of wholes, and the first criterion of differentiation is its direction, either toward isolation of pseudo-autonomous, and unrelated, parts and shrinkage of structure, function and vitality, or toward growth, that is, restructurization of autonomous, and related, parts.

"Let us try, before we go on, to exemplify this thesis by commenting briefly on the positive and the negative aspects of aggressiveness in interpersonal relationships and in that of social change.

"Entering into a meaningful relationship requires as a rule a direct attack upon, and breaking through, one's own as well as the potential partner's resistance. The ego systems of both of them must be loosened up, as it were, prior to the restructurization of their elements in the context of the relationship; this means that temporarily each ego loses part of its determining function, or, in other words, that the individual is threatened with partial ego loss. In such a situation courageous aggressiveness is needed to overcome the structural reaction of anxiety: the ego must be ready to 'take the risk' by attacking its own as well as the other ego's tendency toward staticness which is liable to manifest itself— in this case—as a tendency toward self-identification. If the latter prevails and the ego recoils upon itself, the other, negative, aspect of aggressiveness is liable to appear, in the form of affective negation of otherness and as a tendency toward rigid and isolationist protection of the ego's narrow frontiers. Depreciation of, attack upon, and in extreme cases even destruction of, the other ego—conceived of as a source of danger—are the expressions of negative aggressiveness, in contradistinction of readiness for change through interpersonal relationships, that is, to attack upon any statically defined ego frontiers which, in this case, is the main expression of positive aggressiveness.

"In the process of social and cultural change and of adaptation to new conditions positive aggressiveness expresses itself in the individual's readiness and ability to break-up his system of habits and patterns into isolated elements while relating them selectively to the demands of the new social and cultural constellation to which the individual finds himself exposed; and negative aggressiveness expresses itself in affective negation of the old patterns while taking over part of them meaninglessly, that is, without relating them to the new reality, or, alternatively, in violent and destructive denial of the new patterns and values while, at the same time, losing that identity feeling which gave meaning to the old ones. Here, the expressions of positive and of negative aggressiveness should be interpreted as symptoms and indications of the relative presence or absence of flexible identity.

"To sum up: we can define positive aggressiveness as the ego's readiness and ability to attack any static frontiers and to transcend itself while remaining self-identical; and negative aggressiveness as destruction of otherness out of fear of ego loss, resulting in a perversion of identity into rigid and isolationist staticness.

"We now understand why it is more difficult to identify positive than negative aggressiveness. We have defined positive aggressiveness as forceful dissolution of an extant whole into independent elements capable of combining with other independent elements to form a new whole on a relatively higher level of integration. Normally, however, this dissolution is only a transitional phase immediately followed by, and related to, the process of restructurization. Hence, the character of uninterrupted continuity attaching to any process of normal development, growth or change, a character which makes difficult, if not impossible a clear distinction between the constituent phases of this process, including that of "dissolution". Pathological processes, on the other hand, tend to produce results which are static or automatically inductive and therefore more easily recognized as symptoms of destructive aggressiveness. It is the compulsiveness inherent in every expression of negative aggressiveness and not only the disturbing effect it exercises that accounts for the widespread tendency to identify aggressiveness with its negative aspects only."

Let us now, briefly, analyze the structural conditions of negative and of positive aggressiveness. For a more detailed analysis, the reader is referred to our paper (31) quoted above.

Negative, destructive aggressiveness requires: (a) a feeling of "destroyability" by superior forces in the environment or by uncontrollable unconscious complexes, which, as a rule, appear as parts of that environment; (b) a need for heightening the feeling of ego potency by eliminating the "threat from without"; (c) lack of inner mobility.

We exclude from the present discussion the psychopathic variety of aggressiveness which is characterized by absence of the first and the third conditions: the psychopath does not feel destroyable because he has succeeded in perverting, as it were, the structurally given dichotomy of ego and non-ego into an all-including ego reality and, therefore, does not feel *anything*, neither love nor hate, neither being threatened nor being in need of self-protection through aggressiveness. Even though he may commit murder and rape, he is not aggressive.

The second condition may be eliminated by certain organic states (usually of the cerebral trauma type), by an extreme and overwhelming intensity of reality dangers (in which case flight, fear, despair, or apathy are more likely to appear than aggressiveness), or by an equally extreme autonomy of unconscious forces invading and inundating the ego. It is obvious that in all these cases aggressiveness becomes not only meaningless but also structurally impossible. (Sham rage of the variety described by Cannon (16), uncontrollable irruptions of the psychotic variety, and quasi-aggressive but unintentional panic reactions should again be excluded from the symptomatology of aggressiveness.)

It may sound strange to say that aggressiveness, this seemingly dynamic reaction to threat and danger, is based on lack of mobility, that is, on overstaticness. Even if we exclude psychopathy, neither the normal nor the organic, neither the neurotic nor the delinquent varieties of aggressiveness seem to fall into the category of overstaticness. And yet, they are all characterized by the ego's more or less radical inability to transcend the rigidly defined and established boundaries of its self-conception. We shall see how positive aggressiveness is primarily different in this respect.

Mobility is closely linked with another element, of differentiation rather than of definition: the degree of ego participation. We know that the latter is liable to be lowered not only by certain organic factors but also by certain developmental changes that are, as a rule, being accompanied by ego weakness. It is the degree of ego participation that determines the fate of aggressiveness and thereby also its quality, the degree of its negativeness. (Suppression, for instance, which requires a higher degree of ego participation than does repression, allows aggressiveness to survive, at least in phantasies and conscious desires, and therefore prevents certain negative consequences of uncontrollable transformation through repression.)

But lack of mobility is not only one of the structural conditions of negative aggressiveness, it also tends to become more extreme through the latter,* resulting in defensive overstaticness. The latter may, then, lead to counterattacking the threatening aggressor, but may also set in motion a process leading over defensive increase of rigidity to a kind of imagined anticipation of destruction, by which the ego gradually destroys *itself* in order to escape the need for giving up its rigid self-perception.

Before describing the symptoms in which *negative* aggressiveness manifests itself, we suggest the following analysis of the structural conditions of *positive* aggressiveness. It requires: (a) a feeling of ego permanence and identity in the face of change factors operating from within and from without; in other words, a feeling that the ego's synthetic ability offers protection against the non-ego's superiority; (b) ego mobility, that is, a capacity for self-transcendence, for adaptive changes, for adequate defense, for growth (an ego feeling itself secure knows that nothing ever is final); (c) an experience of the non-ego as resisting, as a challenge to its activity (without which the two first conditions lose their normative

---

* Here, again, the third law of configuration (see pp. 87 ff.) is proved. The results of a certain causal factor (aggressiveness in our case) intensifies that factor (lack of mobility in our case).

meaning);* (d) readiness not to rely only on what Jung calls "the dominant functions" but to live in communicative contact with the *alter ego* and thus to remain open to the manifold intimations of change and growth which the non-ego (the external reality as well as the "reality of soul") offers.

To sum up: Negative aggressiveness, which aims at destruction, at dissolution of wholes into unrelated parts, is the reaction of an overstatic ego to the feelings of objective destroyability from without; in this reaction the ego, knowing itself not to be its own master, tries to reestablish and to heighten its feeling of potency through eliminating the threatening foe who is being experienced as external or is being externalized. In negative aggressiveness, the ego, though knowing itself to be the object of the non-ego, has preserved sufficient organizational strength to relate, as reacting subject, to this non-ego, but does not possess sufficient mobility to relate simultaneously to its own frontiers as objects of attack, of change and transcendence.

Positive aggressiveness, on the other hand, which aims at dissolution of wholes into mutually related parts, that is, ultimately, at higher levels of integration, presupposes an ego characterized by both a strong feeling of identity and a high degree of mobility, an ego whose experience of the non-ego as resisting (not as threatening) becomes a challenge to its own integrative and synthesizing function. It requires an organizationally strong and energetic ego which is ready and able to relate simultaneously to the non-ego and to itself, both being subjects and objects. While the non-ego is experienced as subject and the ego as object of the non-ego in both positive and negative aggressiveness, the difference between the two lies in the way the ego relates to itself. In negative aggressiveness the ego operates as subject of reactively destructive externalization; in positive aggressiveness, as subject of actively synthetic internalization (which is only another way of saying that in positive aggressiveness the ego is an object not only of the non-ego but also of itself).

What are the main manifestations of negative and of positive aggressiveness?

The former can be classified according to the object of aggression which may be the ego or the non-ego (we then speak of autotropic or of allotropic forms), according to the degree of ego participation, and according to the modality of aggressiveness (character traits and attitudes, phantasies, isolated acts). Autotropic aggressiveness finds its expression in self-hate and self-destruction (in action or in phantasy), where the degree of ego participation is *high;* or in failure patterns, in feelings of inadequacy,

---

* "Resisting" does not mean "attacking." Whereas in the latter the non-ego is experienced as a subject only and the ego as an object only, "resistance of the non-ego" describes a relationship in which both are experienced simultaneously as subjects and as objects.

of insecurity, of inferiority, in day-dreaming, in apathy, in pseudo-retardation, etc., where the degree of ego participation is *lower*. Allotropic aggressiveness, on the other hand, manifests itself in negativism, misanthropy, destructive ideologies, sadistic tendencies (both sexually and morally), extreme egocentricity, criminality, in isolated acts of assault and cruelty, theft and disobedience, or in impotent phantasies of potency—all indicating a relatively high degree of ego participation; when the latter is lower, certain character-neurotic symptoms or isolated offenses, fits of temper tantrum, aggressions against substitute objects or aggressive dreams are liable to appear.*

All of these symptoms have in common absence of vitality, of growth potential, of mutuality; they are characterized by their functional inadequacy and their lack of reality-adaptedness, as well as by their automatic inductiveness.

Positive aggressiveness, on the other hand, expresses itself in attitudes and actions which show the reverse characteristics—of vitality, mutuality, reality-adaptedness, and mobile autonomy. It manifests itself in socially desirable attitudes, abilities, and actions such as physical and mental persistence, goal-directed determination, consistency, courage in the face of unknown tasks and situations, constructive analysis (meaning the ability to dissolve whole-contexts in order to reorganize the elements meaningfully), goal-directed forcefulness in ideological or in professional activities for which the ego functions serve as instruments and "partners of realization" rather than standing in the center of motivation and relatedness. The list could, of course be enlarged, but for our present purpose these few examples may be sufficient.

Any attempt to classify the symptoms of positive aggressiveness according to those criteria that we have suggested should be used for a classification of the negative symptoms would be contrary to the former's essential elements of definition. Neither allotropic nor autotropic phantasies of heroism, for instance, indicate positive aggressiveness *per se*, but must often be included in the group of ego-related day-dreams which jeopardize rather than support ego efficiency. Autotropic aggressiveness manifesting itself in ascetic acts or attitudes, to give another example, should not be evaluated positively, unless the presence of ego-transcending motives and goals can be proved (whatever the value area may be to which these goals and motives belong); in their absence, ascetic acts and

---

* It may be argued that the symptoms mentioned here differ markedly among themselves as regards the degree of organizational ability required for their production. Character-neurotic defenses certainly require more ego strength than, say, the emergence of aggressive dreams, aggressiveness against substitute objects more than temper tantrums. But organizational ability is not always and not exclusively a function of ego participation, which, in contrast to the former, presupposes consciousness. It is this factor of consciousness that is equally absent in all the abovementioned symptoms of allotropic aggressiveness.

attitudes not only become indicative of *negative* aggressiveness, but, at the same time, the genuineness of their autotropic character becomes doubtful.

This leads us to the central question in an analysis of aggressive behavior: Is what we here call positive aggressiveness only the result of socialization, conditioning, sublimation, that is, of a long process in the course of which basically destructive (negative) tendencies are being tamed and transformed, so that in the end, the social value of the individual's actions and attitudes becomes the sole criterion of distinction? Or are relative interrelatedness of the two basic life tendencies and the ego's readiness and willingness for self-transcendence conditions and expressions of a *structurally different* type of aggressiveness?

It is obvious that the *expressions* of negative aggressiveness, in reaction to unavoidably frustrating experiences, appear earlier in life than those of positive aggressiveness, whose emergence depends on the existence of an ego functioning as the center of synthesis and consciousness. But this is not identical with saying that the *structural conditions* of positive aggressiveness appear later in life than those of negative aggressiveness. In fact, in the very term "structural conditions" temporal priority of the positive, meaning the normative, condition is implied. On the other hand, the extent to which these conditions become determinants of ego development or give way to the crystallization of opposite, negative, conditions, depends on such environmental factors as early mother-child relationships, sociocultural patterns, presence or absence of compensatory forces of education, etc. (not to speak of constitutional dispositions and thresholds). What we have said in Chapter 2 about defective mother experiences in the infant (see pp. 18 *ff.*) and in Chapter 5 about negative structurization (see pp. 66 *ff.*), may be sufficient to make our present thesis comprehensible: absence of a feeling for rule and regularity, lack of basic trust and of the experience of nearness, make interrelatedness of the two life tendencies, make polar relationships between the ego and the non-ego, difficult if not impossible. Which is only another way of saying that aggressiveness is bound to find primarily negative expressions, if early relationship experiences in configuration with congenital dispositions obstruct the development and consolidation of structural conditions of positive aggressiveness (as defined above).

But on the other hand, *complete* absence of the conditions that are conducive to the emergence of positive aggressiveness is very rare indeed. These are the exceptional cases in which no educational endeavor is capable of counteracting the then unavoidable radical retreat into rigidity or destructiveness, or of transforming negative into positive aggressiveness. In the vast majority of individual developments, it is the life-inherent tendency of opposite principles to relate to each other, rather than to exclude each other, that explains the possibility of transformation and of sublimation. The latter possibility would not exist, were not its final result structurally present before education starts.

"It is 'present' in individually different degrees, depending on a number of constitutional and experiential factors which combine into causal constellations from the very moment of conception. The more it is present, the smaller are the chances for negative aggressiveness to become deeply structurized, in reaction to frustration, and the better are the chances for positive aggressiveness to become an autonomous ego modality as the result of educational transformation of negative aggressiveness" (31, p. 272).

What we have said in the preceding paragraph about the essential elements of each of the two types of aggressiveness can also serve as a "criterion of distinction between sublimational transformations in which the originally negative aggressiveness continues to manifest itself in its characteristic symptoms, and those in which the structural basis of aggressiveness has been altered by sublimation" (31, pp. 272 f.).

This leads to the last point of our brief analysis, the meaning of the concept of *unconscious* aggressiveness. Psychoanalysts devote much, in fact most, of their interpretations of seemingly normal or of obviously abnormal behavior to the problems of so-called unconscious aggressiveness. The most nonaggressive character traits and attitudes, such as apathy, depression, shyness, ineffectiveness, fatigue, and general retardation are being presented in the psychoanalytical case histories and theories as manifestations of repressed and unconscious hostility, the discovery of which is believed to bring about radical changes in attitudes and behavior; perversions and addictions, neuroses and character neuroses, psychosomatic illnesses and habit disorders—everywhere, repressed or displaced aggressiveness is held responsible for the pathology. But since every act of aggression presupposes, as Fenichel has said (27, pp. 38 and 86), *intention* to destroy, unconscious aggressiveness means the existence of intentions of which the ego is unaware and which are often dramatically opposed to what the individual consciously wants to do or to achieve (neurotic delinquency, manias, or compulsion neuroses being good examples for this inner condition).

But important as the distinction between conscious and unconscious aggressiveness may be for the clinician, we should not forget that aggression is in almost every case a *conscious act* (we disregard for the moment such aggressions as may emerge in psychotic states or epileptic fits), although its *motives* may be unconscious, and its *meaning* may be radically different from its appearance. Ego participation is perhaps stronger in the *conscious* act of aggression not only because consciousness means intentionality, coordination, control, but also because unconsciousness means division of ego energy between reality distortion and defense, between two self-contradictory needs, that of destroying the threatening non-ego (threatening in its attractiveness or in its superiority) and that of increasing its own potency feeling. But even with its higher degree of ego participation, conscious aggressiveness, too, is rooted in a deeply unconscious feeling of objective destroyability by forces from within that are represented by forces and figures without.*

We should not lose sight of this basic identity of conscious and unconscious aggressiveness when trying to transform negative into positive (and to preserve the originally positive) aggressiveness through education and therapy, through socialization and sublimation. Such transformation always implies strengthening the aggressive individual's consciousness, his awareness of the hidden meaning of behavior and, ultimately, his readiness to accept objective destroyability without fear.

6. DIGRESSION: ANXIETY AND NEGATIVE AGGRESSIVENESS

If the frustrating or threatening aggression of the superior non-ego is defined as a basic condition for the emergence, in an overstatic ego, of both anxiety and negative aggressiveness, the question inevitably arises: what are the essential differences between these two reactions to frustration? Attempts have been made to reduce this problem of differences to one of—congenitally given or ontogenetically crystallized—types. However, as both anxiety and aggressiveness appear—though in different forms and degrees—in every individual either simultaneously or alternately, and as anxiety determines the fate of aggressiveness and *vice versa*, typology, at least as an exclusive instrument of differential interpretation, would seem to be inadequate. In any case, no such interpretation should be attempted before we are able clearly to compare with one another each of the structural elements of the two phenomena under discussion. We therefore propose, first to summarize the elements of anxiety which we have tried to analyze in an earlier paper (29).

Anxiety, we have said there, is: (a) fear of ego loss, (b) following the disturbance of staticness, through (c) environmental frustration, (d) developmental change, or (e) reactive regression and its concomitant dedifferentiation. The ego in order to experience anxiety must be (f) organizationally weak in addition to feeling (g) that it is not its own master and (h) that it is unable to return to staticness. In other words: anxiety is the

---

* When ego participation decreases below a minimum, aggressiveness becomes impossible. Extreme lack of ego mobility may manifest itself in helplessness, withdrawal, despair, apathy; the ego may lose all hope of ever being able to restitute or heighten its feeling of potency, and completely ceases to be a subject of relationships. We may sometimes be able to trace back such behavior to childhood repression of allotropic aggressiveness, but we should no longer speak here of autotropic *aggressiveness*, because (and to the extent that) the ego has ceased to participate in its acts of self-denial.

affective reaction (i) to the feeling of helplessness in the face of superior forces which threaten total or partial annihilation. The ego feels defenseless because (j) the threatening foe has, as it were, penetrated its inner precincts and because (k) it is self-related in feeling threatened.

If we now compare these elements of anxiety with their counterparts in negative aggressiveness, we arrive at the following conclusions:

(a) While in anxiety, fear of ego loss follows an environmental or developmental disturbance of staticness and expresses itself in the feeling of inability to regain or reestablish staticness, environmental or developmental frustration elicits, in aggressiveness, alongside with the feeling of objective destroyability from without, a rigid tendency to maintain and defend the ego state (and status) by eliminating the frustrating "attackers" through counterattack.

(b) While in anxiety, fear of ego loss may lead to regression which in turn is liable to increase anxiety, aggressiveness usually prevents regression (though it may appear as an epiphenomenon of regressive primitivization).

(c) While in anxiety, a passive and organizationally weak ego feels itself to be helpless and defenseless in the face of forces threatening from within (though usually projected and appearing "without"), negative aggressiveness presupposes an ego strong enough organizationally to react to the feeling of destroyability (from without) by trying to heighten its potency feeling through its externalizing aggressiveness.

(d) While lack of ego mobility and relative isolation from each other of the two basic life tendencies are common structural elements in anxiety and in negative aggressiveness, anxiety is characterized by the feeling that expansion comes from within, as a threat to staticness which the ego feels unable to maintain or restitute; and negative aggressiveness is characterized by the feeling that expansion comes from without, again as a threat to staticness which, however, the ego feels able to eliminate. In anxiety, staticness is experienced as depending on the non-ego, and in aggressiveness, on the ego; whereas expansion is experienced, in anxiety, as happening "within," and in aggressiveness, "without."

(e) While in anxiety, the ego is more or less cut off from the non-ego but continues to relate to itself (though in a self-destructive way), in aggressiveness, the ego continues to relate to the non-ego (though again destructively only), but is more or less cut off from itself.

Like any other dichotomy, these, too, are meaningful as abstractions only. In reality anxiety and aggressiveness always appear jointly, though always in different proportions of intensity. Nonintegration of the two basic life tendencies, their relative isolation from each other, the universality of environmental and developmental frustration, and the maturationally and experientially conditioned weakness of the ego as center of synthesis and organization—all explain the universality of anxiety and negative aggressiveness. Their simultaneity is the necessary outcome of the fact that the frontiers between ego and non-ego are never absolutely defined; in other words, the distinctions, formulated in the foregoing paragraph, between "within" and "without" and relatedness to the ego or the non-ego, have relative validity only. In almost every individual and in almost every life situation, neither constitutional predispositions nor specific relational experiences in the different stages of the child's development preclude coexistence of anxiety and aggressiveness. Hence the many possibilities of anxiety being modified under the influence of aggressiveness and, *vice versa*, by way of contamination, transformation, compromise, etc., whenever one of the two has become more or less structurized as a predominant reaction pattern. Aggressive denial of anxiety or anxious denial of aggressiveness, passive or resentful denial of both, and compulsive coexistence of both are the typical constellations which allow for a classification of almost all behavioral pathologies.

DENIAL OF ANXIETY AND MAINTENANCE OF AGGRESSIVENESS

Here belong the cases of "showing off" in aggressive acts, attitudes, identifications, or ideologies which are easily recognized as clumsy and often infantile attempts to drown, as it were, the underlying anxiety in the loud hubbub of aggressiveness. The lower the degree of ego participation, the more will these attempts be successful.

DENIAL OF ANXIETY AND OF AGGRESSIVENESS

(a) The most extreme and radical result of this two-way denial is apathy, the formation of a kind of protective crust around the ego. ("Nothing can hurt the ego and there is no need for action.")

(b) Inactivity is a less intensive form of apathy, and a higher degree of ego participation is required in order to maintain the protective crust by inactivity than by apathy.

(c) The degree of ego participation is still higher in a third type of denial of anxiety and of aggressiveness, represented by certain forms of resentment. "The world is aggressive; I could, if I wanted, counterattack, but I am not going to give in to aggressiveness. If I am not aggressive, I am superior to the aggressive world; if I am superior, I need not be frightened; and the less anxiety, the less need for aggressiveness." (The price to be paid is the feeling of being discriminated against, wronged and injured, in which both anxiety and aggressiveness return under disguise, as it were.)

MAINTENANCE OF ANXIETY AND DENIAL OF AGGRESSIVENESS

This "solution" appears in two basically different forms:

(a) Anxiety may be maintained, intensified and perpetuated by the very denial of active or counteractive aggressiveness. The result may be self-limiting or self-negating depression or despair, in which the ego continuously anticipates, as it were, destruction from without and makes no attempt to heighten its potency feeling by counterattack. (This form of behavior should not be identified with similar forms of autotropic aggressiveness manifesting itself, for instance, in autosadism or ineffectuality, in which the ego does not deny its aggressiveness but only changes its object by way of inversion, more often than not betraying its truly allotropic character by the pressure it—directly and indirectly—exercises on the environment.)

(b) Anxiety may also be maintained, intensified and perpetuated by choosing symptoms or character traits and attitudes (such as, for instance, stutter or enuresis, compulsive overprotection or overgoodness) which, while seemingly unaggressive, make it possible for anxiety to survive, particularly in the form of anxious expectations.

COEXISTENCE OF ANXIETY AND AGGRESSIVENESS

Aggressiveness, in order to be able to coexist with anxiety, must provoke, by and in the very act of destruction, fear of being cut off from the non-ego (which would make aggressiveness impossible). This fear, in order to be able to coexist with aggressiveness, must reinforce the latter by creating and maintaining tensions. Thus, anxiety, which is fundamentally fear of being unable to return to staticness, becomes, in the coexistence with aggressiveness, fear of, or flight from, staticness; and aggressiveness, which is fundamentally protective elimination of the forces that threaten the ego's staticness, becomes, in coexistence with anxiety, compulsive destruction of staticness. (Elements of this constellation can be found in almost every case of kleptomania, compulsive sex aggression, etc.)

7. DELINQUENT BEHAVIOR

The distinction between allotropic and autotropic aggressiveness and the discovery through psychoanalysis of the dynamic connection between the two—one transforming itself into the other—has led to a far-reaching identification of contradictory behavior forms as indicating the same defense mechanisms. It is particularly the concept of reaction formation through which *nonaggressive* (or *antiaggressive*) behavior is explained as basically (or genotypically) aggressive. Thus, the essential difference between neurosis and delinquency is being reduced to one between modes of solving the same tension problem.

Impulses may find satisfaction in different ways, through reactive transformation of their goals, through idealizing vindication, through isolation from the rest of the personality (whereby gratification without taking responsibility for the aggressive outcome is being made "legitimate").

Acting out of neurotic impulses, characteristic of the so-called neurotic character (5), aims, we are told, at avoidance of displeasure rather than at the attainment of pleasure, although neurotic conflicts persist (for instance in accident proneness).

Thus, the concept of neurotic character approximates what Freud (44), Reik (111), Aichhorn (3), and others have described and analyzed as the criminal out of unconscious guilt feelings, who commits his offenses in order to be caught and punished (actually for his unconscious guilt-provoking oedipal strivings). The ego-alien way of such aggressive acts, unconsciousness, and compulsiveness are common characteristics of both (coexistence of instinct and superego gratification makes them comparable, says Fenichel (27), to the so-called cyclic personality).

Perversions, psychoanalysis claims, are also a variety of neurotic behavior, appearing as the result of pregenital fixations and strong castration fears in persons with constitutionally increased sexual excitability of certain erogenic zones, which operates as an anxiety-weakening factor. Guilt feelings after the need is satisfied also seem to indicate the basically neurotic nature of perversion.

Finally, psychoanalysis speaks of impulse neurosis as it finds an expression in manias, addictions, and particularly the so-called instinct-ridden character—*Triebhaft*, according to Reich (110). Oral fixation is said to be the decisive factor of determination. Fenichel claims that these forms of delinquent behavior are distinguished from compulsion neuroses *without* antisocial symptom manifestations by their ego-syntonic, though irresistible character (as against the ego-alien nature of the latter). The instinct-ridden character, this extreme variety of impulse neurosis, comprises, according to Fenichel, a number of delinquency patterns which have little more in common than the inconsistency of their symptom manifestations and the resulting inner tensions. But whatever the legitimacy of the clinical concept may be (which to the present writer seems rather doubtful), it is evident that here, too, psychoanalysts speak of a neurotic variety of aggressiveness with its typical elements of compulsiveness and unconsciousness.

The question, then, arises whether there exists another, clearly and unambiguously non-neurotic variety of delinquent behavior, either one essentially linked with externalization or with primary aggressiveness. Our answer is that such varieties indeed exist in what we have described elsewhere (28, 34) as primary waywardness, in contradistinction to primary behavior disorders and neurotic delinquency. We propose briefly to describe these modes of delinquent behavior, in preparation for an attempt to classify *all* forms of delinquency according to the criterion of asocial *versus* antisocial behavior.

WAYWARDNESS

This is a form of asocial behavior characterized by the polymorphous nature of its symptom manifestations, their passive occurrence character, the low degree of ego participation, naive identity with impulses, ability to enjoy a life outside society whose laws are nevertheless being recognized and avoided.

To quote from an earlier book (34, p. 70): "The wayward child is in every respect the opposite of the neurotic, including the neurotic delinquent. He... is driven by lust for, rather than by fear of, is after the 'haveable' contents of the world rather than after his parents' love... without fear of ego loss or love loss. He is... not compulsive." Reactive, uncontrollable and unstructured aggression may give way almost without inner logic to equally reactive and unstructured, superficial and noncommital attachments, to parents and strangers alike. He is sexually promiscuous without deep-rooted needs and certainly not out of genuinely perverted inclinations. He is allergic to every framework of socialization that may demand some sort of ego transcendence. He steals to satisfy some ever-present and ever-changing external need. His consciousness does not grow through the almost unlimited multitude of stimulations to which he is exposed in his street life. He does not learn, although he may, at least initially, be of normal or even of above average intelligence. He prefers to live and to act in groups, although he is unable to identify with any group canon, even that of a gang.

Growing up under the externalizing conditions of extreme poverty and educational neglect,* in a family atmosphere devoid of personal, intimate relationships, hence also of ambivalence tensions and inner conflicts, and therefore not conducive to internalization of parental images and values, growing up in an atmosphere of parental indolence and moral laxity, the presence of certain extravert tendencies in the child—these are the principal causal conditions required for the emergence of waywardness.

Waywardness seldom persists into adulthood. The wayward child may undergo a process of " 'delayed maturation' (55) under the influence of reeducational measures or of... life events.... But he may also glide into a criminal career, in which case it is likely that the earlier behavior was wrongly diagnosed as waywardness" (34, p. 74).

In adults, waywardness sometimes emerges under the impact of disappointments, isolating experiences, and a preexisting ego weakness. It is less polymorphous in its symptom manifestations, and the personality is liable to disintegrate gradually, under the influence of personality deficiencies which may have been latent for many years before. But absence

---

* This aspect will be discussed in a subsequent volume.

of inner tensions and extreme passiveness characterize them as well as the wayward child and enable us to diagnose them as against cases of neurotic character disorder or of psychopathy.

NEUROTIC DELINQUENCY

We have already mentioned the tendency in psychoanalytic theory to explain delinquent and neurotic behavior with the help of the same mechanisms. It is against this monistic and unifying approach that we claim the existence of waywardness as an independent, basically non-neurotic, form of asocial behavior. Neurotic delinquency does exist, of course, but nothing would be more futile and more removed from reality than to overlook and eliminate the basic difference between neurotic and non-neurotic forms of delinquency.

When we analyze offenses of a symbolic-substitutive or of a manic-compulsive character, we have to ask what unconscious tendency the offense expresses while trying to cover it. The neurotic offender is not reactive to environmental stimuli but is compulsively bound to his unconscious needs. He does not live with his impulses like the wayward child or adult, and is therefore unable to enjoy their satisfaction. His compulsiveness manifests itself in every phase of his acting out. He attacks whom he loves or he attacks someone else, someone who is "not meant" but serves as a substitute for the one he does not dare to attack. He steals symbols, not realities. His sexual offenses are, as a rule, compulsive, perverse, and accompanied by strong anxieties and guilt feelings. Sadistic acts are not, as in the wayward, naive demonstrations of strength and independence, but are expressions of irrational dependence on unconscious fears. Homosexuality, if it appears, is the manifestation of unresolved oedipal conflicts and not the chance result of undifferentiated drives and needs. Groups do not fulfill the function they fulfill in the life of the wayward (to strengthen a basically weak feeling of trust and security); but, to the extent that the neurotic offender seeks group contacts at all, he uses them—again—as substitutes, for maternal protection and paternal guidance, or as medium and area for his perverted sexual drives.

He fears his love and his hate, he fears his dependence and his independence, he escapes into punishment, since only through punishment can he liberate himself from his compulsion to be bad and to do things infinitely more wicked than his offenses. Hence the striking absurdity of so many of his offenses. Unlike the nondelinquent neurotic (including the compulsion neurotic) he has given up struggling against his own badness, he accepts it as an unalterable fact and "knows" that he does not deserve love. And again, unlike the neurotic who has replaced guilt by fear of love loss and by his suffering, the neurotic delinquent *suffers* from guilt feelings (of oedipal origin) because and to the extent that he is reality-related.

COMPULSIVE DISSOCIALITY

Here is the place to analyze a basic concept in any theory of deviant behavior, that of compulsiveness. We do not accept Fenichel's claim (27) as to the ego-alien nature of compulsion neurosis as against the ego-syntonic (though irresistible) character of what psychoanalysis calls impulse neurosis, including neurotic delinquency, mania, addiction, perversion, and unrestrained acting out of impulses. It would seem to us that the distinction between ego-alien and ego-syntonic behavior is inadequate, because it does not take sufficiently into consideration the difference between the three elements in the ego's attitude toward its tasks: directedness toward the action, ego participation (in planning, execution, and control) and ego emphasis (in the act). We shall try to show (in a later study) how every pathology is characterized by a specific profile, that is, by different intensity-degrees of each of these three elements. Suffice it here to point out that a certain behavior can be ego-alien, and the degree of ego emphasis (in the act) can nevertheless be so high that the impression of ego syntonicity is created. In another case, a certain behavior appears to be ego syntonic, but the degree of intentionality may be very low, so low, in fact, that the diagnosis (of ego syntonicity) becomes meaningless.

What, then, are the essential characteristics of compulsive dissociality against those of compulsion neurosis beyond the dimension of ego-syntonic and ego-alien behavior, and in what respect do the former differ from other, non-neurotic forms of delinquency?

Compulsiveness is a negative concept. It means inability to avoid committing a certain act or thinking a certain thought, irrespective of whether or not this act or this thought is experienced as irrational, immoral, undesirable. The causes of compulsiveness may be organic, sociocultural, or developmental.

The first essential element of compulsiveness is determination by factors transcending the ego's power of conscious control and synthesis (heteronomy). The second element is the contradiction between a relatively low degree of ego participation in, and intensive directedness toward, the action through which tension discharge is achieved. (Heteronomy *without* this second element is present in mentally defective or brain-injured individuals but does not indicate compulsiveness.) Rigidity, meaning fixatedness to a certain behavior pattern, is the third element, though a high degree of intelligence or creativity may make the underlying compulsiveness unrecognizable.

In compulsion neurosis the two first-mentioned elements often obliterate the third one. This is the case when repressed tendencies suddenly break through the compulsive defense system, without, however, restoring the ego's freedom and elasticity, this precondition of genuine reality adjustment.

In perversions and impulse neuroses (which we prefer to call forms of *compulsive dissociality*), compulsiveness is in evidence. But the allotropic character of those disorders requires a higher degree of ego participation and, at the same time, of directedness toward the action than does compulsion neurosis. It is this increase in both that may give the impression that the impulse neurosis is not as ego-alien as the compulsion neurosis.

We quote from an earlier book (34, p. 47):

"A normal person, when excited, feels his impulse as ego-syntonic and, at the same time, as part of the non-ego; he may temporarily identify with the impulse without becoming identical with it.... Not so the pervert and the impulse neurotic who, at the time of their excitation, lose their ego-identity.... In this respect they are ... comparable to the compulsion neurotic who is as helpless in the power of his (defensive) symptoms as they are in that of their impulses.... When we compare compulsion neurosis with perversions or impulse neuroses, we will find that in the latter ... rigidity tends to affect the total personality less than in the former. It expresses itself in ... periodic tension increases and compulsive tension discharge and not in defenses as in the compulsion neurotic with his fearful avoidance of sexual gratification. But although the nondefensive nature of pervert and impulsive activities may give the impression of lesser rigidity, the compulsive and the impulsive neurotic are equally rigid in their fixedness to one specific mode of symptomatic behavior."

From a comparison of what we have said about waywardness with our present analysis of compulsiveness it should be evident that the two are contradictory patterns of behavior. The former is the delinquent variety of externalization, and the occurrence character of life events and actions, so characteristic of defective internalization as well as of waywardness, precludes compulsiveness. True enough, the externalized individual is, as we have said, "tied" to what is known to him or, better, to the illusion of knownness, with its concomitant perceptive distortion of reality; but this kind of pseudofixation is not comparable with genuine developmental fixation of the neurotic variety, fixation to an early phase of development, with its concomitant dedifferentiation and compulsiveness. True enough, the degree of ego participation is as low in the externalized individual, and particularly in the asocial behavior of the wayward child and adult, as it is in the compulsive delinquent; but ego directedness to the delinquent act is as weak as ego participation in the former, whereas its intensity is an essential element in compulsiveness of all varieties. And heteronomy means something essentially different in both cases, since it is the *outer* non-ego, the environment, that determines the individual in the first case and the *inner* non-ego, the unconscious, in the second.

HATE AND DESTRUCTION

We are now going to discuss the clearly aggressive variety of delinquency, the one most frequently studied in childhood and adolescence as "antisocial character" (51), as "primary behavior disorder" (101), as "children who hate" (109), as "affectionless thieves" (13), while the same variety of delinquency is liable to appear in case analyses of adult criminals under the heading of guilt offenders or "psychopaths" (although such diagnoses are often unfounded). Ego weakness, insufficient internalization, and negation of human relationships are the structural elements of this behavior. All imaginable offenses appear, from early childhood, or, at the latest, from the latency period on, as symptom manifestations. Lack of parental love or emotional disappointments can usually be found to be responsible for its emergence. The presence of neurotic admixtures does not preclude a diagnosis of primary aggressiveness, since neuroticizing factors participate to a varying degree in the causal equation. A few remarks should be added here on the essential causes and symptoms of this variety of delinquent behavior:

Growing up in the ambience of parents who do not give the child sufficient love to make him feel secure is the source of many, and the most difficult, pathologies. Here we have in mind the not infrequent case in which a feeling of protectedness may take root in the infant but not deeply enough to prevent the simultaneous emergence of fear of love loss. The growing child's existence, then, will always be threatened by the danger of abandonment. The slightest reinforcement of his insecurity through the parents', and particularly the mother's, failure to protect him may then be interpreted by him as a confirmation of his previous suspicions, and he may react by rejecting his seemingly rejecting adults (the violence of his rejection being directly proportional to the intensity of his preceding insecurity).

When the cause of the parents' incompetence is their preoccupation with the "haveable that they have not," with want, and particularly when this preoccupation emerges after a more or less sudden change in the family's social and economic conditions (after immigration to a new country, for instance), not only may the child experience the loss of parental support as confirmation of his previous suspicions and his basically negative life conception, but he may at the same time form an impersonal relationship to everything non-ego, objects and persons alike; for, he feels, it is the material object reality that now has invaded his parents' consciousness and deprived him of his already precarious place in their mind.* *His hate reaction will therefore have to guard him against personal relationships in order to spare him the experience of another disappointment.* The earlier in life this reaction to the confirmation of previous suspicions and insecurity takes place, the more radical will be the

---

* When the real or imagined change in the parents' attitude toward the child is the direct or indirect result of their preoccupation with some personal problem (conflicts, resentments, anxiety, disappointments), anxiety and inner tensions are bound to emerge in the child's soul, and the behavioral result will be some sort of "person-related" neurotic compromise rather than unambiguous hate reactions.

impersonality of hate and destructiveness; the later the crisis, the greater will be the chances of ambivalence and inner tensions producing neurotic admixtures to the hate reaction.

Not relational inability but negation of relationship; not passive reactiveness but anticipatory intentionality; not gradual loss of potentials, as in externalization, but using (and often even developing) them "in the service of hate"; not unconscious quest of punishment but conscious need for maintaining a negative conception of life—these are the essentials of primary aggressiveness in children and in adults alike.

Group intoxication, particularly in children and adolescents, paradoxically combined with a strong tendency to overestimate their own power of determination; loudly demonstrated resistance to any restriction which the environment may try to impose on them, together with readiness and ability to accept "controls from without," once the intoxicating group-relatedness is effectively obstructed; some kind of compulsiveness in provoking the environment into aggressiveness and "badness" and forcing those whom he hates and attacks to prove his guilt (often with an extraordinary acuity of argumentation)—all these attitudes and patterns are but means through which the aggressive delinquent tries to prove to himself and his environment that he is invulnerable. *It is this central characteristic of aggressiveness that makes the here-described delinquent into a prototype of aggressiveness*, essentially differing from the externalized and the neurotic individual as well as from all other types of delinquents, including the psychopath.

PSYCHOPATHY

This clinical concept covers a number of aggressive *and* nonaggressive behavior patterns. We have tried in a separate study (34) to define and delineate the unit against others (some of which, like Alexander's "neurotic character" (5), Reich's "impulsive character" (110), Bowlby's "affectionless thief" (13), Bender's "affectless child" (8) have been suggested within psychogenetic theories of development in order to make the concept of psychopathy as a constitutional disorder redundant).

We have suggested that psychopathy should be defined as constitutional inability to establish polar relationships; it is based on a structural (primary or secondary) inability to experience anxiety, on ego inflation and on a conception of the non-ego as (potential) property of the ego, to be incorporated at will. We have said that the common causal element in all forms of psychopathy, in addition to the conditions mentioned here, is a structural predominance of the life tendency toward expansion over that toward staticness; and the differential element accounting for the crystallization of subunits of psychopathic behavior are type conditions (extraversion or introversion) and the traumatic impact of specific earliest deficiencies in the mother's relationship to the infant.

Among these forms are some that cannot be subsumed under the general concept of aggressiveness (the imposter and the "queer saint," the oscillating and the drifting, the shallow attachment and the unstable, mirroring varieties). But even the brutally destructive, the explosive, the egocentric, and the paranoid varieties (which we have subjected to a psychodynamic analysis in the abovementioned study) differ essentially from all other forms of aggressive behavior insofar as the feeling of objective destroyability and the need to heighten the own potency feeling by eliminating the threat of destruction—those basic elements in aggressiveness—are absent where, as in psychopathy, ego inflation and structural inability to feel anxiety determine the basic attitude towards life.

CLASSIFICATION OF DELINQUENCIES

We now return to the issue mentioned at the beginning of our discussion of delinquent behavior: how to classify its different subunits as expressions of asociality or of antisociality.

The *asocial* individual does not participate objectively, through polar relationships, in social tasks that require ego transcendence, either because he is *able to live without* the non-ego or because he is *unable to live with* the non-ego. The *antisocial* individual needs the non-ego, though for destructive purposes only, either to prove to himself and to his environment that he is independent or in order to take revenge.

The asocial, as a rule, does not hurt others intentionally, although he may do so inadvertently. Here we find waywardness in children and in adults who as vagabonds, drunkards, happy-go-lucky solipsists enjoy their existence; here we find extreme introverts living outside or beyond reality; here we find egocentrics withdrawn from social contexts, displaying antisocial yet not primarily aggressive behavioral manifestations.

While all these patterns indicate ability to live without the non-ego, escape from the world out of fear of its threatening superiority, neurotic immaturity and infantility, or other forms of neurotic reality distortion and the ensuing acts of unlawfulness, indicate *in*ability to live with the non-ego, to establish and maintain dialogic relationships with the environment and the unconscious. Here belong those representatives of waywardness and delinquency whose life is a continuous quest for a long-lost paradise of completeness, of maternal unity (and we should be careful not to diagnose them too quickly—as psychoanalysts tend to do—as cases of reaction formation and early repressed aggressiveness).

But none of these forms of deviant and delinquent behavior should be classified as expression of *antisociality*.

The difference between asociality and antisociality can be defined as one between two modalities of differentiation between the ego and the non-ego; it is inadequate in the first case, while it is normal but frightening in the second. Hence the passiveness, the indolence and the avoidance tendencies in the asocial individual; the intentionality, the hatred, and the ego emphasis in the antisocial individual.

The psychopath and the pervert, whose antisocial behavior indicates a deep-rooted need to prove their independence of the non-ego, consider the human environment an *object* only to be used at will, while in primary aggressiveness (in the "revenge type" criminal) the non-ego is considered a *subject* to be destroyed. Ego *emphasis* is strong in both subunits of antisocial behavior; ego *participation* is lower in most manias and perversions (the "independence type" delinquent) than in primary aggressiveness (of the "revenge type" delinquent). It is in the first group considerably lower than the ego's *directedness* to the act (a constellation that constitutes the compulsiveness so characteristic of the acts of this group of delinquents), whereas ego participation and ego directedness are more equal in intensity in primary aggressiveness with its lesser degree of compulsiveness.

The neurotic delinquent, particularly the guilt offender with his unconscious intention to receive punishment, has in common with the asocial the inability to live with the unconscious and a tendency to escape from the inner into the outer non-ego. He has in common with the antisocial, compulsiveness. Ego emphasis is considerably lower here than in all other forms of antisocial behavior, but also lower than in the wayward child and adolescent with whom the neurotic delinquent has in common a higher but still relatively low degree of ego participation. The intensity of his directedness to his delinquent action is similar to that to be found in primary aggressiveness.

This list of dissocial behavior patterns is, of course, far from complete. Not only have we omitted those patterns that are liable to emerge under the powerful influence of different forms of brain damage, of mental defectiveness, or of psychotic disorders, we have also left out the variety of mixed forms of delinquency that makes both individual diagnosis and classification difficult. As we have already mentioned above, we shall come back to this problem in a later study, when delinquency will be analyzed in greater detail.

8. Summary

Our brief phenomenological analysis of delinquency patterns, and the survey of varieties of human behavior which forms the subject of this chapter, are both incomplete. We have included neither a discussion of feeblemindedness in its different forms, nor of alienation, nor a detailed analysis of the many subunits of externalization or of neurosis. Why, the question may then be asked, was it necessary to add the chapter at all before going into the main problem with which Part 2 is concerned— phases of development and the causal significance of environmental factors?

The justification of this fragmentary presentation of behavioral outcomes lies in the fact that the three pictures here analyzed, those of externalized, neurotic, and aggressive (including delinquent) behavior, are not only forms of deviation from the norm but are also, and primarily, constituent elements in every *normal* behavior. There is no internalization of concepts, values, feelings without islands of externalization (such as expressions of primitive undifferentiated habits) or without the emergence of more or less deep anxieties which, in turn, lead to neurotic or to aggressive reactions. There is no single case of pure externalization (though we shall try to depict the varieties of externalization as ideal types in a subsequent volume). Not only is every child exposed to contradictory educational influences and is therefore forced into a variety of reactions, but the life process itself with its phasal peculiarities is bound to produce inner conflicts that may, then, be "solved" by way of neurotic, character-neurotic, psychosomatic, or even psychotic systematizations. However normal a child may be, no human being will be spared those more or less temporary disruptions of inner balance and of interrelatedness between the two life tendencies that make aggressive reactions understandable.

Understanding human behavior means understanding the interaction of structural, environmental, and developmental factors as well as the necessary partiality of the outcome, that is, the coexistence of contradictory modes of behavior and the link between this coexistence and the individual equation of factors. Not only these factors but also the behavioral outcomes exist in configurations only. A definition of the former (which we shall try to give in Chapter 8) includes the latter.

8

Phases of Development

1. THE FIRST PHASE OF CHILDHOOD

We have already analyzed the essentials of this phase at the beginning of the present study, when we tried to explain the genesis of differentiation and the structural significance of the mother for this early process of differentiation. We have also mentioned, in Chapter 5, dealing with the problems of structurization, that earliest life events are decisive for the final crystallization of congenitally given dispositions into what we call the unalterable constitution, both in the positive and the negative meaning of the terms. The Swiss biologist, Portmann (107), speaks of the first year of the human infant as the postuterine period of the embryonic development. Not only the infant's absolute dependence on his mother, his symbiosis with her, but also his extreme susceptibility to whatever happens in the maternal environment, seems to justify the hypothesis that the first year is a direct continuation of, actually "belongs" to, the embryonic period. Students of the problems associated with early hospitalization (4, 12, 117) have shown that the child's congenital disposition often undergoes radical and in the end irreversible changes in the absence of the experience of adequate personal relationships and interpersonal regularity with an unambiguous mother figure. Psychosomatic reaction patterns have been brought into causal connection with certain types of "mother-child interaction" (53). The most divergent forms of neurotic and character-neurotic disorders are explained by psychoanalysts as the results of regressions to the so-called oral phase, as patterns of "distorted orality" (27). Practically all forms of later psychoses are connected, in some way or other, with oral frustration and fixation, not to speak of the noncongenital forms of psychopathy (34).

All these and other claims regarding the decisive role of the first year of life are based on the presumption that regularity and consistency in the child-mother relationships are the prerequisites of healthy development. Structural factors are certainly no less responsible for the differences between the pathological outcomes than the specific form in which lack of regularity and consistency of the infant's mother experience appears in the individual case. Thus, a structural predominance of the life tendency toward staticness may favor the emergence of psychotic disorders under the same conditions of maternal deficiency that are conducive to the emergence of psychopathic states when the life tendency toward expansion is structurally predominant. Extravert or introvert reaction patterns account not only for variations of one and the same pathology,* but also for different degrees of vulnerability and susceptibility to certain pathogenic factors that may be active in the environment. The level of intelligence, thresholds of frustration-bearance, love needs, and other factors play a similar role in the interpretation of the first phase of development.

On the other hand, the infant is capable of reacting differentially, already at this earliest stage of development, to the parents' value system and life orientation. Not the observable attitude—for instance, indolence or rejection—but the underlying motives and needs determine the specific behavioral effect the parental, and particularly the maternal, environment may exercise on an infant with his specific structural dispositions and reaction patterns (cf. pp. 97 ff.). Preoccupation with the "haveable" (under conditions of poverty), or with personal problems, or with ego-transcending ideas and values may all produce early experience of the mother as the "absent one," and yet different, even opposite, processes of development will be set in motion.

These developments may be positive or negative, may lead to an improvement or to a deterioration of what the neonate brings with him in terms of endowments and patterns. Although most of the studies and hypotheses mentioned so far refer to *negative* changes only, there can be no doubt that, once we accept the thesis of changeability, we have to admit that positive changes may take place, and in fact, do take place as well in this early period of extreme plasticity, (cf. footnote, p. 69). Moreover, qualitative changes in the congenitally given type condition occur, extravert or introvert tendencies turning into their opposites under the impact of type-contrary environmental conditions, and sometimes leading to what Sheldon (115) calls "dyscrasias or incompatibilities between morphology and manifest temperament" (cf. p. 61).

We shall now try to define the structural function of this first phase of development.

Although we speak of the first year of life as if it were a functionally and maturationally definable unit, we know from observation of the infant's development that this phase comprises a number of more or less distinct subphases. Many psychoanalysts, and foremost among them the representatives of the British school (69, 84), regard the eruption of the

---

* Variations sometimes so extreme as to justify classification as different clinical pictures.

first tooth, approximately at the age of six months, that is, the experience of "pain without remedy," of "badness" and of "aggressiveness," as a dividing line between the two subphases of the oral stage. (Abraham (1), of course, preceded them.) On another plane of developmental analysis we find the claim that after the age of six months separation from the mother causes less severe damage to the child's constitution than before (12, 85, 117). In again another context, Spitz (118) calls the age of two to three months the stage of the "smiling response," that is, the end of the stage of primary narcissism and nondifferentiation, and the beginning of interhuman relations (although the objects are still interchangeable). At the age of eight months (6-10) the child reaches what he calls the "anxiety stage": unfamiliar figures evoke reactions of displeasure, the child has discovered his love object and, with it, also fear of love loss. Similarly, though on a different theoretical basis, Hartmann (60) sees "intentionality" emerge in the third month and "true comprehension" at the age of six months. Gesell's (54) and Bühler's (14) descriptive findings regarding the child's behavioral development in the course of the first year of life are well known. So is Piaget's analysis (106) of the stages in the first-year development of the child's intelligence, to which we shall refer soon.

Speaking of the infant's tasks, we call the first two months a period of *primary learning*. It is in these two months that the child ordinarily learns how to bring into a relational context his two basic experiences, those of the "mother as part" and of the "absent mother." The result is, at the age of two or three months, an ability to experience the mother as the near one whose regular return can be expected. The first symptom of this experience is what Spitz calls the "smiling response," and he is right in ascribing to this "exchange of signals" anticipatory character. We also agree with Hartmann when he says that intentionality begins at this age (the primary learning is purely associative).

It does not seem justified, however, to speak of "exchangeability of objects," only because the "smiling response" can be evoked by any friendly person approaching. Normally, we have said (p. 21), the mother limits the infiniteness of possible encounters with the world of objects and processes by endowing them with maternal character. The infant's world is normally a mother-world. But this does not mean that the mother is exchangeable for other persons: without the regular return of one definable and recognizable figure, that of the mother (or her *permament* substitute), a normal smiling response does not come forth, and its place is taken by that shallow attachment or that apathetic withdrawal that characterizes institutionalized infants (as Spitz has so convincingly shown).

What, then, happens between the emergence of the "smiling response" and that of anxiety over the possible loss of the love object (and the affective discrimination between the "near" mother and the "stranger")?

In these five to six months the child learns: (a) how to observe a more and more receding object environment (which means: the beginning of active differentiation between ego and non-ego); (b) how to manipulate certain objects in his immediate reach (a kind of play with "presence and absence," though on a basis of impersonal objects only); (c) how to move his body and establish associative bridges between observable and "feelable," outer and inner body movements (which gradually leads to the emergence of the body image (114); (d) how to establish and maintain contacts with a more and more receding, that is, separated, human environment; and (e) how to relive experience in imagination and thereby, again, to differentiate between an outer and an inner world.

It is self-evident that the infant will be successful in all these learning activities to the extent that differentiation between the growing ego and a bodily, a material, a human, a psychic non-ego takes place. This process, so we claim, is a necessity of life, because it is rooted not only in the dynamic polarity between stimulation and rest but also in those two of the patterns of orality that are biologically connected with feeding: swallowing the food as prototype of accepting, shutting the mouth (and turning the head) as prototype of refusing and rejecting what comes "from without."

But this process can, and indeed will, be delayed and disturbed even at the beginning of life to the extent that the primary mediator of the non-ego, the mother, does not relate herself to the infant in a relationship of unambiguous polarity—which happens when she is preoccupied with the "haveable," with herself or with her unconscious, when she is indolent, rejecting, or absent.

Under such conditions, directedness and intentionality in the infant's relationship with his environment are liable to remain weak, and his mental acts will lack coordination (which is based on intentionality). This is only another way of saying that the organizational strength of the growing ego is exposed to the danger of nondevelopment or of shrinkage whenever the infant does not have a chance of experiencing the mother as personally related to him.

On the other hand, the infant must liberate himself from that symbiotic mode of existence with the mother in order to reach the stage of intentionality from which ego development starts. The primary "adualism," to use Szondi's term (120), which explains why the child is able to react specifically to the mother's conscious and unconscious attitudes, this "participation mystique"* is as vital for the emergence of a "basic sense

* We use Levy-Brühl's expression (91), as Jung and his pupils have used it, for the purpose of interpreting individual rather than group developments.

of trust" (23) as it is dangerous for the emergence of what we call the experience of "nearness" (see pp. 20 ff., where we explained why we prefer the latter to the former term). True enough, the first signs of intentionality which, according to Hartmann (60), appear at the age of three months—approximately the same age at which, according to Spitz (118), the "smiling response" appears—do not contradict or preclude the continuation of symbiosis with the mother; in fact, this symbiosis is indispensable for a long time still, so that the infant may gradually learn how to experiment with, and how to achieve, differentiation. But while it goes on, and while it makes distantiation from the universe of objects more and more possible, less and less dangerous, the very emergence of an ego pole of intentionality and relationship limits its generality, its exclusiveness.

Bowlby (12, p. 48) quotes those students of early separation who feel inclined to see the middle of the first year as the "critical age" for the structurization of functional damage caused by institutional care. This would mean that at the age of six to eight months the infant has reached the relative end of symbiosis. Other research students, and among them Bowlby himself, consider the damage caused by separation from the mother in the second half of the first year much more serious than that caused in the first half of the first year. They believe, it would thus seem, that the period of symbiosis with the mother comes to an end after the first year of life only. The weakness of their position lies in the inductiveness of their method: they confine the material from which they draw their theoretical conclusions to one case only, that of maternal deprivation. We must, however, take into consideration a number of other life events as well, if we want to evaluate adequately the pathogenic significance of such factors as separation from the mother, events which we can study only through observing all kinds of infants in all kinds of problem situations, in their somatic history, in their sensorimotor, perceptive, and apperceptive development, in their anxieties and fears, as they appear in the family and not in the institution.

When we do this, we cannot but agree with Klein (84), who emphasizes the importance of that crucial experience of pain and badness that emerges with the first tooth and is accompanied or followed by what Spitz has described as the anxiety stage, when the infant reacts differently to familiar and to nonfamiliar images. It is the stage of differentiation and objectification in yet another sense. Hartmann (60) sees here the first signs of "true comprehension," and Piaget (106) of "deliberate adaptation to new situations" (though still dependent on repetitions rather than on spontaneity), of a much more pronounced directedness toward outside objects, of transition to genuine intentionality.

This configuration of emotional and cognitive discoveries justifies seeing in the age period of six to eight months the demarcation line between two subphases or periods in the first year of life. In the second half of this first year, intentionality determines the actions of the infant, exploration of the unknown starts, and the dimension of the future becomes a reality; the child shows the first signs of an ability to anticipate (106). It is in this subperiod of the first year of life that the infant learns not only how to observe objects as separate entities and how to manipulate them for the purposes of familiarizing himself with "absence" and "presence," not only how to "move toward" an independent object and thus to establish contact with a non-ego, but also how to relive experience and how to approach a changing present in the light of these recalled and revived experiences.

The question of the psychodynamic priority of emotional or cognitive aspects seems rather futile. The neglect of affective elements in the development of the ego and its functions and the exclusive concentration on the cognitive aspects of the growth process, as we find it in Piaget's writings, deprives most of his findings of their value in a dynamic theory of behavior. The neglect of the cognitive at the expense of the affective-relational aspects in psychoanalysis (of all shades, with the exception of Hartmann and his co-workers)* produces a most sterile division into libidinal development and the so-called conflict-free areas of psychic phenomena, which are thus left out of the field of psychodynamic explanations, and forced into the role of secondary derivatives of an "as if" nature.

We suggest a synthesis: our concept of nearness (making possible trust *and* differentiation, preparing the ground for relationship *and* abstraction) is a concept to the point. So are the concepts of anxiety and aggressiveness, of staticness and expansion, of inner and outer non-ego, etc. In the area of ego development, we maintain, a phase becomes meaningful only when its analysis makes the cognitive data relevant for an understanding of emotional and relational problems (and *vice versa*).

2. The Second Phase of Childhood

The second phase is characterized by the emergence of what Erikson (23) has analyzed as "sense of autonomy." Its genetic roots are the relative maturation of certain sensory and muscular functions and the growing ability to give and take. On closer examination, we see that these two elements supplement each other and depend on each other: sensory

---

* Hartmann himself is somewhat hesitant and apologetic with regard to his concept "conflict-free areas" (of perception, recall, thinking, language, intention, motority, productivity, etc.). These areas, he says, "in general contribute less to psychoanalytic technique than the study of conflicts and defences" (60, p. 9). And yet, they are indispensable for a proper evaluation of human development. Would it not, then, be appropriate to question the adequacy and, even, the legitimacy of that "technique"?

and general somatic maturation manifests itself in improved muscular and sensorimotor coordination and in expanding mobility as well as in the experience of being stronger than another, younger, child (*cf.* Bühler's observations (14)). To the extent that the boundaries of relevant (because reachable) reality widen, more activity is required, and the feeling of responsibility and autonomy grows stronger. To the extent that this happens, the boundaries of reality widen again. To the extent that the child becomes aware of the fact that no state is final, that change is inherent in the very process of life, he will again feel challenged to mobilize energy in order to bring about change actively.

It is essential for an understanding of this second phase of development to bear in mind that, in contrast to the beginning of life, when change was structurally associated with non-ego and staticness with ego (see p. 10), change now becomes part of an actively manipulating ego and, as such, is a source of satisfaction (in Freudian terms, the reality principle "serves" the pleasure principle, and *vice versa*).

On the other hand, it is this growing activity and autonomy that helps the child find the courage which he needs to establish relationships of give and take, of *mutuality*. For, only to the extent that the child experiences his ego as bearer of his own activity and intentionality, will he be able to perceive the other person as directing his own activity and intentionality, when he "interferes" through commands and prohibitions, through support and guidance, through reward and punishment.

Although elimination and its libidinal concomitants are undoubtedly important problem areas in this period, the psychoanalytic monism, its libidinal ideology, as it were, is inadequate: there are many other tasks which bring the child in contact with the adult world and make it mandatory for him to solve problems of emerging autonomy and mutuality.

"Retaining" and "eliminating" are not identical with their physiological variety, of retaining and eliminating feces (nor, for that matter, with their oral precursors). Grasping and holding an object, releasing and dropping it, keeping the breath and pushing it out, playing at holding on and letting go in language, both before and after its conversion into a tool of communication, keeping a hold on a more or less separated and differentiated non-ego by observation, and eliminating it by not looking at it, by avoiding it, muscular tension and relaxation—all these and many other antithetic expressions of growth in the second phase of development are as important as, if not altogether more important than, the activities and feelings related to the process of defecation.

Nor are they less erogenic in the meaning of psychoanalytic libido theory. And—what is more important still—their erogenic character, the libidinal satisfaction and tension they make possible, is much more

directly and meaningfully connected with the development of consciousness, of the ego as the center of consciousness and of later character
dispositions, than are anal activities and processes. To make the latter
meaningful for the understanding of ego development, we have to translate the original, sexual, content into more general concepts of mental
life, as Erikson (23) has tried to do by using (sometimes rather doubtful
though always very ingenious) analogies and "similies."* Synthesizing
the "conflict-free" and the "anal" areas, on the other hand, renders
possible a much more comprehensive understanding of later developments, normal and pathological, because it allows for a uniform method
of interpretation.

One of the most important functions of this phase is the learning of
ambivalence, that is, of the coexistence of contradictory, *prima facie*
mutually exclusive, feelings or evaluations. Although this learning process is intimately connected with bowel training, it has other, no less
decisive, experiential roots as well: Wherever an ego activity is interrupted by adult intervention, after the primary differentiation between
the ego and the non-ego has already taken place, the affective negation
of the interruptor which is then bound to emerge, is a "position" of the
ego, is a vital attempt to retain autonomy in the face of coercion from
without. (This becomes particularly evident in the *Trotzage* at the end
of the period.) At the same time, however, the ego may negate its own
position for the sake of positing its negator.

This formulation is not meant to be an excursion into Fichtean
idealism. It is but an attempt to define ambivalence genetically. Erikson
(24) contends that the individual's love-hate rate is being determined in
this stage of development. It seems a rather extreme statement in view of
the fact that many subsequent experiences may radically alter this rate
maturationally or reactively; but it would seem correct to say that the
individual's ability to bear, to "live with," ambivalence comes into being
during this phase. Ambivalence, far from being identical with conflict
or from being a pathological symptom, is in fact a constitutive element
of the healthy personality. It is the precondition of adequate emotional
relationships, and it protects against the danger of "either-or" feelings
that indicate repression of the nonlived, the negated aspects of life.

*Ambivalence thus guarantees rationality. It is rooted in the child's
experience that the good adult is bad, the beloved one hateful; that the
object of his own aggressions, of his own badness, is identical with the*

---

* One wonders when reading his similes whether the "gain" of remaining in the fold
of psychoanalytic theory is worth the effort, particularly as the most important question
(of the relationship between "conflict-free" and libidinal areas) remains unanswered.
Erikson, incidentally, seems to be aware of the problem: he uses the psychoanalytic
terms in quotation marks, he speaks of general patterns, of dimensions and approaches
that are "not restricted" to the erogenic areas (of the mouth, the sphincter, etc.).

object of his own love. This, however, means that the child comes to know that he himself, too, is good in spite of his negative feelings. Which, in turn, is the foundation of social learning, of adjustment, of socialization. For only where there is faith in his own basic goodness can the child allow himself to be bad without becoming identical with his badness (as is the case in primary behavior disorders) or escaping into all kinds of inadequate defenses (as is the case in phobia or in compulsion neuroses). And only then does he become ready for partial renunciation of temporary ego positions in order to gain additional recognition and love.

Here again, we see the close connection between social learning and abstraction. Self-distantiation from a given ego position, a state in which the individual finds himself at a given moment, requires, as we have said above, courage and trust in the ultimate permanence (what we call, at a later stage, the identity) of the ego. Only when "badness" and "goodness" are experienced as modalities of that self-identical ego, can one of the two aspects be relinquished temporarily without fear of identity loss. Whereas temporary renunciation of an aggressive drive or need, for the sake of a beloved adult, then means experimenting with a partialized ego, temporary renunciation of goodness, for the sake of satisfying some no less "beloved" drive or need, means experimenting with separation, with individuality. This partiality of existence and the accompanying experimentations with contradictory attitudes and behavior can be called the socializing factors of ambivalence. We shall come back to analyzing its effect on cognitive processes where life conditions impede the development of ambivalence.

Needless to add, this learning requires adequate educational attitudes on the part of the immediately relevant non-ego, the mother, the father, other members of the family. Most later psychopathologies—with the exception of constitutional psychopathy, psychotic processes, or psychosomatic dispositions—are rooted in this second phase, irrespectively of whether and to what extent disturbance of the *basic sense of trust* has prepared the ground for such pathological reactions. The reason this stage is decisive for their development is not difficult to find: it is at this stage that the ego emerges as the coordinating and synthesizing center of consciousness. This means that, on the one hand, there has now emerged an inner agent of structurization, which, on the other hand, is still in the process of crystallization, hence vulnerable and changeable. We maintain that the central area of structural and functional character formation is the area of ambivalence.

Ambivalence is *preceded* by structural differentiation and polarization (the ego gradually emerging in the process of relating itself to the non-ego in its various aspects). It is *followed* by speech communication, which not only presupposes separation, distance, and an increasingly conscious tendency to reestablish contact and unity, but also helps transform the simultaneity of contradictory feelings and evaluations into a series of alternating, distinguishable states. Were it not for the dynamic element of ambivalence tension and the inherent incentive of resolving it, speech would only continue to fulfill its functions of self-expression and perhaps also of communication, but would hardly become a tool of conceptual differentiation, of thinking as "inner speech." Ambivalence, we maintain, is a prerequisite of thinking.

In addition to autonomy, mutuality, and ambivalence, the child learns in this second phase of his development *functional aggressiveness.* We do not accept the psychoanalytic term of anal or oral "sadism"—an illegitimate anachronism and inadequate for the proper evaluation and understanding of the functional aspects of aggressiveness.

Aggressiveness, already at this early age, has two different aspects and functions: that of reactively defending a recently won and therefore still precarious ego position against the dangers of non-ego intrusion, of being limited and negated by the non-ego; and that of conquering a still unknown, a new ego position.

The child may refuse to accept an adult directive; he then shuts himself off from the intruder, does not recognize objective resistances on the part of a human or a material non-ego; or he violently eliminates a "foreign body" that has been forced into his system by the will of an outside ego; or he obstinately holds on to an object, a state, an attitude which the environment tries to take from him or to change.

To understand these behavioral manifestations as oral or anal patterns is inadequate, because, as we have said, this conception unnecessarily limits the area of ego functions to certain biological processes, while relegating to the level of secondary processes all that is immediately relevant, both causally and symptomatically, for the growth of consciousness and for the development of the ego as the organizing center of consciousness. It seems to us much more adequate to interpret the manifestations of aggressiveness that emerge in this phase as expressions of the normative interaction of the two basic life tendencies, that toward staticness and that toward expansion. Defensive aggressiveness serves the first tendency, insofar as it renders possible systematization; conquering aggressiveness serves the second tendency, insofar as it renders possible change from within, change as an ego activity and an ego process.

The medium through which this constructive, expanding aggressiveness expresses itself, is, first and foremost, the child's *play activity:* it both requires and stimulates *imagination,* which can be defined here as the ability to see and try out the various ways in which a manageable reality detail may be fitted into varying contexts. In order to make such shifting of details possible, breaking up of the whole-context within which a specific detail first appears is necessary. Such dissolution, however, requires aggressive energy and courage (*cf.* pp. 122 *ff.*). Hence the differences in the level of imagination that characterizes the play activities of children, according to the amount of vitality, energy, and courage they are able to muster.

The most important area in which the child's constructive aggressiveness shows its effects is that of *intellectual functions*. Aggressiveness is required in every phase of intellectual behavior: in the resistance against deflecting forces of affect, drive, impulse; in the readiness to try out new ways, beyond the well trodden ground of associations and memories (originality); in the "intending" of a specific goal; and most of all, in the very process of abstracting from the multitude of incidentals in order to find the best solution.

However, not only aggressiveness, but autonomy, mutuality, and ambivalence as well are present in the child's intellectual activities during this second period. Piaget (106) mentions experimental "modification" of specific movements, watching the effect and inventing new methods, as characterizing the second year of life; he calls inner coordination and representation the achievements of the following years. They require not only differentiation between subject and object but also readiness to relate to the objects of cognition, that is, the beginnings of mutuality and autonomy (and this in spite of the fact that the child is not yet able "to take the role of the other"; in other words, has not yet overcome his cognitive egocentricity). Ambivalence is present in the very coexistence of contradictory facts in the child's consciousness, facts determined by contradictory needs and drives. It is the resulting ambivalence tension that supplies the incentive for the continuation of intellectual development from the phase of beginning objectification to growing differentiation and intentionality.

3. The Third Phase of Childhood

In the first years of life the child's world is—normally—a mother-world, even though with progressing maturation he increasingly experiences changes and growth, separation and polarity. The maternal character of reality is independent of the child's sex. At the age of three, however, sex difference enters the child's consciousness, as the result of both external experience and maturation of the ability to feel sexual excitation as *specifically* connected with the penis or the clitoris (whereas before these were only two "accidental" zones of excitation, among others).

This is the age when the *father* is being discovered and maternal universality thus comes to an end. The world is from now on separated not only into an ego and a non-ego—a process which is already taking place in the first months of life—but also into male and female. It is the age when the *paternal principle of differentiation* (see pp. 22 ff.), which, as we have said, in some way or other operates from the beginning of life on, becomes associated with, and represented by, the personal father. (Absence of such representation in the institutionalized child or under certain pathogenic family conditions is, as we shall try to show in a later study, one of the causes of mental retardation in the development of thus prejudiced children.)

The child now also becomes aware of the difference between male and female sex organs. It is unimportant whether this awareness starts with the own body and serves as an incentive to observing other children's organs, thus *leading* to the discovery of "penis-carriers" and "penisless" beings, or whether chance experience *precedes* awareness of the own body and sets in motion increased interest, self-stimulation, and processes of excitation, which have become maturationally possible in the meantime. What counts is the fact that both the boy and the girl now become aware of the uniqueness (hence the "preciousness") of the penis which does *not* exist "dually" and is "showy." That it supplies pleasant feelings when manipulated only increases its value for the boy, but does not explain the girl's penis envy, as she possesses an equally potent supplier of satisfaction in her clitoris.

The elements of the psychoanalytic theory are well known. The penis, Freud claims, is of central importance to the boy as an organ of penetration and return into the mother; its loss is feared, because the father may punish the little competitor by cutting it off; threats to this effect are voiced frequently, when the boy is found masturbating; the girl is envious of the boy, blames her mother for having prejudiced her, feels less anxiety, because she has nothing to lose, and less inhibitions, fewer "qualms of conscience" over taking the father away from the mother.

Without entering into a discussion of whether or not castration fear can be presumed to be universal and independent of ontogenetic evidence to be adduced from individual observations and case studies, and without discussing the psychoanalytic "penetration theory," we suggest the following modifications:

The boy reacts to the discovery of sex differences by fearing his beloved parents, the mother no less, and perhaps even more, than the father. He *knows* her to be different from himself, just as he *knows* the father to be essentially equal, though infinitely more "potent" (*cf.* our comments on pp. 26 ff., about sex differences as structural determinants). From this twofold certainty springs a twofold uncertainty and anxiety. On the one hand, a threat is implied in his mother's otherness, a threat to his own sexual identity: perhaps he must give up his penis to become like her? (Here, a new edition of ambivalence appears: a conflict between his love of the mother and his love of the penis.) Castration fear is not, or at least not only, a result of a threat; but it is also, and mainly, a result of *structural* conflict. On the other hand, the father, representing his "self-in-future" and driving him into the future, as it were, deprives the boy of the pleasures of staticness which he seeks in the realm of the mother.

The girl, upon discovering the sex difference, comes to experience, painfully, her lack of wholeness and this experience, in turn, strengthens her (structurally given) tendency to seek wholeness from without, by receptive contact with, by supplementation through, the male. She uses much fewer defenses than the boy, as she has not so much to fear. But on the other hand, she now starts to develop aggressive tendencies of incorporation, and the active mutuality of give and take is liable to be more and more replaced by a passive tendency of "snatching and receiving." Differentiation is not so much of a challenge to her as it is to the boy.*

Here is the place to refer to our structural analysis of sex difference in Chapter 1. In the light of that analysis and on the basis of the concept of the paternal principle of differentiation, we would interpret what psychoanalysis calls the "oedipal situation" as follows:

Unlike the boy's way of experiencing otherness—already through the experience of the "absent mother" (AM) in the earliest phase of his development—that of the girl is liable to remain below that level of intensity that is required for the emergence of a feeling of separateness, of "standing opposite" the non-ego (even the "absent mother" continues to be, at least structurally, "present"). Hence the relative weakness in the girl of the paternal principle, that is, of the tendency to overcome otherness activity;† hence the lack of a sufficiently strong motivation for changing the non-ego's essential strangeness by way of introjection (instead of submitting to it receptively); hence the girl's oedipal tendency to see in the father—as representative of otherness—a desirable object of possession, a precious part of her external reality with which to supplement her ego. In other words: we consider inadequate that part

---

* Preference of the male in our—and for that matter in practically every—society acts as a factor of social reinforcement of prestige and stress: belonging to the preferred sex is considered an advantage, but at the same time means increased tension for the boy when he tries to live up to the patterned expectations of his environment; it means increased envy and resentment for the girl. It is therefore not by chance that the mother's reaction to her son's masculinity, her female resentment with all its emotional and educational implications, assumes its aggressive or (aggressively) overprotective forms in this third phase of the boy's development with its typical sex differentiation. (More on the problem of maternal resentment and its impact on the boy's development will be said in the second volume.)

† "Separating" is not felt to be an effective weapon against "separateness," when the latter is not felt as a danger or a threat.

of the oedipal theory according to which the girl's effective strivings toward her father are simply a reflection of her inability to identify with him. Without the presumption of a *structurally* weak paternal principle of differentiation in the girl, her relative unawareness of the non-ego as of something that she should transform into a part of her inner self remains unexplained.

In the psychic structure of the boy, on the other hand, staticness contains, as we have said (p. 27), otherness, and, as a result, the *mother* becomes his object of possessive strivings. In his case, too, the countersexual parent fulfills a function of supplementation, but not, as in the case of the girl, of supplementing the ego by parts of an external and insufficiently separated non-ego; in his case, "possession" of the mother supplements his essentially incomplete unity feeling (incomplete because his identity feeling, mediated as it is through the experience of the "mother-as-part", already contains an element of otherness and oppositeness).

These tendencies toward supplementation through the countersexual parent obviously influence the development of the boy and of the girl in essentially different ways: differentiation prepares the ground for introjection of the father and protects the son against the danger of self-alienation that threatens from him as representative of the future and of change; introjection furthers objectivity, initiative, and autonomy, while at the same time protecting against the maternal danger of being drawn back into a stage of lesser differentiation. Without introjection the boy will not be able to mobilize the energy which is required for the development, not only of his intellectual but also of his relational abilities.

In the girl, on the other hand, the so-called oedipal situation has an entirely different function: unless she comes to experience the mother as a threat, a threat to her growing autonomy, she is liable to remain "contained" (imprisoned) in her. Tension and conflict thus help the girl on her way toward differentiation, for which she is structurally less prepared than the boy. Not the father, object of her libidinal strivings, but the mother is the girl's first object of relationship, provided she succeeds in experiencing and recognizing her as separate, as different, as non-ego. (One could almost say: what is a danger for the boy—self-alienation—is a structural necessity for the girl.)

Thus, we understand that differentiation far transcends the areas of sex, of libidinal tension and satisfaction, vital as the latter undoubtedly are for the child in this third phase of his development. *The so-called oedipal strivings are manifestations only of his general tendency to dissolve complex situations into their constituent elements, to discover the essentials of each of these elements and later to synthesize them in new meaning contexts. These are the structural functions of the third developmental phase.* Although they presuppose differentiation between the ego and the non-ego and ability to perceive the non-ego as independent counterpole of relationships, they also *help develop* differentiation and polarization.

The three fields in which the structural functions of this phase must be applied are: the family, the kindergarten group (at least in our culture), and the universe of cognizable facts, the dichotomies of life and the laws of reality.

The parents are only now being discovered as "a couple," to quote Ophuijsen (101); but at the same time the child feels provoked into attempts to separate this parental unit into individually different objects of relationships. In other words: individual relationship becomes possible only *after* the child has experienced the parents as a unit—one from which he is excluded. Recognizing the father's and the mother's essential and distinguishable qualities is the "method" through which the child not only maintains differentiation (that is, dissolution of the whole into its elements) but also establishes new whole contexts, those of individually different relationships, with the mother and with the father as individuals.

In the kindergarten group the child finds himself constantly exposed to situations in which he is challenged into differentiation and synthesis, particularly by his spontaneous and organized play activities. These activities help the child not only to consolidate his prior phase achievements (particularly autonomy and mutuality) but also to apply his objective learning to the day-to-day problems arising out of his family conflicts and his need for reality orientation and adaptation through thinking and imagination (provided someone is there to help him structurize his experience).

It is this last area of application in which the structural function of this developmental phase is most in evidence. The child feels himself confronted with the incomprehensibility of the fundamental life issues: birth and death, past and future, ego and non-ego. He feels challenged to penetrate into the secrets of cause and aim, of the laws governing the objects and events which he encounters,* that is, to differentiate and to internalize.

It requires courage and confidence to accept this challenge. Not every child is equally prepared and able to do so. For, in every act of separation—and, as we have stressed already several times, no synthesis is possible without prior differentiation—a danger is inherent inasmuch as it

---

* It is irrelevant here that the laws he finds, establishes, believes in, imagines, are not those of "adult" science. What matters is the fact that the child feels impelled to find *some kind* of law, of organization, that is, some means of differentiation and synthesis.

compels the child to stand alone in the face of the unknown. Every separated reality element, every isolated phenomenon, object, or event is at first "unknown," at least until the synthesizing ego succeeds in finding a place for it in a new—real or imagined—context. Not always does it fit naturally into this new context (then another danger emerges, that of confronting a distorted and *therefore* threatening reality). But even when the synthesis is successful and effective, a period of anxiety precedes it: fear of losing the protective unity feeling which the yet weak and dependent ego needs so very badly. It is the normative early experience of the "mother-as-part" which, paradoxically, explains both the fear of unity loss and the courage to separate a whole into its components.*

Here, another essential element of the so-called oedipal phase, the guilt feeling, must be interpreted in the context of our structural analysis. Guilt is, in the last instance, always a feeling of insufficiency and helplessness, elicited by separation from a whole context, that is, by individualization. Guilt is therefore universal and unavoidable, its developmental root lying in the "discovery of the father." Oedipal strivings would not cause guilt feelings were not the disposition so to react created by the separation of parental wholeness into an individual father and an individual mother. Hence, one might even say that certain *oedipal strivings and conflicts are the result, not the cause, of guilt feelings.* This holds good in particular for the boy's affective attachment to his mother, which can be interpreted as an attempt to restitute the lost unity feeling on the basis of a mother-son relationship (the rejection of the father being a secondary, though unavoidable, result of the restitutional attachment to the mother).

Similarly, guilt feelings may be the *cause* (and only secondarily also the result) of masturbation. We believe that only after the discovery of sexual duality, and the existential guilt feeling accompanying this act of separation and differentiation, masturbatory activities are able to provoke guilt reactions, but that these reactions are secondary reinforcements only of the original, primary guilt reaction to sex differentiation. We also claim that masturbation in the oedipal phase is a means to alleviate preceding guilt feelings, a means to recreate a kind of "uroboric" unity stage.†

Normally, we may now say in summing up the present analysis, *separation* is the essential, structural, function of the third phase in the child's development. Anxiety and guilt over separation are unavoidable,

---

* This is only another way of formulating what we have said about the normative integration of the two life tendencies, that toward expansion, here represented by the courage to differentiate, and that toward staticness, here manifesting itself as fear of unity loss.

† We use the term in the meaning it has in Neumann's writings (96).

and the question is not how to avoid them, but how to mobilize the courage needed in order to live with them* and not to give up the developmental function. *Both, to live without anxiety and guilt and to rely on distorting defenses (neurotically or aggressively), are deviations from the norm.*

We have already emphasized (p. 151) that in our opinion neither the so-called psychodynamic approach to the child's development, as advocated and practiced by psychoanalysts, nor Piaget's epistemologic approach (106) make the concept of "phase" meaningful for the interpretation of functional development. To reduce thinking and problem solving, moral judgment and language behavior, play activities and imagination to the level of epiphenomena of libido processes does not do justice to the *essence* of these ego manifestations. Neither do we accept Hartmann's negative term (58) of conflict-*free* ego areas: there is as much conflict and tension in language and in thought, in judgment and in play, as in the emotional and relational fields. Thinking is as dangerous as loving; both require courage to be aggressive in separating whole contexts and trust to be capable of reestablishing new whole-contexts (in relationship—or in conceptual activities).

On the other hand, the inadequacy in Piaget's intellectualistic approach to the problems of phasal development is no less evident. Not only does the child as a living entity disappear there behind the multitude of functional analyses, but many vital areas of functioning, such as those of family relationships, of feelings, of sexual strivings, are not included at all (and rightly so, we may add, since they cannot be reached through methods of reduction to cognitive levels). This, however, is more than incompleteness; it precludes an adequate interpretation even of those functional developments that *are* included in Piaget's research.

It is through mutual application of dynamic to cognitive and of cognitive to dynamic categories that we believe the phases of development become meaningful for an understanding of behavior.

4. The Fourth Phase of Childhood

The next phase of development is that of learning. The area of consciousness grows through the reception and assimilation of knowable facts and connections between facts, through the training of skills and through the strengthening of the ability to concentrate, that is, through the extension of the subjective time span. While reception and assimilation of facts helps delineate the borders between the non-ego and the ego, training of skills and growth of the subjective time span make the ego more courageous in its relationships with the non-ego.

* We refer to Tillich's analysis of guilt in his book, *The Courage to Be* (121).

This is also called the *social* phase in which, as Piaget (105) has pointed out, the child gradually experiences the significance of the rules of social behavior by actively manipulating and modifying them in his "society of equals." The child needs his "equals" in order slowly to learn how to give up dependence on his adults, though for a long time to come this learning will be only by way of experimenting with independence. It is precisely because objectively and realistically he still needs his adults, that the "society of equals" offers him the opportunity for such experimentations, through which he learns how to take responsibility not only for his actions but also for his thoughts.

The growth of consciousness and of autonomy depends, at least in our society, on three conditions:

(a) That the tensions aroused in the previous phase by the "discovery of the father" and, through it, of sex differences and of existential polarities in general, that the anxiety and guilt feelings over "separation," differentiation, and individualization abate, thus setting free mental energies required for the acts and processes of impersonal, objective, and receptive learning;

(b) That the experiences of polarity and of mutuality, this heritage of previous phases of development, now become applicable to the tasks of cognition; that the child gradually becomes aware of polarity and mutuality as of general life-regulating principles and thus learns how to evaluate objectively the non-ego as well as the ego;

(c) That the essential meanings of events and objects are being explained as manifestations of the non-ego through actively guiding representatives of that non-ego; in other words, that objectivity is being "learned" with the help of another ego, on which the child can *rely*, preferably one outside the area of intimate family relationships and representing objective reality.

It is evidently not by chance that the family—in the Western middle class stratum at least—now starts to delegate a large part of its educational responsibility to anonymous agencies such as the school. The child's readiness to learn within more anonymous groups is not only the outcome of a biologically conditioned—and testable—process of emotional and intellectual maturation; it can also be interpreted as the result of preceding separation activities: *at the end of the third phase of development, the child's world is one of separated elements which require synthesis through learning.*

Freud (48) explains the "passing of the Oedipus complex" and the ensuing decrease or disappearance of early sexuality in the so-called latency period, as the outcome of repression set in motion by castration fear (though he does not deny the causal role of maturation); and he sees in the superego and in the ego's learning capacity the heirs to oedipal tensions. In order to counter the argument that the universality of castration fear cannot be explained ontogenetically he suggests his "archaic rests" theory, a personalistic version of the Jungian theory of archetypes. We suggest, in the place of this theory of "repression out of anxiety,"* the hypothesis that *differentiation, the essence of the third phase of development, gradually reaches a stage where "life with separated elements" (and not only with those of the parental unit) becomes unbearable, and a change into another, nonpersonal, mode of dealing with, and relating to, these elements becomes imperative: this is the condition out of which cognitive initiative is born.* Introjection of adult precepts, values, and concepts is a by-product only of this initiative. Its results are: growth of consciousness and of the ego pattern (in thinking, judging, evaluating, acting, behaving) and, at the same time, repression of ego-alien contents and strivings.

Thus, we understand why the child is now ready to leave—more, why he *must* leave—the intimate area of the family in order to learn, why learning *requires* the school as a counteragency, different as much as possible from the family. Its otherness, its relative impersonality, is a safeguard against illegitimate interference of previous—personal and emotional—modes of differentiation with the learning processes. This, however, does not mean that the child, at least in his first school years, can do without constant confrontation of his school experiences with his parents' reactions.† On the contrary, division of the educational functions between the family and the school, which renders possible objective learning as well as a variety of partial identifications with extrafamilial values and "hero figures," requires communication of the school experience *to* the parents. Though it is true that separating the parental unit into independent father and mother figures (in the third phase) prepares the ground for (partial) separation of the school-entering child from his parents, it is equally true to say that the "feeling of togetherness" (to use Fromm's term, (52)), becomes all the more important in the fourth period of the child's development, the more meaningful his learning experience will be.

There is no contradiction between our two statements (about the division of educational functions and the child's need for togetherness with his parents), if only we do not confuse the concept of "togetherness" with those of "containedness," of "fusion," or of "unity." Togetherness means coexistence of separate individuals relating to each other in

---

* Which, Freud says, has the disadvantage of fitting the structural situation of the boy more than that of the girl.

† A problem which today, when most parents are unable or unwilling to cooperate with the school, necessitates far-reaching reforms of curriculum and methods! We have dealt with this problem in an essay (36), "School Without Parents," from which we shall quote in Chapter 9 (see pp. 217 *ff.*).

give-and-take relationships based on trust; it therefore *presupposes* separation of the ego from the non-ego. Its ultimate aim is communication and, through it, recreation of unity; it therefore presupposes delegation of the formal teaching functions to an agency *outside* the family so to make true communication possible. We can say that it is the *structural function of the fourth phase of development to make the child's ego into an agent of synthesis.* The decrease of inner tensions that are characteristic of the preceding phases is both a condition and a result of this synthesis.*

It is generally presumed that in the third stage of development the child is yet unable to distinguish between phantasy and reality. The child "is" what he imagines, says Erikson (24), whereas later he "is" what he learns.

In this respect, too, the third phase, that of separation and differentiation, prepares the ground for the following, the learning phase. The child's imagination, we maintain, is experimentation with reality, at a time when the channels connecting his weak ego with the inner non-ego, the unconscious, and consequently also those connecting the inner with the outer non-ego, are still open. In this third phase imagination is the mental activity best suited to isolating from each other elements of the child's complex reality, to construing relational connections between these elements and filling the connections with experiential associations. The fact that the child is not yet able clearly to distinguish between inner (phantasied) and outer reality does *not* justify the conclusion that he is unable to manipulate the representational elements of his reality; it only means that he manipulates them irrespectively of whether they are "within" or "without."

At the end of the third phase, however, the child already becomes aware of the fact that there is a difference between facts shared with others and facts of a private world of dreams, phantasies, wishes, feelings, thoughts, and values (although, as far as he is concerned, this private world will, for some years to come, continue to infringe upon reality by claiming general validity). Learning in a relatively impersonal environment, the school, playing with a view to testing out and applying to reality newly acquired knowledge and skills, and, most important, the processes of internalization which lead to the emergence of inner agencies of judgment—all these contribute toward more definite and more objective separation between phantasy and reality. They not only help rationalize previous (irrational) anxieties and guilt feelings and thus diminish inner

---

* When discussing the third phase (see pp. 159 *f.*) we said that it is characterized by differentiation *and* synthesis. But in the preschool phase synthesis is implicit only in the separation processes and activities, whereas now it becomes gradually a conscious ego function (see also p. 166).

tensions, but they also make the child increasingly capable of relating differentially to his inner and to his outer realities.

The phase here under discussion should be subdivided into at least two periods. During the first, learning, in addition to its cognitive function, protects the growing ego against the danger of regression to those stages in which separation and differentiation, the precursors of analytic operations, were accompanied by anxiety and guilt feelings. The child's plays, too, fulfill rationalizing functions in this first part of the learning phase. As regards internalization of parental images, the first years after the end of the so-called oedipal phase are again a period of experimentation rather than of structurization. The gradual formation of inner agencies requires frequent confrontation of (partial) achievements with the external reality of the parents, even though it may mean an occasional return to the tensions of the preceding phase. Internalization (introjection) should not be misunderstood as an "all-or-nothing" process which "produces" the superego as a defense against oedipal guilt and anxiety; it is a process of years during which the relationships between the ego and the non-ego slowly change (so that in the end the ego becomes subject-object of an internalized non-ego).

The second part of the learning-phase could be called the period of abstraction. Normally, learning, both intellectual and social, has by now enlarged the factual basis of orientation, the *massa apperceptiva*, to such an extent that the principles of subject-object relationships (polarity and mutuality) which the child previously experienced in their *personal* significance, become applicable to his problems of *objective* learning. In other words: the processes of learning will from now on be influenced less than before by personal associations; analysis will no longer be associated with the danger of separating the parents; internalization has advanced to a point where it can become a general method of transforming observable and touchable facts into concepts. *This is the phase of achievement (23), of autonomy in the meaning of the term as used by Piaget (106); it is the phase in which the ego crystallizes as an inner agent aiming at synthesis* (synthesis of ego patterns, defensive and otherwise, of interrelatable facts, of facts with meanings, of learning with behaving, of thinking with imagining).

5. THE FIFTH PHASE OF CHILDHOOD

Anna Freud's explanation (41) of the adolescent's contradictory behavior is well known. Sexual maturation, she claims, revives the oedipal conflicts; the newly acquired ability to translate sexual drives into action makes them all the more dangerous, as the ego is not yet strong enough to cope with drive demands in a realistic and reality-adapted manner; hence, the need for particularly powerful and effective defenses.

Such a defense is the "escape" from the parents, their affective negation; it allows negation—by way of suppression or repression—of the "sexually dangerous" direct contact with them; it allows denial of that inner moral force, the superego, that owes its emergence to the introjection of parental images and values; hence, uninhibited drive gratification *outside* the family group becomes legitimate. But it also allows, following the negation of parental values and thereby of generally accepted traditions, a new discovery of reality, on the level of principles.

This last consequence of "avoiding the parents" is not identical with Anna Freud's defense mechanism of "intellectualization." In fact, it is more than a defense; the adolescent, at least the one who has grown up in the emotional tension climate of a western middle-class family, substitutes realistic relationships with the ego and the non-ego by his tendency "to live with principles." Its intensity is not only proportional to that of his libidinal strivings, but is determined by a number of structural factors and by the adolescent's intellectual and emotional experiences.

The tendency "to live with principles" finds its expression in the coexistence of those seemingly self-contradictory attitudes that are mentioned in every theory of adolescence: cynical coldness with lyrical fervor; ascetic denial of, and uninhibited indulgence in, libidinal gratification; philosophical speculations about the fundaments of life and reality along with demonstration of commonplace banalities; etc. It is precisely through these contradictions that the adolescent proves his independence of the either-or of life, his ability to rise above the laws of logic. On every level he seeks to replace the concrete with the abstract, the friend with friendship, fair behavior with justice, the way towards realization of a task with anticipation of the goal.

Both the coexistence of self-contradictory attitudes and the flight into the abstract preclude defining adolescence as a preparatory or a transition period; they show, on the contrary, that it rather constitutes an *interruption of developmental continuity*. It then follows that we *cannot* accept Erikson's thesis of identity formation being the normative function of adolescence. Identity in the meaning of the term as suggested by Erikson (25), is *not* attained through gradual integration of all previous identities and identifications (and it is even open to question whether and to what extent those identifications with frequently changing hero figures, that are made possible or at least facilitated by the adolescent's separation and self-distantiation from his parents, exercise a positive or a negative, a clarifying or a distorting influence on the development of later identity). On the contrary, the identity prepared in each of the preceding phases of development (through growth, through experience, through learning, through identification) is now "being taken out" of its reality continuum (so that we often fail to recognize in the adolescent what he used to be as a child). It is precisely this interruption of continuity and this *principalization* that explain the danger of psychotic personality disorders in adolescence (as well as a number of other typical deviations).

Not only are the oedipal problems now being repressed, but also the post-oedipal past is liable to become irrelevant or, at least, to be reinterpreted in the light of the unrealistic present; and the future is regarded as a perpetuation of a consummate present; it is experienced as already known, hence also as capable of being anticipated: principles are eternal, are beyond the dimensions of time.

It is this unrealistic time concept that makes of adolescence a period of *staticness*. The adolescent himself, it is true, tends to indulge in exactly the opposite illusion: that his "life with principles" is an essentially dynamic existence which is contradicted by the adults as the guardians of traditional values and demands, hence as restricting representatives of a dangerous staticness. (He imitates, it is true, his frightening or disdained adults, but this imitation does not necessarily mean identification; it rather shows his endeavor to continue into adulthood his "life with principles" without need for adaptation or submission to the socially accepted norms of behavior and judgment).

The illusion of finality is the central symptom of adolescence. Included in it are all the other essentials of this age, the interruption of continuity, the abandonment of reality in favor of principles, the staticness. It is this illusion of finality that, on the one hand, impedes genuine self-confrontation with the family past and the personal future, with social reality and demands, and, on the other hand, renders possible enlargement of the individual's value system and structurization of new attitudes and qualities. It is precisely because the illusion of finality is *not* based on an objective identity feeling that the adolescent's value system is capable of growth and change, that ego transcendence becomes possible (though it is open to question, as already said, to what extent each of the "new" attitudes and qualities that emerge in the adolescent's personality is genuine, hence positive by the criteria of a later emerging identity).

Closely connected with the illusion of finality is that of *creativeness*. The adolescent's defensive independence of the objective givens in his physical and social environment, of the traditional norms of behavior and judging, of every genuine polarity, explain his arrogant belief in his ability to recognize the essence of, and thereby to master (if not to recreate), reality.*

* Here, again, the close connection between developmental and pathological (psychotic) negation of reality becomes evident.

But it would be a mistake if we were to conclude from what we have said here about the interruption of developmental continuity, the illusions of staticness, of finality and of creativeness, that these concomitants of the adolescent's "life with principles" precluded intelligent behavior. On the contrary, principalization is conducive not only to irrealistic attitudes but also to cognitive acuity, to deep insights, to originality (provided, of course, the adolescent is intelligent). Scientific thinking, command of the "formal operation" methods (to use Piaget's term (106)), and familiarity with the dimensions of the future and the possible—all these characteristics of the intelligent adolescent are the outcome of his intercourse with principles. In the less intelligent adolescent, on the other hand, the same tendencies and illusions are liable to degenerate into ego-inflational signs of falsity and stupid irrealism.

And yet, it is a sadly known fact that even the most brilliant adolescent often turns into a most uninteresting, most trivial adult. How, then, we ask, does the adolescent find his way back into the leveled out, dull world of the adult? How should we explain the fact that this return as a rule manifests itself as a more or less sudden transition from one extreme to another, as a radical resignation, a sacrifice of the life with principles for the sake of a trivial adaptation to the social environment?

In order to understand this return we should bear in mind that a life with principles is not only absurdly impracticable, but also—in the long run—most unsatisfactory. Abstraction as an exclusive mode of orientation isolates man not only from his environment but also from himself, from the own ego; the latter will be an object of self-transcending ego consciousness only to the extent that it remains in dialogic relationship with the—physical and social—non-ego. Where this relationship is replaced by adolescent abstractness and unrealistic principalization of life, the experience of *deadlock* and the concomitant existential despair (following failures in relationships) become unavoidable. Three ways lead out of this despair: suicide, psychotic withdrawal from reality, or giving up the abstract mode of orientation, that adolescent "life with principles".

The third solution is the rule. Usually, the constitutional and the experiential conditions of development are such as to make reconnection with parental values practicable and reassuring. But it is not easy to return to a reality which the adolescent has been neglecting or even treating with contempt for a number of years. His integrity is likely to suffer damage in the process. The triviality, obscurity, and meaninglessness that characterize the existence of most adults in our era with its cold ideals of objectivity, average, and compromise, are regrettably incompatible with the almost unlimited multitude of childhood potentialities. They certainly are in sad contrast to the adolescent's life with principles, with its often repellent, but always disturbing and exciting, intensity of feeling and living. The question then arises whether this loss of intensity and vitality is really unavoidable.

The answer is in the negative. Left to their own resources, only very few adolescents, only the most gifted ones, it is true, will be able to remain self-identical in their return to reality. Adolescence is, as we have said, an *interruption* of the identity continuum; only in his return to adult reality is the "returner" being forced into an integration of his previous identities; return to adult reality thus means at the same time a return to the own past, to the ego roots. This return, however, is not comparable with that of a person who, when awaking even after a particularly intensive dream experience, as a rule finds his way back to, reestablishes contact with, his ego identity without great difficulty. The adolescent, upon "awaking" from his illusions, needs self-reflection and self-confrontation with the experiences of his past in order to achieve the now required integration of his identities; he needs this self-reflection and self-confrontation precisely in the face (and because) of those many adjustment and achievement demands that now assail him. This need, however, is almost incompatible with the external adjustment ideals of our extravert culture and is therefore liable to be neglected. As a result, the search for identity is given up or, to put it more correctly, a pseudo-identity is being built up through repeated self-adaptation to intellectual, vocational, social, and relational tasks, from without rather than from within, and is at best being supported by a gradual development of sublimative or reactive character traits.*

We do not agree with Erikson, whose analysis of adolescence as the period of identity formation may be correct, when we consider the life history of creative men or of individuals whose functional differentiation makes constant attempts at integration necessary, but not when we think of the average citizen of our culture. For the latter, the transition from adolescence to adulthood is a result of environmental influences and demands rather than of the integrating activity and initiative of his ego. This is the principal cause of that loss of vitality that so often characterizes the postadolescence period of development in our time.

Here, an important educational conclusion is warranted: the adolescent, as a rule, needs educational support and guidance in order to discover the traces of his identity not only in the early stages of his development,

---

* What psychoanalysts (*e.g.*, 27) call "sublimative" and "reactive" character traits and what they try to explain as the result of successful or of defensive repression, emerges, it is true, already in the preceding phase of the child's development and in any case before adolescence. But these character traits become part of the individual's personality structure only when life offers a variety of opportunities to "use" them in different and ever-changing reality contexts that require variation and adjustment.

but also in his identity-alien adolescent behavior. It is precisely in the critical stage of transition to adulthood that he needs such support and guidance in order to let his earlier experience and behavior become relevant for his future development. In other words: the adolescent needs adult help for his self-reflections and his self-confrontations. It depends on the quality of this help and guidance, whether and to what extent his life with principles and his existential illusions will be allowed to act in the now following adaptation stages of young adulthood as suppliers of energy; whether the ego will be able to use the experiences of all preceding stages of development, of nearness, of mutuality, of differentiation, of synthesis. The young adult must learn that reality can be recognized and mastered neither from without alone (through receptiveness and self-submission) nor from within alone (by way of anticipating potentialities), but that his ego and the non-ego (in the various connotations of the concept) are equal partners in a dialogic relationship. This learning requires help; when it fails to come forth, the formation of a heteronomous pseudo-ego is almost unavoidable.

One of the most vital manifestations of the transition from adolescence to young adulthood (which incidentally takes place at individually and culturally determined different age points) is the functional maturation of intelligence. It is the function of the educational environment (the family, the school, the group, the place of work) to provide opportunities for intellectual, vocational, and social objectivization which the young adult needs to solve his problems of thinking and behaving in a goal-adapted and yet individualized, autonomous way. Abstraction, originality, perseverance, resistance to emotional interference will now become modes of intelligent behavior only when systematically supported by the educationally relevant environment. Without this support, the adolescent patterns of ego-inflational principalization and staticness will either continue to determine the individual's thinking processes, even after they have already proved their nonviability, or will give way to adult "triviality."

We must not forget that all we have said so far about adolescent development and transition to adulthood applies to the middle-class family of Western society only. For it is only in the tension-charged, affective atmosphere of this family type that retreat into a "life with principles" becomes possible and dynamically meaningful. On the other hand, the social order of which the middle-class family is part and expression, supplies, as a rule, those educational services that the adolescent needs to find a realistic way out of his sterile principalizations into adequate adaptations to the adult world. As a result, many of these adolescents do preserve at least some of the intellectual originality and acuity of the insight into reality connections "behind the scene," which is being fostered by the very tendency to live with principles, and they become "normal adults."

We shall try to show in Section 6 of this chapter what this concept of normalcy means, in what respect childhood and adolescence prepare the ground for it, and how its meaning changes in the third part of life with its inversive tendencies. But before going into a discussion of the phases of adulthood we must at least mention the impact of cultural and social conditions on the transition to adulthood.*

It is only the middle-class adolescent of our technologically oriented society who enjoys what Erikson (23) calls the "moratorium," that is, the (doubtful) privilege of spending the years between childhood and adulthood in socially sanctioned social irresponsibility in order to prepare himself for a vocational or professional function. Already where this preparatory period forms part of a social plan, as in certain totalitarian regimes, its moratory character is weakened, and this not only because collective responsibility is being emphasized, but also because under such conditions of social planning little room is left, as a rule, for the emergence during childhood, of those intimacy ties with the parents that are liable to drive the adolescent into his "life with principles." When social conditions require the child to participate in his adults' labors and concerns from early life on and the personalistic climate of the family is thereby being reduced to a minimum, a moratory existence and a life with principles are *ipso facto* excluded.

In all these and similar cases, transition to adulthood means something essentially different from what it means for the middle-class adolescent after his life with principles has come to an end. It is the absence of intrapsychic tensions resulting from intensive emotional relationships within the family circle that makes imitative adjustment to the adults' style of life relatively easy. One of the almost unavoidable results of this type of adjustment is: weakness of autonomy, of mobility, of empathy.

This, then, leads up to the question of how to evaluate the individual and social achievements of adulthood. What is a healthy adult? What are the criteria of normal behavior, at least in Western society? Can we formulate such criteria to be valid for *all* members of our society, irrespective of social class differences (if not of cultural differences)?

---

* We shall analyze in the second volume the phases of development of children growing up under the externalizing conditions of extreme poverty and educational neglect, of a life in plenty, of certain culture crises as produced by the educational ambiguity and value-vacuum of our time, the sudden transition from so-called primitive to technologically sophisticated and differentiation-oriented societies, and under other sociocultural conditions. It should therefore suffice to add here a few remarks only in order to make our subsequent discussion (on adulthood) appear in the proper perspective.

6. The Concept of Normalcy

All attempts to define the norm of behavior by way of induction, that is, of summarizing observable factors statistically, and to identify "norm" with "average," are irrelevant for a meaningful interpretation of man. Not only does such a method require "dissolving" mankind into an almost unlimited number of subgroups, each with its specifically calculated average (until in the end the method is bound to defeat its set purpose); but there is no way from observation to interpretation, unless the latter precedes the former in the form of *criteria* of observing, if not of evaluating behavior. An analysis of these criteria, however, leads ultimately to the formulation of *ideal* norms, provided we dare to base such an analysis on a phenomenology of essentials.

We suggest the opposite approach: to define normative behavior according to those elements of structure which we have analyzed, at the beginning of the present study, as elements of ego-non-ego relationships. Normal, healthy, behavior, we claim, (a) presupposes the ability and readiness in the individual to place himself at the disposal of trans-individual tasks, that is, to transcend himself, to establish and maintain free contact between the ego and the outer and the inner non-ego, the physical and social environment, on the one hand, and the unconscious (or, in the last instance, with the depth zones of the psyche), on the other; (b) while at the same time being capable of organizing (assimilating and accommodating—in Piaget's language—internalizing and integrating) the stimuli and the directives sent out (given) by the non-ego.

Normal behavior thus pressupposes openness *and* ego strength. Neither one is sufficient to guarantee normalcy. Ability and readiness for self-transcendence may be motivated or even dictated by the collective environment or by the unconscious to the exclusion of the initiative of the ego as the organizing center of consciousness; in this case self-transcendence indicates character disorder, usually of a compulsive nature. Needless to add, organizational ego strength alone, far from indicating a healthy personality, as a rule is but a form and a symptom of egocentricity and rigidity.

Normalcy manifests itself in creativeness, in the courage to face new and changing conditions, in empathy and love, and in the ability to evaluate reality objectively, though the thus evaluated reality may be found to deserve negation and transformation.

It may be maintained that these qualities—creativeness, courage, empathy, love, objectivity—require inner tensions; that they are, in fact, but means of resolving these tensions, that is, of reestablishing inner balance. Such a claim would not contradict our above mentioned definition of normalcy; for the coexistence of its two elements, openness and organizational ego strength, constitutes a state of *tension to be resolved*, a challenge and not a final achievement.

This raises an additional question of defining the normal adult: imbalance between functions within one specific area (the body, the intellect, the feeling) or between these areas may act as a stimulus for achievement and certainly for creativeness, and it will be nevertheless correct to claim that health means *balance* of functions and of functional areas (provided, we should add, the functions do not sink below a certain minimum of functioning, since balance on such a low level of over-all functioning would mean structural absence of both openness and ego strength).

Achievement made possible through imbalance and tension may be of objective social or spiritual value, but the personality of the achiever would nevertheless *not* be healthy or normal. The genius who lives with the inner rather than with the outer non-ego, who is, therefore, open to the non-ego in part only, and whose organizational abilities may be strong enough for the purpose of objectifying and forming his visions, but not for the purpose of accommodating himself to his own views of life, leave alone to his environment, is not normal according to the criteria of normal behavior as suggested here. It is this very *lack* of balance between openness to the world without and the world within, between the fields of application of his ego strength, and often enough the rather marked discrepancy between partial functions in this or that area, that accounts for both his genius and his lack of normalcy.

Is our definition of normal behavior valid for *all* cultures and social strata or for a very limited segment of humanity only? There is no culture in which the individual is not required to be able and ready for self-transcendence; but not in every culture is the individual expected to place himself at the disposal of transindividual tasks *autonomously,* that is, without being determined primarily or even exclusively by the outer or the inner non-ego, the collective reality or the unconscious. On the contrary: in many cultures it is precisely the opposite method of realizing the transindividual task, subordinational and heteronomous acceptance of the prescribed way, that makes realization legitimate. In these cases, autonomy is replaced by internalized heteronomy, that is, by conscious acceptance of, and identification with, the cultural canon and pattern.

We come now back to the question of how childhood and adolescence prepare the ground for transition to adulthood, and to what extent the criteria of normalcy as analyzed here are applicable to those pre-adult stages of development as well.

There are periods in the child's development in which ability and readiness for self-transcendence are not only precluded by the exigencies of the assimilatory growth process but are even counterindicated, periods in which openness is dangerous; others in which dependence on the inner or the outer non-ego is so extreme that the organizational control and competence of the ego is bound to be inadequate. But taken as a whole, childhood is a period of *growth in balance:* body parts and organs become increasingly proportionate, related to each other and to their functions (excluding, of course, pathological deviations and disorders); the same applies to the components of intelligence, which grow not only operationally, as separate functions, but also interrelatedly, so that, at the end of childhood, a functional optimum of intelligence emerges. But more than in any separate function or area the process of growth in balance becomes evident in what we call social, emotional, behavioral maturity.

This maturity, which finds its expression in a relative balance between inner and outer realities, between receptiveness and activity, between the two life tendencies (see pp. 7 *ff.*), but also between partial functions in each functional area, emerges, strangely enough, after the end of that period (of adolescence) that we have analyzed as one of discontinuity, of retreat from reality into a life with principles, of illusions and despair. We have described the transition into adulthood as loss of vitality, as a process of sinking into adult "triviality." How are these negative qualifications compatible with our present claim that the mature balance between different functions as well as between different functional areas —though, of course, somehow present in each stage of normal child development and, in fact, constituting its normalcy—emerges only after adolescence has come to an end? Could it be that maturity and radical adaptation to adult standards are essentially linked together? So that maturity would be jeopardized whenever a young adult is *not* ready to give up and to overcome his adolescent illusions?

Whereas the answer to this question is self-evident (fixation to adolescence, as any fixation, being *identical* with lack of maturity), the conclusions from it are far from being self-evident. Would it not seem to follow that radical renunciation of all adolescent qualities, attitudes, and values and acceptance of adult "triviality" are *prerequisites* of maturity? So that this negative qualification would appear to be an essential element in the definition of maturity? Or is maturity conceivable *without* this precondition (which in any case cannot claim universal validity since it depends on the presence of certain sociocultural conditions)? And, to reformulate our basic question: what is the relationship between the two concepts, normalcy and maturity?

We suggest the following answer, first to the last question: Of two equally immature children passing through a crisis situation or being exposed to equally strong factors of frustration, one will show more normal reactions than the other to the extent that he will be capable of compensatory achievement, of balancing contradictory forces or functions. When these two children face the same learning or problem-solving or adjustment task (and both are of equal intelligence), the one may be called more normal than the other in his approach to the problem with which both are faced, when he will be more "task-oriented," that is, more capable of ego transcendence and of keeping apart the different function areas of his existence.

Whereas these elements of normalcy can be found in any definition of the mature personality, *maturity requires more than normalcy;* it requires self-distantiation, value-orientation, capacity for dialogic relationships with persons, objects, and events which emerge only with growing age (and only in individually different degrees). But maturity in this sense is different from the variety we had in mind when mentioning the strange discrepancy between postadolescent "triviality" and maturity, which marks the beginning of social independence and adjustment.

In other words: we should distinguish between *phases of growing maturity,* from postadolescence to senescence. Notwithstanding sex- and culture-conditioned differences in the essential characteristics and in the relative length of each of these phases, it would seem that there exist at least three distinctly different periods in adult life, comprising the third and fourth decades (ages 20 to 40), the fifth and sixth decades (ages 40 to 60), and old age (age 60 and over). In each of these phases, maturity means something different, according to the different life tasks and the different biological conditions of man passing through them.

This differentiation contains an answer to our preceding question: whether loss of vitality after adolescence is a precondition of maturity. It would indeed seem correct to say that radical adaptation to adult standards characterizes the first phase of adulthood; but we should add that it begins considerably later for the sons of middle-class families (or their equivalents in socialist societies with their new class stratification), when they prepare themselves for a professional career and thereby are being forced into another kind of moratorium, than for other middle-class young adults and certainly for the sons of lower class or rural families whose responsible participation in their elders' life concerns often starts much earlier, as we have already pointed out. But it would be a mistake to identify this radical adaptation to adult standards, and its concomitant vitality loss and triviality of life style, with maturity. The emergence of the latter depends on a later revision of values, usually appearing in the second half of this phase. (Such a generalization, however, would seem to be rather dangerous. The individual level of intelligence and of integrational abilities, the intensity of the adolescent irrealism, the sociocultural patterns of the group in which the individual has grown up and is living, and other factors determine the onset of that revision that marks the beginning of genuine maturity development.)

In the following we shall try to sketch very briefly the essentials of each of these phases of adulthood with their (class- and culture-conditioned) patterns and functions. Here we wish to refer only to two different conceptions of development after adolescence: According to the one this development is but a structural decline (whose ill effects are described by psychologists, for example, Wechsler (123), as a gradual decrease of *intellectual* mobility, or by physiologists and neurologists as *physical* dedifferentiation). Other, more philosophically oriented psychologists not only emphasize compensatory or maturational processes resulting in the gradual emergence of a mind capable of reaching deeper and seeing wider into reality and its meaning; some of them go so far as to ascribe to what Jung (76, 77) calls "the second half of life" the function of correcting the ill effects of functional specialization (which is bound to take place in the first half), as if this process of integration through correction were something going on automatically, following inherent energetic laws of compensation.

The two positions do not exclude each other: when adjustment to the environment, achievement of status, procreation, and relationships with other egos are the essential tasks with which the individual is faced in the first of the three periods of adulthood, different functions are required than in a later period when—normatively—man is confronted with the *inner* non-ego more than with the outer environment. Thus, the decline of those functions that are vital in the first period, particularly those that indicate intellectual and social mobility, not only does not contradict the integration hypothesis, it actually confirms it; for, that decline of functional vitality can be interpreted as one of the structurally necessary conditions of the compensatory turn toward the inner non-ego which characterizes the second period of adulthood. As long as functional mobility enables us to cope, more or less effectively, with the tasks of adjustment to, and intercourse with, the outer non-ego, the intellectual, emotional, and physical functions that are needed for this purpose are not available for the establishment and maintenance of adequate (polar) relationships with the *inner* non-ego. On the contrary, relative disruption of contact with the inner non-ego is a precondition of man's ability to make proper use of his functions for the purpose of adjustment to the environment.

7. The Phases of Adulthood

We begin this analysis by referring the reader to our earlier discussion of the concept of the inner non-ego (see pp. 35 *ff*. and particularly p. 38 *ff*.). There, we have mentioned the growth of the unconscious as a concomitant of internalization, every process of habit and pattern formation, of resolving inner conflicts, of mobilizing defenses entailing selective repression and elimination of certain realities and thus producing new non-ego contents to be internalized. We encounter the same problem when considering the phases of adult adjustment.

The issue is more complex than it would seem from Jung's thesis (76) according to which the (personal) unconscious owes its crystallization to the unavoidable neglect of *inferior* functions and to the exclusive reliance on the *dominant* functions in those periods of life in which man's principal task is adjustment to the environment. Not only is it open to question whether those functional preferences are congenital dispositions or develop through reaction to the changing conditions of environment and organism and are therefore less constant than Jung would want us to believe; neglect of inferior functions is only one of the factors that constitute the personal unconscious, and the others—first and foremost those studied by psychoanalysts as defense mechanisms—often *determine* the intensity of that "neglect," at least secondarily. Moreover, the transpersonal components of the inner non-ego (see our discussion of that concept, pp. 55 *ff.*) are inseparable from the personal components and determine the adjustment process no less than either the functional preference or the defensive reactions to environmental frustrations.

But a still more decisive argument against Jung's simplifying concept of compensatory development relates to the lack of phasal differentiations: subsuming infancy, childhood, adolescence and the first 20 years of adulthood under one concept, that of the first half of life, is not only meaningless (as is the use of any excessively wide concept), it also obviates an answer to the crucial questions of how adult adjustment to the external non-ego, the physical and social environment, is being prepared through functional growth during childhood, through adolescent irrealism or—maturationally and socially conditioned—inadequacy and through relative renunciation of adolescent radicality. This, however, is the essential question which must be answered if we wish to understand not only the essence of adult adjustment but also that of the revolution of the so-called second half of life.

Functional growth during childhood produces the prerequisites of adult adjustment: conceptual clarity and ability to differentiate between separable reality elements, simultaneous orientation toward a phenomenon and its hidden meaning, mobility in thinking, in judging, in acting, ability to abstract from the own ego and its positions, in order to cognize and recognize universally valid laws.

All these properties are normally much more strongly in evidence at the beginning than at the end of adolescence. What intervenes is not a process of binding together, as it were, "all the converging identity elements" (to use Erikson's words (25)), but a retreat from maturity. We maintain that *adolescence anticipates the inward movement of the second half of life, while the functional growth that takes place during childhood is a kind of anticipation of adult adjustment. And we suggest that the essentials of adulthood should be defined by way of translating childhood achievements into the language of adjustment and the adolescent's denial of adult adjustment demands, his illusions of permanence, finality, and creativeness, and his intercourse with principles into the language of later inversive movements.*

The areas of primary adult adjustment are work, marriage, and group affiliation. Cultural and especially economic factors (such as class identification) determine the extent to which the individual's attitude toward each of them is instrumentalistic, self-realizational, or self-transcending. Work may be perceived as an instrument for providing the subsistence means and/or as a source of satisfaction through self-expression and/or as a vehicle of creation; marriage, as an instrument for the satisfaction and the regulation of sexual and other basic needs, and/or as a field of intimacy and love relationships, and/or of parental self-transcendence; group affiliation, as an instrument for safeguarding and protecting economic and other personal interests, and/or as an area of affect discharge, distraction, and tension, and/or as a means for creative self-transcendence (whether we think of political, of vocational, of avocational, of religious or other groups). Change from one to the other mode of perception is the rule, and each individual usually shows different attitudes to his various fields of adjustment at one given moment and in different phases of his development.

Although such potent environmental factors as the historical constellation, the cultural patterns, the social conditions into which an individual may have been born, in which he has grown up and lives, determine the relative frequency in a given population of certain types of attitudes toward the problems of adult adjustment, it is nevertheless the personality that determines the individual varieties and variations of behavior. Anxiety over the threat of change, that is, the type-conditioned and experience-conditioned degree of mobility, of openness to the non-ego, of security, is the decisive factor.

It will be the function of the following chapter to analyze the impact which each of the many environmental factors may have on the process of adjustment in the various phases of development. But while these factors in the *pre-adult* phases account for the formation of the personality of which adjustment is a symptom, they determine, in the first phases of *adulthood,* how the adjustment process is modified, notwithstanding the influence of personality factors.

When we say that childhood achievements "anticipate" adult adjustment, we do *not* refer to the similarities that allegedly can be found between the child's anxieties in the face of new and unknown situations such as transition to the impersonal atmosphere of the school and to the equally impersonal atmosphere of the work place, or the establishment of relationships in the society of equals (at school, for instance, or on the streets) and in adult groups; what we have in mind becomes clear when we recall what we have said about the essential functions of the various phases of childhood and particularly of the learning phase.

This is the period of learning when consciousness is being enlarged through reception and synthesis, the period of growing clarity, differentiation, mobility when meaning is being discovered behind the facts, when abstraction gradually becomes the vehicle of transition from personal to universal truths and laws. The very same tasks lie before the young adult when he is faced with problems of vocational and social learning, of adjustment to work and groups. Adjustment in these areas could, in fact, be defined as a process of gradual substitution of individual by transindividual task orientations and modes of operation. Differentiation (between individuals, between tasks, between methods of approach, between facts and meaning) and readiness to distantiate oneself from any momentary ego position (mobility and abstraction) are the preconditions of this "substitution" in the areas of work and of group life.

The same applies to the establishment of personal relationships, including love and marriage. Here, too, the first stage of adulthood resembles childhood more than adolescence, provided, of course, the individual has succeeded in overcoming, in the main, his adolescent irrealism and despair. The first period of adulthood supplies a new edition, as it were, of that society of equals through which the child learns that he is responsible for the discovery of—reversible—rules and laws. The adult now learns, in and through his relationship experiences, that he is responsible for mutuality. The fact that he often enough fails in this specific learning task and that, as a result, many personal relationships bear the character of infantile ego-relatedness and lack polarity (and dialogue), does not disprove our thesis but only comes to show that transfer of childhood achievements to the tasks of adult adjustment is a slow and difficult process, and that in most cases it is the partiality of early achievement, that is, partial failure and fixation in certain phases of childhood development, which is reflected in those partialities and limitations of adult adjustment, in work, in group contexts, and in love and marriage relationships.

Exactly as adjustment in the development of intelligence and other ego functions during childhood goes through the stages of assimilation and accommodation (to use Piaget's terminology), so adult adjustment in the three main task areas goes through the stages of receptiveness (assimilation) and synthesis (accommodation). Courage based on the experience of nearness and trust, ambivalence based on the coexistence of contradictory experiences and contradictory needs (protection and separation, goodness of love and badness of pain, mutuality and aggressiveness), differentiation based on ambivalence and courage—these achievements of the various childhood phases before the onset of adolescence are the essential elements in both, assimilation of experience and accommodation of the ego to the tasks of work and relationships.

It is because these childhood achievements are indispensable for adult adjustment that adolescence must be renounced. Not only despair over the nonviability of a life with principles and an existence in illusions drives the adolescent out of his irrealism, also the future coming toward him in the process of maturation forces him into transition. The same intensity with which adult values and demands and, with them, the achievements of the preceding phases of development, are depreciated by the adolescent, now characterizes the young adult's tendency to live up to the standards and ideals of his elders.

It may be argued that this is perhaps typical of transition from adolescence to adulthood in the Western middle-classes only and that even there imitative tendencies are often much less in evidence then continued radicalism of the adolescent type. Whereas this is undoubtedly true for many sons and daughters of middle-class families who prepare themselves for one of the liberal professions, it would not seem to be correct to draw even from their demonstrated radicalism the conclusion that they are *not* adjustment-oriented: care-free demonstration of independence serves, more often than not, as a means only to cover up inner acceptance of adult values, as if open admission of such identification meant betrayal of something sacred. And betrayal it is indeed, not so much betrayal of adolescent illusions and principles as betrayal of a life from within, which has to be repressed to make adjustment to adult reality possible.

The more genuine the motivation of professional learning is and the higher the intelligence of the learner, the less important become both adjustment to adult values and demonstrated radicalism. Still different is the attitude to preparation for professional careers in a social order in which such learning and training is considered of socially equal value with that of the actual execution of functions: there, learning is already "adjustment."

In the majority of human careers, however, that is, in most lower class and in most rural families, the beginning of adulthood is almost undefinable in terms of age, and the slowness and gradualness of transition finds its expression in the absence of adolescent interruption of continuity and in immediate utilization of childhood achievements for adult adjustment. The less marked the adolescent crisis, the less urgent becomes the need for adjustment; its beginnings are not much different from its later stages, since so little depends on the individual and his initiative, so much on anonymous processes, on patterns, on group conditions. The same holds good for traditional family settings in general, irrespective of class differences. And it is well known that, irrespective of class or culture, adolescent interruption of continuity and subsequent radicalism of adult adjustment are as a rule much less characteristic of girls and women than of boys and men.

All these conditions have one element in common: less emphasis, in the development of the individual, on differentiation than on whole perception, less on paternal values than on maternal. Here, acceptance of reality as such, intuitive and emotional rather than cognitive orientation are considered the proper ways of coping with the tasks of adjustment. All these conditions are conducive to the preservation of continuity.

We can now correct our initial statement about the transition from adolescence to adulthood by formulating the following law: *In its first stages, adult adjustment, being a recapitulation of childhood achievements, shows a tendency toward radical imitation when a preceding adolescent irrealism has to be counteracted and held in check; to the extent that such adolescent deviation is less pronounced or even absent, adult adjustment proceeds smoothly, gradually, and without tension.*

The phase of adult adjustment is divided, we have said, into two periods, the first one being that of adjustment proper, when the *individual* gradually assimilates social norms and expectations in his work, his married life, his group realizations. The second period, however, is that of fulfillment, when the individual knows "the rules of the game," plays it accordingly, modifies the rules following the command of his individual life style and his by now crystallized identity—sometimes successfully, more often failing in his attempts at individuation.

This is the time of life when the unlived parts of the self begin to make themselves felt, not yet aggressively or even destructively but nevertheless strongly enough to make man doubt the wisdom of adjustment, or at least to make him ask what values hide behind the protecting wall of social achievement. His adjustment may be strong enough and his ego may be effective enough to guard the gates against the inner non-ego, those unlived parts of the soul, those "inferior functions," those "repressed desires and strivings," those areas unknown, whose exclusion from consciousness had been one of the preconditions of his adjustment to the external non-ego, the physical and social environment. The vague feelings of hidden values, the questions, and the doubts may even be repressed as soon as they emerge; but once raised they must be answered if adjustment is to be maintained. Repression of those portents of coming changes produces somatic, intellectual, or emotional disorders that are bound to weaken, if not to destroy, the foundations of whatever adjustment the individual may have achieved.

It would of course be utterly misleading to define this second period of adulthood as one of "coming changes." Type factors, structural givens such as the degree of the ego's organizational strength and its openness to the non-ego, but also sociocultural patterns and, last but not least, the very level of adjustment achievement and the satisfaction derived from it—all these factors determine the crisis character of the phase here under discussion. It may be almost absent—in men with a marked structural tendency toward systematization, for instance, particularly when they are strongly receptive extraverts. However, not only they, but others too are more or less immune against change from within. In fact, even changes that *do* begin to announce themselves in this second part of the adult adjustment period do not, as a rule, lead to radical personality changes, at least not to such changes as may be visible to outside observers. On the contrary, there are more adults who now reap the harvest of their previous adjustment than who search for another identity or suffer from what they are. Malcontent, not with fate or with the conditions of life but with one's own identity, is rather exceptional (when we exclude introvert neuroses).

This is one of the reasons why, in contrast to our thesis (according to which the second part of the adult adjustment period leads toward the midlife crisis and to compensatory changes in the following phase), the generally accepted philosophy of man, at least in our Western culture, puts emphasis on identity in Goethe's meaning of the concept ("*geprägte Form, die lebend sich entwickelt*") or, as Erikson (24, 25) defines the concept ("sameness in variety and in change"). Seeming changes are being interpreted as indicating "revivals" only of early repressed parts of the personality which had been excluded by the adjustment-oriented ego and had consequently been forced into latency, irrespectively of whether their past exclusion from consciousness had been a structural necessity or had only *produced* their gradual alienation from the meanwhile emerging and crystallizing identity.

Here, let us recall our discussion in Chapters 4 and 5 of identity (see pp. 54, 65, and particularly 79 *ff*.); of identity proving itself through change and self-transcendence only (so that it might be defined as "change in sameness" rather than as "sameness in change"); of identity owing its emergence to the "category of sameness" and its growth to the impact of the non-ego; of the difference between reactive change on the one hand, which has been shown by psychoanalysts to prove the underlying identity ("sameness"); and radical change or sudden appearance of another behavior and reaction pattern, on the other hand, which may be interpreted as the manifestation of a parallel (unconscious) ego development going on simultaneously with the main stream and suddenly producing another identity; of the discrepancy between what we consider part of our identity when we are young and the way we later interpret certain manifestations of our juvenile behavior as ego-alien, as nongenuine, as worthless, even as deviant.

When we combine these statements, we see that the difference between the stronger emphasis on sameness in the individualistic and personalistic orientation and the emphasis on change and self-transcendence in the structuralistic and transpersonalistic orientation is not unbridgeable. We reject the definition suggested by the individualist of the congenitally given identity nucleus (*geprägte Form*), as a unique, individual configuration of dispositions and potentials, a configuration which develops and materializes in the life span to the extent that external conditions favor this development and materialization. The life-inherent tendency toward balance (Piaget) or homeostatis (Cannon) or compensation and *unio oppositorum* (Jung) implies the presumption of a predifferential unity—and wholeness—stage which is the prototype of sameness and identity. Hence, the return to that stage, after individuation has reached its peak toward the end of the adult adjustment phase of development. Adjustment requires functional specialization, progressive restriction of the infiniteness that is the primary unity stage, elaboration of individual methods of assimilation and accommodation. This partiality creates structural tensions which make the midlife crisis necessary.

We have maintained that there is some essential similarity between adolescent irrealism and life with principles and the inversive movements of the postadjustment period of adulthood, called by Jung the "second half of life." The question will then be raised again: What happens in those many cases in which there has been little, if any, adolescent tension and crisis? Will this relative absence of adolescent tension influence the intensity of the midlife inversion?

If the connection between the two crisis periods would be of a psychodynamic order, a law of proportion would make sense (just as Anna Freud (41) tries to account for the intensity of adolescent defenses by referring to the two factors of relative drive strength and relative ego strength); we could then make personal factors of constitution and experience responsible not only for the intensity of adolescent retreat from reality into principles but also for adult adjustment reactions as well as for the later midlife inversion.

If, however, the intensity of adolescent irrealism *cannot* be explained satisfactorily as a function of the personal life history alone but becomes intelligible only when these biographic factors are seen in configuration with transpersonal factors, such as a structural need for ego transcendence, then the connection between the two crisis periods takes on the character of opposites: While adolescent predominance of principles over reality could be interpreted as an exercise in ego transcendence without which social adjustment and adult development in general would be unthinkable, the midlife inversion may be interpreted as a slow process of gradual withdrawal of mental energy from adjustment and achievement and of using it for self-transcendence. Adolescent ego transcendence means inflating the ego into the role of the personal realizer of external truths and values; the *midlife* inversion, on the other hand, means finding and paving the individual "path into the law," to use Kafka's expression (79), the individual variety of transpersonal truths (which now becomes more important than adjustment and achievement, than universally valid abstraction and personally valid reality). Adolescence, even when it is *not* a period of violent upheavals, is characterized by contradictory attitudes. In the later years of life coexistence of opposites no longer produces tensions and no longer elicits attempts to replace that coexistence by compromise, balance, or solutions.

Every achievement of earlier phases of development—nearness and differentiation, mutuality and aggressiveness, autonomy and ambivalence, taking-in and synthesis, life with principles and illusions of finality—takes on a different meaning in the phase of inversion. Courage no longer grows out of the experience of nearness but rather grows out of the confrontation with the absolute; differentiation is no longer needed for cognitive or for relational achievements but is an ever-present challenge to rediscover unity contexts and meaning; giving becomes more essential than mutuality as a means and an expression of ego transcendence; aggressiveness no longer serves as an instrument of eliminating threats of destruction or of heightening a feeling of ego potency, but more and more becomes a means for the construction of new whole contexts; autonomy is increasingly replaced by recognition of dependence, ambivalence by readiness to live in a world of opposites; and in every area of life man now feels the need to create in order to prove his identity by self-transcendence (although this need may produce despair rather than creations). *Genuineness rather than adjustment is the ultimate value in the "second half of life."*

Needless to add, the foregoing is an "ideal type" construction only, and in reality we will find more failures than successes, more cases of neurotic inability to accept the demands of advancing age than cases in which the inversive movement produces genuineness.

8. Senescence

It would certainly be superfluous to add here another essay on senescence to the almost endless list of publications on the subject. It seems nothing has remained unsaid, and most statements have been repeated all over again in different forms about both the inevitable loss of functional efficiency and the compensatory tendencies manifesting themselves with growing age.

We may, however, ask how the—positive and negative—characteristics of old age as they are defined by gerontologists fit into the model of developmental phases as suggested in the present study. The biological definition of senescence as the period of tissue degeneration and of lowered homeostatic efficiency could also be formulated in terms of changes taking place in the ratio between the two life tendencies and in their interrelatedness, in the degree of the ego's openness to the non-ego and its organizational ability, in the general level of thresholds and sensitivity.

Whatever the individual presenescence constellation of the two life tendencies may have been, it is self-evident that the tendency toward expansion becomes weaker in the course of involutional changes. And yet, it is not so much this involutional decrease of the tendency toward expansion, as it is the simultaneous decrease in the ego's organizational strength and the resulting low level of interrelatedness between the two life tendencies that characterizes old age. The inversion taking place, according to Jung, at midlife (that is, long before old age) means: changes in the contents and the aims of life but *not* in the degree of the individual's vitality and in the intensity of his goal-directedness. The involutional changes of senescence, however, as a rule limit not only the aging person's reality area but also his vitality and goal-directedness.

The dialogic relationship with the non-ego now gradually becomes more monologic in character: the external as well as the internal non-ego, the environment as well as the universe of memories, of ideas, of dreams, of images, "speaks" to the ego more than it is being "answered," is an object of observation and contemplation rather than of "discussion."

Theoretically, there is, of course, no end to the process of the non-ego's self-realization with the help of the ego (as its aim and instrument). If the ego would be capable of maintaining dialogic relationships with the non-ego and responding adequately to its ever-changing intimations, senescence would not be a period of loss of function. This, however, only means begging the question, since loss of functions is a biological necessity, the onset of which can perhaps be delayed but not eliminated, the ill effects of which can perhaps be eliminated—through drugs, operations, diets, exercises—but never for more than a limited period of time. Hence, the "dialogue" between the ego and the non-ego must come to an end. *Normatively, senescence is the period of life during which the aging individual's ego gradually ceases to be an object responding to the non-ego without and within, during which man becomes a subject only facing himself and going toward "his" death.* This, however, is but the norm. In reality, we encounter "deviants" more than "normals": men and women trying to escape into false communications, as it were, into some kind of reactiveness in the face of a reality which never ceases to fascinate them and to keep their ego in captivity, men and women who pay for this unwillingness, and for their inability to live as subjects only, with never-ceasing fear of death.

9

Environmental Factors: The Wider Environment

1. THE CONCEPT OF ENVIRONMENT

Environment as a causal factor in normal or abnormal development can be defined as: (a) the totality of acting and reacting persons (parents and other family members, friends and neighbors, teachers and other authority figures, chance acquaintances and strangers), (b) each being conditioned in his actions and reactions by his own constitution, life experience, cultural patterns, social status, and personality structure, (c) and acting within and from within a given natural, social and cultural reality, (d) which exists independently of, contains and transcends, the existence of these persons, (1) as the totality of the *general* geographic and climatic conditions, economic order, historic constellation, social pathologies, collective ideologies and patterns, and (2) as the totality of the *specific* conditions of neighborhood, social institutions, etc. encountered by the individual.

The causal effect of the latter *specific* conditions cannot be evaluated properly, unless seen in the context of the *general* collective conditions. Both, however, cannot be evaluated properly unless related to the personal figures living in, and acting out of, this totality of conditions. The actions and reactions of these figures, on the other hand, must be related to their personality structures as well as to their reality, in order to become meaningful for the interpretation of a specific individual's behavior and development. This, in short, is a configurational definition of the concept of environment.

Each of its components can and, indeed, must be described in isolation, if we want to avoid the use of ambiguous concepts and to understand the possible meanings of each in the analysis of individual cases. It is customary to speak of natural, historic, and economic conditions, of the quality of training facilities, of the positive and the negative stimuli operating in the environment, of cultural values, patterns, conflicts, and changes, of the family structure and composition—all of these being facets of the one factor called environment. They must be described and defined *in abstracto,* that is, as quasi-independent partial realities, but *should not be measured*

188

as such or, for that matter, "added" to each other in order to produce answers to the questions of individual developments.

What we have said about the fallacies of the pluralistic approach in general (with its ambition to establish objective laws of causation by way of calculating correlation coefficients) holds good also for the components of the factor called environment, both in the causal equation of an individual and in a phenomenological analysis of behavioral units. It would be meaningless to discuss the relative weight of environment in a specific clinical picture unless we defined this factor specifically, that is, as the specific constellation of its component factors.

Each environmental factor, however, has an objective and a subjective meaning. It is primarily the second aspect with which we should be concerned in any causal interpretation of behavior, as only the *reaction* to objective factors produces behavioral results (one more argument against the quantitative methods of factor analysis!).

Often enough, it is true, we may discover omnipotent factors at work in the environment. Let us mention only a few. A radical disruption of family life after war and revolution may create mass problems of waywardness in children; certain cultural patterns may be responsible for the emergence of rigidity in all members of a specific group, irrespective of other environmental factors; extreme poverty* sets in motion, much more frequently than conditions of economic security, processes of externalization. But even these seemingly overriding factors depend for their causal effectivity on the mediation, as it were, at least of the parents, whose relational and educational attitudes determine the child's reactions to the first-mentioned factors, that is, the individual variations.

No environmental factor becomes causally relevant and significant unless it is *represented* by specific persons (outside) and *transformed* into an integral part of the developing personality (inside). So formulated, the concept of *personalistic* interpretation means the opposite of *objectivistic* rather than of *structural* interpretation. We claim that any objectivistic theory of behavior based on a conception of environmental factors as parts of an external non-ego is bound to be inadequate. Environment is a causal factor mainly "from within," but as such it is part of an inner *non-ego* (an inner environment), whose assimilation and integration determine the process of development.

Natural, historic and economic conditions are represented in the causal equation by inner patterns of thinking, feeling, and judgment; objective conditions of learning and training, by habits and expectations; stimulations "sent out" by the environment, by positive and negative inner tensions and drives. The family structure operates as a causal factor through the medium of the self-conception it produces in the child.

* Effects of poverty will be discussed in detail in a subsequent volume.

No partial factor lends itself better to explaining the structural approach than that called "the parental environment." We leave aside in this context the determination of the child's heredity, and thus of his fetal reaction patterns, by the parents; or the determination of the child's intrauterine and birth experience by the mother's somatic structure and state of health, her psychosomatic attitudes toward life and motherhood, or her reactions to the acting and reacting fetus. For we are not interested here in analyzing the ways in which the child's constitutional nucleus, including its hereditary and its congenital components, crystallizes and emerges (see pp. 90 ff.). But when the parents react to the neonate's actions and reactions according to their own expectations, satisfactions, and dissatisfactions, and according to the manner in which they experience their own sociocultural and personal environment, they determine the child's personality structure *from within and from without.*

We have already tried to explain the structural meaning of the parents in our analysis of the maternal and paternal principles (see pp. 22 ff.). Here, a few remarks may be added with a view to showing how the parental environment "without" is *related* to the parental environment "within."

In psychoanalytic theory the superego is the result of a process in the course of which parental demands and prohibitions are being introjected, though it is not *identical* with these introjections insofar as constitutional factors (of selection) participate in the process. The theoretical orientation of psychoanalysis is, however, purely genetic, and there is no room in it for the assumption of structural equivalents of environmental factors (48).

Jung (73, 76) speaks of the archetypal significance of the father and the mother, meaning that they are two constituents of experience and as such precede all individual experience, although they depend on the latter to be "actualized" by them, to become "operational."

Klein (84), though defining the parental, and particularly the maternal figures in similar terms, explains the universality and the inevitability of certain basic infantile modes of experience (such as that of the devouring mother) through reduction to the biological necessity of frustration.

Both Jung and Klein ascribe to the "real" parents the role of representation and concretization of universal and transpersonal factors of the psychic reality, that is, of structural factors, in addition to their role as actual and individually definable persons.

We maintain that the relationship between the personal parents and their inner equivalents is *not* only one of introjection and internalization, that is, of transformation into inner images or inner agents, but rather one of correspondent entities: *environmental factors such as the parents exercise their causal effect in the individual's development only through the medium of their structural equivalents.*

The same applies to all other environmental factors. Not only must they, as we have said above (p. 190), be represented personally and be transformed into "parts" of the developing personality (mainly by way of internalization), they must also, in order to become causally effective, appeal to their structural equivalents, actualize them. In other words, no environmental factor becomes causally effective, unless there is a response from its structural equivalent. Lack of such a response may be due to deficiencies either in the structure or in the environment.

(It will be clear by now that the terms "personalistic" and "transpersonal" (see pp. 55 *ff*.) each have a twofold meaning. We call an interpretation personalistic *both* when it is based on ontogenetic reduction of behavioral results to purely personal antecedents, and when it is based on the presumption that no environmental factor determines a behavioral outcome without being represented, in the environment, by a personally definable factor. We call an interpretation transpersonal *not only* when it is based on the presumption that every personally definable causal factor— such as an attitude or a reaction—is determined by a number of collective, hence transpersonal, factors, *but also* when it is based on the presumption that environmental factors operate causally only through the medium of their structural equivalents, that is, from within. Paradoxically, we could call the second type of the personalistic interpretation "transpersonal" insofar as it recognizes the importance of the external non-ego; and we could call the second type of the transpersonal interpretation "personalistic" insofar as it places the ultimate responsibility for the causal effect of an environmental factor in the psychic structure of the individual being determined by the environment.)

2. NATURE AND CULTURE

The concept of *natural environment* refers to the climatic and geographic conditions of the individual's life space, which could almost be called *constitutional elements of reality*, insofar as they, at least indirectly, determine group averages of behavior, the expected degree of individual activity, affectivity, clarity, decisiveness, and continuity in action. The natural environment is, thus, one of the causes of the cultural and educational patterns, although it would be wrong to overrate its causal importance as such. The comparative study of cultural and educational patterns shows that similar patterns may emerge under different climatic and geographic conditions, and different patterns under similar climatic and geographic conditions. The same studies, however, show that these conditions directly and indirectly influence social processes, customs, beliefs, and habits, and the way in which they operate.

In the individual's development the factor is liable to play a decisive role when he is suddenly transferred to radically different conditions which require readaptation. Failure of the organism to solve its readjustment problems adequately affects the ego's integrative power and, as a result, the individual may become more susceptible of frustrating social factors or of tension-creating occurrences and particularly of social pathologies that are characteristic of the new society. The more frequently the organism fails in the changed environment, the more intensively is the individual liable to become aware of his dependence on the external conditions of his existence.

But climatic and geographic conditions are not only part of the individual's sociocultural environment, although it is undoubtedly this sociocultural aspect of nature that should be emphasized in any etiological study of environment. Before entering into a detailed analysis of *culture* we must try to answer some more specific questions concerning the connection between certain climatic and geographic conditions and the emergence of certain attitude preferences in certain groups, such as tendencies toward externalization, internalization, neurotic or aggressive reaction patterns.

It may well be that certain climatic conditions, such as regular warmth, act on the human organism as tension-reducing factors and support tendencies toward passivity. Moreover, it is a well known fact that under such conditions people are spending a relatively large part of their day outdoors. Here it becomes evident that the climatic factor under discussion may further externalization, but only when configurated with specific *social* factors: in a rural environment this kind of passivity and living with nature may produce and support tendencies toward internalization, its main manifestations being introspection, contemplation, and readiness for dialogic relationships with the non-ego. In an urban environment, on the other hand, the same factor may operate in an opposite direction, insofar as it strengthens the individual's contact with outside reality as the area of chance occurrences.

The *form* of externality that may result from the impact of this factor will, as a rule, be different from that emerging under conditions of poverty. Certain conditions of nature (monotonous environment, low-tension climate, etc.) direct man's consciousness toward what happens in any given moment rather than toward the "haveable" (this main value in the poverty type of externalization). The relatively low level of inner tensions—which characterizes a passive and receptive life style—may, it is true, turn into a pathogenic factor, if supported by tension-creating, collective or individual, factors; but where such factors are absent, the low tension level is definitely compatible with good relational abilities. Here, man does not depend on the "illusion of knownness" (see pp. 112 *ff.*) as he would under the externalizing conditions of poverty; but his consciousness expands in this case, as in poverty, through receptivity and dependence on chance occurrences rather than through intellectual activity and initiative.

It would, of course, be wrong to conclude that opposite, tension-creating, conditions of nature are *per se* conducive to internalization. On the contrary, the very unpredictability of nature may then produce attitudes of fatalistic dependence on the non-ego to an extent that truly polar relationships between ego and non-ego are again endangered or even obviated. Only in configuration with unequivocally internalizing factors, such as patterns of activating education, high expectation types of cultural tradition, security-providing parents, is a tension-creating natural environment conducive to internalization. In such conditions it is precisely the unpredictability of nature that increases man's awareness of being an ego in front of, and in relation to, an ever-changing non-ego.

Geopsychologists have pointed out that geographic isolation and monotony, both in the narrowness of a mountain village and in the endlessness of a desert, are likely simultaneously to limit and to deepen man's life orientation (66). Paucity of stimulus variations, that is, limitation of man's opportunities to enlarge his *massa apperceptiva* through assimilation and comparison, is bound to restrict extraversive tendencies and mobility while at the same time directing the mental energies inward and forcing the ego into confrontation with the *inner* non-ego. The result is not necessarily genuine internalization. The latter requires a level of differentiation and of polar relationship between ego and non-ego which man may not be capable of reaching under the impact of a narrow or monotonous natural environment. Moreover, it is the infant's earliest experience of maternal reality that determines, here as under any other external conditions, whether group-patterned introversive tendencies will be conducive to repression, to apathetic withdrawal, to aggressive reactions, to hallucinatory recreation of reality. Obviously, the primary experience of nearness and of belonging determine the degree and the type of internalization more decisively than do nature-conditioned group tendencies toward emphasis on communication with the outer or with the inner non-ego. Communication with external realities may be differentiated and ego-related, communication with the inner non-ego may be externalized (for instance, in hallucinatory processes in which a whole group is involved).

But the range of influence of climatic and geographic conditions on the average expected behavior is wider than the antithesis between internalization and externalization would seem to indicate. Erikson (23) tries to explain the differences between the "genital" patterns of the Sioux hunters and the "anal" patterns of Yurok fishermen, in part at least, by reduction to the differences between "openness" and "narrowness" of the habitat. Here, then, the natural environment is seen as a determinant of value patterns and educational practices through which the former are transmitted from generation to generation. In the context of our present discussion Erikson's psychoanalytically oriented interpretation of anthropological data is of interest as an indication of the possible link between nature and deviant behavior: if climatic and geographic conditions are capable of favoring the emergence of certain behavior patterns, it may well be that they are also conducive to the relative frequency or the relative absence in a certain group of neurotic or of aggressive patterns or even of certain subunits of disturbances. In other words, we ask to what extent a group, owing to the natural conditions to which its members are exposed, is liable to produce a relatively large number of what in another group would be called "deviants" (neurotics, aggressives, etc.).*

That geopsychologists (7, 62, 66) are unable to give a clear and unambiguous answer to these questions is obvious, not only because they lack, as a rule, clinical experience and psychodynamic orientation but also because of the inseparability of natural from sociocultural conditions. The maximum that we can therefore expect from an analysis of climate and habitat—in addition to its possible contribution to a configurationally oriented ecology of normal and abnormal behavior—is an at least partial answer to the question of conduciveness: which conditions are conducive to generalized feelings of being threatened and helpless (and therefore to a high frequency of anxiety reactions at various levels of intensity); which conditions are conducive to generalized feelings of being persecuted and injured (and therefore to a high frequency of aggressive reactions aimed at maintaining or restricting individual integrity); which conditions make for loss of initiative and for ineffectiveness; which conditions make for an all-pervading feeling of emptiness. The same questions can, of course, be asked in an opposite direction: which conditions of nature favor the emergence of general security, of general effectiveness, of feeling challenged.

An answer to such questions not only helps in the analysis of individual behavior, normal and abnormal, insofar as it makes psychodynamic interpretations more meaningful and more specific (by adding another level of causation), it also helps to understand more adequately the meaning of sociocultural factors such as educational patterns and value systems, which take on different meanings under different conditions of nature; and we will be well advised not to lose sight of this dimension of meaning in this analysis of the so-called cultural factors of determination.

In the context of the present discussion, the term *cultural factors* means: (a) the social order prevailing at a given place and time and determining group attitudes and values on which the individual's behavior depends;

* We are, of course, *not* concerned here with the problem of individual deviants from a specific group, whom Kardiner (82) has tried to interpret as "atypicals," whatever the "basic personality type" of their specific group may be (*cf.* also Mead's descriptions of the deviant (94)). While this is one of the main problems of *individual* pathology, we have in mind here the social pathology aspect of causation only: how certain *nonhuman* factors such as conditions of nature are capable of producing *human* factors such as value patterns and attitude preferences.

and (b) value and attitude changes following war, revolution, national liberation, migration, economic depression, etc.—changes which are generally believed to produce in the members of the affected group increased aggressiveness and hate or insecurity and fear, restlessness and activism or passivity and indolence, ego inflation or ego loss, and in any case to affect the family as a unit of orientation and guidance.

Let us try to specify this question of pathogenic effect. In which way, we ask, can cultural patterns, in which way can value and attitude changes, be held responsible for prevalence of internalization, externalization, neurotic distortions of reality, aggressiveness? (Cf. Chapter 7.)

It is a well known fact that certain patterns of culture favor, others disfavor, internalization. In the first case externalizing factors that may be active in the environment or in an individual must reach a considerably higher degree of intensity in order to produce externality of behavior than in the second case, in which the general atmosphere of the culture supports externalization. Feeblemindedness, constitutionally conditioned indolence, primary or regressive behavior disorders following certain types of disappointing and frustrating experiences or certain forms of developmental crises, are necessary to counteract the internalizing impact of a culture characterized by differentiation between the ego and the non-ego, by emphasis on autonomy and polarity and, thus, by an all-pervading tendency toward internalization.

Where, on the other hand, ego weakness is a result and a reflection of cultural patterns—such as institutionalization of all life aspects, heteronomy, "tradition-directedness" (112), primitivity, particularly in situations of cultural transition—or of conditions of want or plenty, externalization is much less dependent on the cooperation of other, individual, factors. Although these cultural conditions differ from each other essentially, they have one aspect in common: as a rule, the individual growing up and living under the impact of any of them is *not aware* of his being determined by them; but it is precisely this unawareness, this unconsciousness, that increases his susceptibility to externalizing life factors. In other words, unawareness of dependence and externalization are mutually reinforcing factors.

In some tradition-directed societies, education aims at making the individual *recognize* the absolute superiority of traditionally defined truths, at *making* him dependent on them, at *preparing* him to submit to them in his thinking and in his behavior. Obviously, internalization in the proper sense of the word is unattainable in *any* tradition-directed society; but there is an essential difference between this type of internalized, and other types of externalized, heteronomy. True enough, even in the first type, which is characterized by the individual's awareness of his dependence, the categories of interpretation are those of externality (staticness, chance oc-

currence, extrinsic cause and effect, rather than development, aim, intrinsic cause and result); but the very fact of the individual's self-confrontation with his (cultural) non-ego limits the extent and the radicality of
externalization.

Primitivity may serve as another example. The concept covers different
forms of cultural existence: the "original" pattern, in which the ego is
contained, as it were, in a transcendent non-ego, the pattern that emerges
under conditions of cultural isolation, and the various forms of primitivity
which we encounter in situations of sudden culture clash, of heterogeneity
of values. Here, too, it is correct to say that primitivity is a cause of externalization to the extent that the individual is unaware of the cultural
conditions of his existence. Neither the "primitive as philosopher" (to use
Radin's term (108)) nor the sophisticated individual who reflects on the
ambiguity of his condition, is truly externalized (although we may find
even in their behavior not a few symptoms and indications of externalization). In their case, primitivity has ceased to be a cause of externalization,
and we must look for *individual* factors to understand their *nonexternality*.

(The same applies to the many islands of primitivity in the consciousness
of modern man. Here, primitive behavior may be a symptom of personality
disorders, of lack of integration, or of partial dedifferentiation; it should
not be included in a discussion of *cultural* factors.)

The second group of cultural factors are those subsumed under the heading of *culture change*. We must not lose sight of the fact that *change* is not
identical with *crisis*. Changes of cultural patterns in the wake of a revolution, a national liberation movement, or a migration may manifest themselves as increased chances of humanity and are often conducive to internalization.

It is the sudden appearance of new perspectives that may enable the individual to transcend the patterns of his previous existence, to distantiate
himself from what was self-understood hitherto, from his actuality, and
thus to become ready for polar relationships with the non-ego and thereby
also for internalization. The opposite may, of course, happen as well: that
the new perspectives become visible only in and through the collective contexts in which man experiences them, that his heteronomy thus increases
and, with it, the externality of his behavior and his thinking.

Let us consider the case of an individual who grew up under conditions
of social heteronomy and, as an adult, was transplanted into an autonomy-
oriented society (whether by force of revolutionary changes in his group or
through individual migration). His heteronomy-oriented environment may
have caused him to become passive and ready to accept the social non-ego
as omnipotent, though he may have felt at the same time to be identical
with "his" non-ego and may have acted as if he were master of his decisions
and actions. He may now fail to understand the need for reorientation and

may tend to transfer to the new environment his dependence patterns (though with one significant change: the omnipotent non-ego is now being experienced as responsible for his failures and therefore negated). But the value orientation prevailing in the new society, with its emphasis on personal responsibility, may also help him translate his former *illusion* of internality and mastery into a truly autonomous orientation and thus become a cause of internalization. Apart from personality factors, it is primarily the way in which the autonomy-oriented society interprets itself to its new, heteronomy-oriented, members that determines the externalizing or the internalizing effect of transition to a different value system.

More frequently discussed and better known are the *negative* consequences of historic crises. We know that value disintegration and *anomie,* those frequent concomitants of crises, are liable to eliminate the achievements of previous internalizations, not only in individuals that may be personally affected by them, but also in the group as a whole, in its life patterns. We may then witness a process of regressive externalization: separated from the value system which so far contained him, man feels himself thrown into an outside reality of occurrences that have little meaning behind their plane of appearance; he is neither able nor willing to seek or to recognize their hidden essentiality. More: what his reason fails to conceive, his senses may fail to perceive. And he is apt to include in his consciousness —perhaps by way of external imitation or of material participation—all that he does not understand, as if it were part of his prior experience.*

In what respect differs the ideal type of externalization from the "pattern of externality" as it appears under the impact of cultural transition and crisis? In such transition and crisis man is liable to lose that inner security which he had derived previously from "his" value system, and to feel himself at the mercy of an ambiguous and fundamentally meaningless new environment. This fact explains why externalization in this case will often be associated with inner tensions and anxieties, so that in the end the original pattern of externalization may become almost unrecognizable.†

Here, again, the question may be asked: To what extent can the cultural factor in its twofold meaning (of patterns and of change) be considered responsible for the emergence of certain neurotic or aggressive tendencies in a social or in an ethnic group? It is self-evident that, within the narrow

---

* These are unambiguous signs of externalization, as we shall show in the second volume.

† The effect of an individual's transition to the unaccustomed conditions of a "new" climate is similar. When the organism fails to adapt to these new conditions, a feeling of helpless dependence on external conditions is likely to appear, a feeling which operates as a pathogenic factory through the tensions it produces and through the consequent drain on psychic energy it causes. In such a situation the individual is likely more and more to experience the non-ego as an omnipotent, all-determining reality. Externalization is here a secondary symptom only, indicating loss of ego feeling, of orientation, and of initiative, and presence of a strong fear of the unknown.

limits of our present discussion, we cannot hope to add much to what has been said about these subjects by psychologists, anthropologists, sociologists, and ecologists dealing with the problems of educational and cultural patterns, of change, of class behavior, or with the relative incidence of mental and physical illness and deviations in different social or ethnic groups, or with the relationships between individual and social pathologies, or with the question of the applicability of psychodynamic principles to the interpretation of group behavior. We wish to add only a few short remarks:

Sociocultural patterns of behavior and, even more so, cultural change in processes of transition, are conducive not only to internalization or to externalization but also to a variety of neurotic or aggressive forms of individual behavior, either as characteristics of a certain group (that is, as parts of a "basic personality type" (82), of a "national character," etc.) or as specific hazards to which relatively more members of that group than of other groups are exposed through the medium, as it were, of the prevailing value system and the educational methods. However, such a general statement will become meaningful only to the extent that we relate our analysis of patterns or of change processes to that of the essentials in neurotic or in aggressive behavior, as we have tried to define them in Chapter 7.

We should also beware of widening clinical concepts such as "neurotic" or "aggressive" behavior so much that they cover every variety of normal and abnormal behavior. On the other hand, it should be clear that whatever we say about the behavior-determining effect of cultural conditions (about their conduciveness to certain "preferred" reaction patterns and attitudes) is always an "ideal type" statement; when it comes to verifying such a statement empirically, by observation and research, we find only mixed types of behavior, a "more or less" of this or that reaction pattern and attitude in a more or less large number of members of the group in question.

Defining a given cultural condition as characterized by the essentials of aggressiveness or of anxiety, of externalization or of internalization, means generalizing, means widening the concepts beyond what is empirically admissible, but, at the same time, is what makes a causal analysis of the environmental factor (culture) meaningful. Some of the questions that must be asked and answered in such an analysis can be formulated as follows: What are the forces inherent in traditions, value systems, beliefs, customs, that make it possible or difficult or impossible for the mother to give the infant a feeling of protectedness? What are the elements in an educational pattern that further or inhibit processes of differentiation? What is the intensity of personal as against transpersonal commitments of the individual in each phase of his development? How much is he expected to repress his longings and desires, and why—for the sake of whom or what? Are his anxieties being channeled into beliefs and customs, or is his weak and weakened ego forced to deal with them as an individual only? What amount of aggressiveness does the cultural situation allow, expect, require, or inhibit? In which areas and at what stages of development? Does the culture regard heteronomy or autonomy as the essential property of man and how is either one defined? What situation and what task call for introspection or for introversion; what others require extravert adjustment, and to what extent is the individual being prepared for these attitudes by the cultural agents of socialization and education?

These are, of course, only a few of the most general questions that should be asked if we want to make the factor called culture meaningful as an element in the causal equation of individual development and behavior. They show that not only through its configuration with all the other factors (of constitution, development, and experience) is its causal effect determined, but already its specific nature explains, partly at least, why we may speak of externalizing or internalizing or neuroticizing cultural conditions.

3. Social Conditions

A discussion of social conditions appears as an essential part in every analysis of individual or social pathologies as well as in every sociological analysis whatever its subject may be. Although we are not concerned here with either one, we must try to answer the basic question of etiology: In what way do social conditions, particularly those of poverty and of plenty, determine the individual's behavior in its various phases of development? Let us first discuss the meaning of poverty. This will in part be a repetition of what we have said before (see the section on externalization, pp. 112 ff.).

Under the impact of extreme poverty the life tendency toward staticness tends, as a rule, to gain predominance over the opposite tendency, that toward expansion, even when, in an individual case, the latter was structurally stronger. The most important manifestation of staticness is, then, what we suggest should be called "the illusion of knownness": man is tied (fixated) to the narrow area of the known (or, better, what he thinks is known to him), resists change, and is unable to make adequate use of whatever services society may offer him.* But behind this general staticness and illusion we find different types, different conceptions of the essence of poverty, hence also different causal meanings of the factor under discussion.

For example: One man may accept his condition in apathy, without ego participation, without inner reactions. The second, no less passive, may see in his distress the will of fate or God, which must not be questioned; in this case ego participation and readiness for inner reactions (though *not* for

* Good examples for this kind of staticness are to be found in studies like *Families in Trouble* by Koos (86) or *The People of Shipstreet* by Kerr (83).

practical action) are considerably stronger. A third one tends to see in his condition proof of a personal deficiency to which he may react with lack of initiative, with a feeling of worthlessness, with depression. A fourth one, who may have the conception of distress as a sign of personal deficiency in common with the third, differs from him essentially insofar as he is pre-occupied with resenting his impotence.

Although there exist also fundamentally different reactions, even a strongly developed tendency toward expansion—expressing itself in readi-ness to fight, in "positive aggressiveness" (31)—can be reversed under the devitalizing influence of poverty. We therefore understand why in so many people who live under conditions of extreme poverty the tendency toward expansion, change, and growth will be hindered or distorted by resentment. In the slum quarters of our big cities with their bewildering contrasts, a frequently found attitude is: to see in the conditions of poverty the result of social discrimination—and not to act.

But we maintain that irrespectively of attitudinal differences, poverty is liable to condition man so that reality becomes identical with what he has not, and what he has not becomes identical with the "haveable" (see pp. 112 ff.). Externality of behavior which results from such an orientation is characterized by the ego's relative inability and unwillingness to experience itself as independent pole *vis-à-vis* the non-ego, that is, by relatively weak ego consciousness and by a generally impersonal mode of relationship (feel-ings becoming identical with their precipitating causes, the fellow man becoming part of a world of things to be manipulated).

One of the essential symptoms of externality, we have said above, is the inductive spread of the results of pathogenic factors in an unstructured environment. This inductive spread is all the more dangerous, the less structured and the weaker the ego is. The greater the causal weight of other factors and in particular of certain neuroticizing forms of family disruption and of parental incompetence, the more nonspecific traits are likely to ap-pear in the behavioral picture of externalization, reflecting, and resulting from, feelings of guilt, anxiety, insufficiency and impotence.

Here we must emphasize that in configuration with "opposite" factors (such as a religious orientation, which considers *"not* having" a value, or a *Weltanschauung*, that recognizes nonmaterial values as superior to mate-rial ones) poverty is *not* a cause of externalization. More: without the "cooperation" of at least one negative factor (in itself an outcome partly of want, partly of personality disorders), that of educational neglect, poverty does *not* cause externalization.

It cannot be repeated often enough that there exist other reactions of parents to poverty as well, constructive reactions which not only do not endanger or injure their children's welfare and normal development, but may even—under certain conditions—further it. The fact that the parents' negative reaction to poverty conditions is one of the strongest causal factors in externalization should not make us overlook that it is *not* the rule.

This reservation, however, should not be understood to mean that we consider the *objective* conditions of poverty less important than the *subjective* factor of parental reaction. On the contrary: injury to the physical, emotional and social health of parents and children is almost unavoidable under conditions of extreme poverty. Negative reactions of the parents are therefore understandable, and we should beware of condemning those who so react, because there are others who have enough strength to react constructively! And as regards the child, we should remember that, although the further influence of the damage caused to his health by the hazards of poverty depends, as a rule, on his parents' personality, there are not a few cases in which even the most courageous attitude of a parent cannot make good what objective conditions have destroyed. Here is the place to add a few remarks on the causal meaning of the concept called the *low standard of living*.

It is customary to distinguish between the economic means that may be available to the individual for the satisfaction of his physical, intellectual, and emotional needs and his reactions to these available means. Although the standard of living always results from an interaction of objective and subjective factors, the distinction is essential for the purposes of an etiological analysis of development.

Inadequate utilization of available means may be instrumental to the emergence of an externalized orientation toward the "haveable," not only under conditions of poverty but also when adequate means are being wasted on unessentials or are being used by one or several family members for the satisfaction of their personal needs only. In these cases, however, it is not only the inevitably resulting low (or at least unstable) standard of living that may cause externalization (like any other condition of economic want), but also the affected family member's reactions to negligence and thoughtlessness on the part of those responsible, manifesting itself in the inadequate utilization of available means. Here the resulting poverty does not only (and sometimes not even primarily) condition the child into externality of behavior, but also (and sometimes even primarily) produces resentments and personal tensions which make naive externality almost impossible.

Thus, we see that *poverty* and *low standard of living* are not identical in the causal equation of externalization, or, for that matter, of any form of inadequacy, although both determine the child's development through the medium of the adults' attitude.

The same holds good for the positive case in which the available means of need-satisfaction, though limited and objectively inadequate, are utilized adequately. Here, too, it is the adults' attitude that determines the causal significance of objective conditions. But here, too, the *character* of the result—in this case internalization following the experience of satisfaction and security within the family—depends on *objective* factors: the more frequently the security feeling is threatened by objective distress, the more realistic the processes of internalization and of self-confrontation will be; the more security the economic life conditions of the child provide, the longer the delay of reality testing that society may allow.

To sum up: The subjective factor (of personal reactions) determines the causal significance of the standard of living; the objective factor (of economic realities) is responsible for the qualitative differences of the results.

This law of causation is valid in the opposite case, that of "plenty," as well as in the case in which the available means are objectively inadequate. Under conditions of *plenty* man's conscious orientation is again liable to be focused on the external world of the "haveable," although, in contrast to the person growing up under conditions of want, he experiences the "haveable" not as part of a non-ego but rather as part of his ego. As we have said in another paper (34, pp. 89 *ff.*):

"This dialectic emergence of externalization under opposite conditions, of poverty and of plenty reflects the operation of a common factor in the development of children from lower and from higher class families: because of their orientation toward the 'haveable,' not only their oedipal involvement and conflicts but also the incentive for the introjection of parental images will be weak. The parents, under both conditions, are liable to remain so remote that the child experiences them as strangers who do not evoke strong personal feelings. Thus, the vicious circle of impersonality and defective relationality is being closed. . . . The roots of this separateness lie in the child's earliest mother experience . . . both a poverty-stricken mother's orientation toward that which she has not, toward want and its (temporary) elimination, and a wealthy mother's excessive orientation toward her personal problems, her lack of genuine contact with reality, may support the emergence, in the child, of overdependence on external stimuli, weakness of ambivalence feelings, inability to grow through identification. It is this very similarity between the mother's and the child's externalized orientation which separates them from each other and thus prevents polarization, interrelation, and introjection."

We shall later* try to analyze the development of the child who grows up under such conditions. In the present context, that of defining the essence and the causal effect of environmental factors such as social conditions, we may only add that impersonality is by no means the sole pattern of relationships between parents and children under the conditions of plenty here discussed. But to the extent that the child's upbringing is conducive to the attainment of the sociocultural aims, that is, in our society, of internaliza-

---

* In a subsequent volume, to be published.

tion and autonomy, it is not the factor of social conditions that is causally responsible for the outcome.

This principle applies to every form of class-conditioned patterns of behavior and education. Not only a life in want or a life in plenty may produce the most divergent forms of normal or deviant behavior according to the way in which the "decisive adults" react to their condition (not to speak of the large number of other environmental, constitutional, and developmental factors with which "adult reactions to social conditions" is configurated), but also the life and growth conditions prevailing in most Western middle-class and lower middle-class families are liable to produce internalization or externalization, normal or abnormal behavior patterns, all according to the subjective factor of the adult's reaction to objective givens. While the etiologically relevant element in poverty is the individual's almost exclusive orientation toward what is *not* available as "haveable," and limitless availability is the factor determining the development and behavior of man under conditions of plenty, the middle-class family is characterized by its mobility orientation with all the tensions and expectations and fears resulting from it.

But neither the orientation toward the "haveable" nor that toward the "available" nor that toward mobility is an only and all-exclusive determinant in these class conditions. We shall give in the next section an example of how to differentiate between different attitudes toward want and poverty that are *not* conducive to externalization as defined in Chapter 7. Similarly we could show how typical middle-class or lower middle-class parents may be capable of either *avoiding* the tension climate liable to be produced by their mobility orientation or of *transforming* it into a stimulus of internalization. In these cases, however, the environmental factor called "middle-class patterns of living" *per se* would lose its identity, as it were, and in any case its causal weight in the individual equation, whereas the compensating factors in the parental personality or in other environmental conditions would have to be stressed. This is only another way of saying (what we have emphasized in the chapter on "Etiology") that a partial factor may be *defined in abstracto* through its essential elements (the phenomenological approach) but *operates* only through a specific configuration of partial factors, both "horizontally" and "vertically" (the clinical approach).

We now ask: What happens to a child who grows up under conditions of poverty *without* being exposed to the externalizing influence of parental impersonality and their orientation toward the "haveable"? What is the causal meaning of one of the most decisive social conditions—poverty— when the significant adults in the family group and in the community are capable of ego transcendence, that is, when their mind is directed toward some kind of transindividual values, when want becomes a symbol or a stimulus and, in any case, leads away from its objective representatives, the "haveable" goods, to self-experience, to reflection, to some sort of creative effort? Similar questions could and indeed should be asked with regard to other social conditions as well. The following analysis, therefore, should be regarded as an example only of how etiological research of environmental factors should proceed. (It can also serve as an example of how to define a factor dynamically and differentially.)

4. Poverty and Ego Transcendence

We distinguish between the following four levels of ego transcendence:

(a) *The first level* differs from what shall be described as the "ideal type" of externalization in that the adults no longer relate themselves exclusively to the "haveable" but have discovered the dimension of their own ego as measurable by some outside value criterion. The degree of ego participation and organizational strength is still rather low on this level but they feel themselves "meant" by their condition. Their reaction to poverty may be apathy, a feeling of worthlessness, or resentment.

In the *apathy reaction* to poverty the non-ego is experienced as "omnipotent nothingness." Nothing can be done to change the conditions of existence, not because a mysterious fate has decided they should thus be, but because life *is* emptiness, *is* nonavailability. Even in those cases in which apathy results from radical repression of aggressive childhood tendencies, emptiness is all that is left after the flame of hatred has gone out (although we must add that there can always be found isolated cases in which a smoldering flame can be rekindled, through release therapy, for instance). The mentally retarded may not be able to *experience* the non-ego as nothingness (simply because he is not capable of any form of conscious experience or self-reflection), but he, too, in his apathy, is unable to relate himself to his world of want as to a world of the "haveable." In other words, even in this extreme case, emptiness can be regarded as a category of ego transcendence.

When poverty and want are experienced as proof of *personal inferiority and worthlessness*, a clearly ego-transcending criterion of evaluation is being applied, whether we call it vitality, power of organization, or ego strength. The fact that poverty is being related to personal insufficiency and inferiority indicates not only a considerable advance over the pattern of externalized behavior with its exclusive orientation toward the "haveable," but also over the apathy reaction with its static mode of experiencing the non-ego as emptiness. Only on the basis of individual case analysis can we decide when, and to what extent, these inferiority reactions to poverty and want are in themselves the results of rationalization, avoidance (by way of self-depreciation), or other defenses, and when they should be interpreted as expressions of genuine inferiority feelings. We shall see later that the pathogenic significance of this attitude toward poverty on the part of the parents depends on its genotype rather than on its phenotype.

As a third form of ego transcendence on this lowest level we have mentioned *resentment* against society being experienced as discriminating and therefore responsible for the individual's helplessness in the face of poverty and stress. Here, the negative affect, though in no way conducive to adequate self-confrontation with reality or even to active planning of change and progress, deprives the "haveable" objects in the environment of their power of attraction, of their character as sources of satisfaction; resentment and hatred make direct enjoyment of "having" almost impossible; thus, they represent again advances over externalization as well as over apathy reactions. Like feelings of inferiority and worthlessness, these introvert equivalents of resentment, the latter, too, prepares the ground for internalization, though not without the help of active treatment interventions.

(b) In the *second* group we find the same three attitudes lifted to a higher level of consciousness and ego participation: fatalism instead of apathy, despair instead of inferiority, conscious rejection of society instead of resentment.

Belief in a transempirical, all-directing *fatum* (sometimes, though not necessarily, deified) transforms poverty into part of a meaningful though transcausal reality in which the ego is deprived of its role as actor and is defined as passive recipient and partner of this meaningfulness. Here, "meaning" means existence—while under conditions of externalization meaning disappears behind appearance. On this still relatively low level of consciousness ego activity is restricted to a minimum, but can be increased through proper treatment measures. The fatalist can be brought to realize that, although activity by no means guarantees change, and although it is not causally necessary for bringing about change, it does not contradict the will of fate. He may even learn to consider activity a value *per se*, irrespective of its possible influence on his fate. But even without such educationally or otherwise induced changes it is evident that fatalistic acceptance of existing conditions is an ego-transcending attitude.

The equivalent of the feeling of inferiority on a higher level of consciousness is *despair*. Regardless of the extent to which the material goods are actually available or not, man experiences them as "unreachable." The world is one in which value is defined as "beyond reach" (so that, what is *in* reach is by definition valueless). Man is at the mercy of those all-pervading forces of negation which—in spite of their all-pervasiveness—rule from without. Poverty is unalterable; not even chance can bring about a change. There is neither the consolation of belief and dependence nor the illusion of selfhood.

Similarly we find on this second level a more generalized conception of *society as hostile*. There is no longer a personal feeling of being discriminated against, no longer a personal resentment—everyone is the victim of society's negative, destructive tendencies. Society is *defined* as the existential negation of the individual. Man knows, of course, that there are others who, unlike himself, do not suffer from want and poverty, whom society—or fate—has treated gently; but this knowledge only confirms and strengthens his conception of society as basically negative and hostile, lacking in justice, arbitrarily changing its temporary favorites. The distinction between society, the enemy, and the individual in his enforced poverty is not affected by the knowledge of inequality; on the contrary, this knowledge only reinforces its sharpness, because everyone who is not of the poor belongs to "society," is on the other side of the fence. Even a definite improvement in his condition does not cause the individual to change his outlook and orientation; it may only arouse his suspicions.*

It is evident that this attitude, which borders on paranoic conditions, implies self-transcendence, though not *per se* in a socially acceptable direction; if supported by appropriate measures of treatment and education, it even makes possible self-transcendence of a much more durable and socially accepted kind, that of the reformer, the fighter, the revolutionary. But these belong already to a third level of ego transcendence.

(c) On this *third* level we find the believer, the creator, the reformer. Here, the ego perceives itself as servant of an ego-transcending idea or value; through its realization he recreates reality. Here, we find the most divergent attitudes toward poverty, all of which have one element in common: poverty may be an unavoidable, though unessential, concomitant of a life with ideas and values, it may be its indispensable precondition, it may be the incentive to action that creates value—but it no longer is in the center of life.

This becomes evident when we consider some of the ways in which poverty is evaluated by *religious man*. He may find consolation in the knowledge that all men are equal before God, poor and rich alike; in other words, that material conditions and social status are accidental modalities only and not indicators of essential qualities. Or he may enjoy his poverty and the suffering it entails because it entitles him to eternal compensation. (The genuineness of such an attitude will be found to be proportionate to the absence of masochistic admixtures, though it will not be too easy to assess their relative weight without deep-reaching analyses.) Poverty may also be experienced as a necessary precondition of personality integration, that is, as a value in itself. In all these conceptions, the meaning of poverty is obviously the reverse of the one defined as *externalization:* In each of

---

* In this respect man in poverty who has adopted this attitude of hostility and dichotomization of reality resembles the aggressive child who suffers from "primary behavior disorders" (101) and who rejects friendly adults in order to maintain his negative picture of the world as hostile.

them, the ego finds itself in polar relationship with a transindividual reality which obliterates the reality of the "haveable" and protects against the dangers of impersonality.

In the life of *creative man,* despair in the face of the non-ego's unreachability (see the discussion of the second-level attitudes) turns into a challenge; he feels responsible for its realization, precisely *because* it is unreachable. But as a result, material want that so often is his inescapable lot not only does not set in motion processes of externalization but, on the contrary, is likely to provoke still stronger concentration of energy on the task of creation which, as already mentioned, can always be understood as an attempt at reconstructing and recreating reality beyond the level of want and having.

Resentment and aggressiveness, on this third level of consciousness, turn into elements of social *responsibility for changing* the life conditions not only of the suffering individual but of all who have a common fate. This responsibility appears, of course, in different degrees of generality, from that of the worker who identifies with his union or his party over that of the fighter for justice and freedom to that of the planner, the organizer, the thinker. It also appears with different admixtures of resentment. But the degree of generality does not essentially affect the individual's attitude toward the conditions of poverty in which he may find himself.*

(d) Apathy, inferiority feelings and resentment against society, fatalism, despair and aggressive rejection of society, religious acceptance, creative transformation and social responsibility for society—these are some of the ways of reacting to poverty that do *not* set in motion processes of externalization. But there is one form, and perhaps the most important one from the point of view of our present analysis, which we have not yet mentioned—the *child-centered reaction.*

When the parents experience their economic condition and react to it primarily as parents, their main concern being the improvement of their children's lot, poverty, far from being conducive to externalization, may actually elicit and support processes of identification with, and introjection of, parental images, attitudes, ideas, and values.

But we must not forget that the parents' concern is not necessarily based on a clear *recognition* of the child's needs and abilities. On the contrary, often the child is but an extension of his parents' identity, their conscious and unconscious strivings and longings, and the plans they make for him are little more than attempts to realize their own day-dreams in and through a powerless object. Thus, they violate the child's identity, and his identifications and internalizations will consequently never produce that inner

---

* In creativeness, the criterion is the scope of reality which the creation reaches, contains and represents, and its power of conviction; in religious belief, it is the degree of polarity between the believer and his object of belief that decides.

mobility that characterizes normal development. (The analysis of some cases of later schizophrenic breakdowns reveals a prehistory of such identity distortions through the parents.)

Only when the parents are able and ready to subordinate their own ego to their child's needs will their struggle with economic pressure, with want and stress, become a dynamic factor of internalization, in themselves as well as in their children. Their objectivity and their readiness to subordinate themselves to the child or to an independent reality indicate differentiation, this prerequisite of genuine internalization (see Chapter 1). This is why we claim that the child-centered reaction to poverty represents the highest level of consciousness (though the social and cultural relevance of the third-level reactions is, as a rule, considerably greater; but we should not forget that we are concerned here with the conditions of child development rather than with the problem of creativeness and values).

EFFECTS OF PARENTAL EGO TRANSCENDENCE ON THE CHILD

We are now going to analyze the specific effects which parental ego transcendence may have on the child's development when he grows up under conditions of poverty. We need not emphasize again that no single factor can be held responsible for any behavioral outcome, but that it operates only in configuration with a large number of other—cultural, social and individual, constitutional, developmental, and environmental—factors. Each of the aforementioned parental attitudes toward poverty, for instance, draws its causal significance from the family culture, from the child's intelligence, thresholds, needs and resistances and from the type of critical experiences he makes in his formative years.

When we nevertheless isolate *parental reaction to poverty* from all other factors, we intend in this way to make a contribution to the understanding of the dynamics of internalization.

The First-Level Reactions

At least the three first-level reactions—apathy, inferiority, and resentment—have, as far as the child is concerned, one effect in common: the child feels left out, unnoticed, because his parents are not free to relate themselves to him directly and intentionally. But apart from this general feeling of aloneness, each of the three attitudes produces a different reaction in the child, a different way of dealing with that basic feeling of being alone.

*Parental apathy,** for instance, helps establish in the child already—and particularly—in the early stages of his development a feeling of emptiness which precludes not only adequate learning of values at the hands of his parents but also the emergence of security, mutuality, autonomy, initiative,

---

* *Cf.* what we have said in another context (33) on apathy in the child as a factor of externalization. This will also be discussed in a future volume, to be published.

that is, the *prerequisites* of learning. We have maintained in another study (34) that maternal apathy in configuration with a structural predominance of the life tendency toward expansion may produce a certain variety of the psychopathic constitution, while the same factor, when configurated with an equally pathological and pathogenic predominance of the life tendency toward staticness may be responsible for personality disorders of the schizophrenic type. Where these extreme pathological conditions are absent, that is, in the majority of cases in which parental (and particularly maternal) apathy is a determining factor, we find one of two different lines of development: It either supports or counteracts in the child an orientation toward the "haveable," produces either externalized behavior or apathy. The result depends primarily on whether the parents' apathy but accompanies an externalizing and externalized orientation toward the "haveable" in themselves or reflects a general personality insufficiency.

In the latter case, the result may be a behavior pattern in the child in which a surface of seeming internalization conceals the underlying emptiness and lack of initiative. This will then be a perfect example of character trait transmission from one generation to the other. Parental apathy often prevents the emergence of tensions and conflicts between the generations, including even the oedipal type of conflict. Internalization of attitudes, values, and ideas, to the extent that it occurs at all, will then not be based on active differentiation and polarization, but on an almost automatic process of induction and imitation.

It seems logical to ascribe to the mother's apathy the effect of a general lowering of the child's mental alertness and vitality, of his psychosomatic tonus, his level of responsiveness, his initiative, and this in particular during the first years of life; to ascribe to the father's apathy later difficulties which the child may have when faced with a task of separation, differentiation, and abstraction. On closer scrutiny, however, and remembering what we have said about the influence of maternal deficiencies on the paternal principle (see Chapter 2), we have to revise this schema of interpretation. The mother's apathy reaction to poverty is much more decisive than that of the father and not only in the first stages of life but all through childhood; its ill effects cannot be offset automatically by a more adequate and a more active and activating father figure (though reversely, weak initiative may be further weakened, particularly in the development of a boy, when the father's apathy deprives him of that support in differentiation and identification that he will badly need at a certain age, the age of learning and achievement).

But parental apathy in reaction to economic stress may, as we have already mentioned, also cause other developments, in accordance with the child's personality factors with which it is configurated. Thus, high intelligence in a child of such parents may be the indirect cause of depressive reactions, while strong vitality and an outgoing temperament may be the causes of aggressive behavior. Similar developments can be observed when the parents' reaction to their economic stress is a strong feeling of inferiority or resentment aganst society.

Parental insecurity and inferiority feelings in reaction to poverty reflect, as a rule, personality traits and tendencies that manifest themselves in other areas of reaction as well. In other words, this is a reaction pattern not specifically related to poverty (unless we consider the reaction to a sudden economic deterioration which may produce inferiority reactions even in a previously more or less balanced individual).

But for the child it again makes a great difference whether his parents are generally insecure persons or whether they concentrate, as it were, their feelings of worthlessness on their failure as providers. While a child will find it difficult, if not impossible, to identify himself with a generally insecure parent, he will be able to feel with him when he suffers because of his inability adequately to provide for the family.

On this first, rather low, level of consciousness, however, feeling is not yet differentiated or articulate enough to evoke differentiated or articulate reactions. As a result, the child is liable to experience his parents as self-related only, as isolated in their inferiority feelings. He may react by depressively losing interest in life, and particularly so when he feels a strong need for parental love and protection. Here, then, depression in the child is reactive rather than imitative or identificational. To the extent that the parents' withdrawal into feelings of worthlessness is accompanied and tinged by open or hidden aggressiveness, it is this latter component of the parental attitude that is liable to determine the child's reactions of anxiety or aggressiveness.

We have called inferiority feelings the introvert equivalent of *resentment* (p. 205). Both, we have added, stand in the way of externalization, because in each some kind of ego relatedness and, at the same time, of ego transcendence is implied and, as the result, the mind is deflected from the "haveable." But the impact of parental resentment on the child's personality development is essentially different from that of the two foregoing reactions.

When the child grows up in a family atmosphere of resentment, in which society is experienced as an eternal source of frustration and discrimination, identification with the parents—to the extent that it takes place at all—is not conducive to autonomy, but is likely to produce in the child a growing inability to establish relationships of polarity and mutuality with his human environment. Mistrust and lack of spontaneity, those almost inseparable concomitants of adult resentment, make their appearance early in the life of a child who experiences them in his parents. Feeling discriminated against means defining himself as unable to determine his fate; hence, internalizing the parental images paradoxically leads in this case to mistrust not only in the non-ego but also in the own ego, lack of spontaneity not only in the face of unknown but also of familiar figures, tasks, situations.

It is the generality of these negative attitudes that clearly indicates the essential difference between this behavior pattern and the one we intend to describe in a future volume as the ideal type of externalized behavior. In our brief analysis of externalization (see Chapter 7) we have spoken of the "moratory" character of the immediate neighborhood in which the externalized individual—child like adult, though the latter more than the former—is less vulnerable and more secure than "outside," in the world at large. This is, in part at least, a result of the externalized individual's almost exclusive orientation toward what he has not, the "haveable." "Outside," it appears in incomprehensible contexts, whereas in the "moratory area," it is somehow "here," available, familiar. In contrast, mistrust and lack of spontaneity, when produced by the impact of parental resentment, do *not* remain limited to the outside world, because they are anchored in a specifically distorted concept of the non-ego, a concept which *precludes* "haveability."

Aggressiveness is a frequent expression of this resentment and mistrust. But it differs in type from the aggressive reactions of an outgoing, extravert child who protests against parental apathy, as well as from the aggressive reaction of a child to the elements of unconscious aggressiveness which may hide behind parental inferiority feelings. While in the resentment type of aggressiveness the child takes over the parents' attitude (though his identification will not necessarily prevent him from turning this imitated aggressiveness against the parents as well), reactively extravert aggressiveness is a means and and expression of self-preservation and of struggling for identity, in protest against parental apathy; in the third, the neurotic, case we find the child "living out" what the parents did not dare to live out in their life, a vicarious realization of parental aggressiveness, a well known neurotic pattern. The degree of conscious ego participation in the aggressive behavior is highest in the first case (that of imitating parental resentment) and lowest in the last one which, correspondingly, shows the highest degree of compulsiveness.

The Second-Level Reactions

For the *fatalist,* we have said (p. 205), poverty is a meaningful though transcausal reality. Whatever exists is, in its specific way of being, meaningful, but the laws of difference and change are incomprehensible. One day, these laws may manifest themselves, so that the facts of existence, of difference and change, will then become explicable even in relational terms; but man does not need this empirical confirmation to feel life to be meaningful—determined, as it is, by fate.

For the child, at least for the one who grows up in a Western, change-oriented and achievement-oriented society, this fatalism contradicts the very laws and dynamics of growth and development. To the extent that he identifies himself with his parents and their value attitudes, he is liable to fail in those of his tasks of learning and group adaptation in which initiative and causal understanding are of the essence. He may not feel frustrated by his relative failure, just as his parents do not feel frustrated by their condition. But the more frequently he comes in contact with representatives of other, more activistic attitudes, the better are the chances that he will discover the connection between success and initiative—a discovery that may estrange him to his parents and their fatalistic acceptance of economic stress. Paradoxically, it is this estrangement that may set in motion delay of processes of differentiation long after they take place normally.

The danger of this parental reaction to poverty will obviously be more acute in urban than in rural areas and in transitional more than in traditional societies, that is, wherever opposite attitudes are being encountered more frequently. Moreover, the danger grows with the child's age and with his maturationally growing sensitivity to differences.

Again we understand why being exposed to parental fatalism in reaction to want and poverty precludes externalization with its direct orientation toward the "haveable."

This holds good still more for the child of parents who react to poverty by *despair*, because they experience their condition as an unalterable result of all-pervading forces of negation. In this respect despair is the opposite to fatalism: the intentions of those forces of negation are as incomprehensible as those of fate; but while the fatalist believes in the meaningfulness of existence, which he accepts, despair is based on *nonacceptance*, and the forces of negation that determine man's suffering are basically meaningless.

To the extent that such parents are at all factors of determination in their children's development and do not completely withdraw from their educational function (in which case neglect may be conducive to externalization or delinquency) it is precisely their negativistic philosophy of life that *prevents* externalization. Here, poverty means not so much want of things "haveable" as it means want of things withheld and unreachable. By way of imitation and identification the child who grows up in such an ambience of parental despair may fail to learn how to show and how to maintain initiative in the face of an objective task of learning or doing; the time span fails to grow, as the parents are likely to discourage—or in any case fail to stimulate—intentionality in the growing child. He does not learn how to enjoy life, as the external world of objects and events will be associated, from the beginning, with the unreachable.

Again, there is a way open to avoidance and escape; but this will not, as a rule, lead to externalization either, because fear of despair, which in this case produces the escape reaction, precludes naive orientation toward the external world of the "haveable." Sometimes the result of escape will be compulsive delinquency, sometimes we may find irrational short-circuit actions or, again in other cases, addictions. All these forms of dissocial behavior serve the purposes of defense and express anxiety, both in clear contradiction of externalized behavior patterns with their typical absence of inner tension and anxiety.

Resentment is based on a feeling of being discriminated against personally. On a higher level of differentiation we find conscious *rejection of society* as the representative of injustice. This rejection may be nothing but a way of rationalizing personal failure, in which case it may be almost identical with what we have described as resentment against discrimination. It may be the expression of a hate ideology which is not incompatible with the responsibility of a social fighter and reformer (see pp. 215 f.). But it may also be a symptom of generalized aggressiveness and hostility or even of antisocial tendencies.

In this last case the impact of the parents' aggressiveness and antisocial reaction on the child's development is not identical with that of antisocial attitudes in general. Reactive aggressiveness does not express itself as frequently as antisocial tendencies *per se* in brutal neglect of the child; it therefore leaves more room for identification. The fact that the child may regard his parents' aggressiveness as justified because they have been mishandled by society, explains the emergence in the child of what psychoanalysts (13, 51) have called a negative superego, and what we prefer to call a negative *social canon:* the child who identifies with his antisocial parents, particularly when he sees in their conduct a protest against social injustice, is likely to accept this conduct as objectively justified not only in his parents but also in others whom he believes to be in a comparable social situation, and not only in others but also in himself. While his concept of social injustice and his tendency to transfer this interpretation of the parents' behavior to others indicate some kind of ego transcendence, the transfer to the own ego could be interpreted as a variety of introjection. But neither the one nor the other leads to genuine structurization: the first is not based on truly abstract behavior but indicates the presence of strong affective components; the second is not based on truly polar relationships. (This is, incidently, the reason we prefer not to use the structural concept of "negative superego.")

Needless to add that the formation of this negative social canon serves also the purpose of rationalizing aggressive tendencies which may be rooted in the child's or the adolescent's personality rather than in his identifications with aggressive and antisocial parents.

When we speak of antisocial children or adolescents whose behavior is the result of identification with his parents' antisocial reaction to poverty, we have *not* in mind the wayward child but rather a more active, intentional type of delinquent adolescent. We intend to describe and analyze in another study the different forms of juvenile delinquency, and shall therefore confine ourselves here to a general statement:* Parental rejection of the child, growing up under the externalizing conditions of extreme poverty and educational neglect are required to produce that specific blend of externalized and delinquent behavior that we call waywardness; the child's and particularly the adolescent's identification with his parents' antisocial reaction to poverty (their conscious rejection of society) is liable to produce a *nonexternalized* type of delinquent and criminal behavior precisely when the child is *not* being rejected by the parents.

The Third-Level Reactions

In the following discussion of the socially accepted and value-representative attitudes of the parents to their negative economic conditions, it would be erroneous to presume that these attitudes—religious acceptance, creative transformation, and social responsibility—guarantee by themselves a positive development of the child, a constructive form of internalization (though they do, of course, preclude, as a rule, processes of externalization).

We have mentioned some forms of *religious acceptance of poverty* as they are known in most different societies, from the United States to Tibet, and in the most divergent periods of history (see pp. 206 *ff.*). How do these convictions affect the believer's functions as educator of his children in an inner-directed or, as we prefer to say, in an internalization-oriented society? Is not belief in the transcendental equality of men prejudicial to the development of the child's ability to differentiate? Is not belief in heavenly compensation harmful to the development of initiative? Is not the belief that poverty is a necessary prerequisite of personality integration incompatible with the educational ideals and principles of present-day culture?

All these are, no doubt, real dangers and obstacles on the path to internalization. Recognition of individual differences in oneself, between oneself and others, and in others; initiative and autonomy; responsibility for change as process and as action; responsibility for development and integration—these concomitants of internalization require a truly polar relationship between the ego and the non-ego, whatever its structural definition may be. And truly polar relationship, as we have tried to explain, at the beginning of this study, requires exchangeability of the subject-object positions. The latter, however, is incompatible with belief in the depend-

---

* Which, incidentally, can be regarded also as an example of the configurational method in differential psychopathology.

ence on a transempirical reality. It therefore seems that at least the two first-mentioned parental reactions to poverty—acceptance through transcendental equalization and acceptance through anticipating heavenly reward—are liable to impede or even to prevent internalization.

But in order correctly to evaluate the assets and liabilities of the religious believer's attitude toward poverty we must consider the third form of interpreting poverty; here, poverty means absence of forces which could draw away from selfhood and wholeness into dependence on external, nonessential, values. To the extent that *this* attitude is present, even the first two elements take on a different meaning.

This distinction between essential and external values is not necessarily related to transcendental criteria—as can be seen very clearly in most of the great religious systems of Asia, but also in many of the basic tenets of Judaism and Christianity. Essentiality here means realization of human wholeness as willed by God and as prescribed by the specific religious tradition, but it does *not* mean heteronomous directedness by God and by tradition. Only to the extent that man succeeds in transforming the way into a set of inner directives can he be called a truly religious individual; only then is his conscious rejection of material, external values meaningful.

In this case, the child learns—through the attitudes of his parents, and not only through their teachings and the directives they give—how to relate his actuality to an objective and objectively defined ideal, provided, of course, the parents' attitude is genuine, free of selfrighteousness and defense mechanisms. Only in this case will poverty not cause repression of the values, which are in the center of life. In fact, nonrepression of the human-transhuman values is the criterion for the genuineness of the religious attitude toward poverty here discussed.

Poverty, we have said (see p. 207), may stimulate *creative man* into evergrowing concentration of his energies on his objective tasks of recreating reality. But his parental functions are only in exceptional cases integrated with his creative capacity; as a rule, he is an insufficient parent, lacking in patience, in responsibility, and in understanding for his children's needs. It goes without saying that in this case the child will be exposed less to the dangers of externalization than to some kind of inner tensions, some kind of difficulty and disorder in his identificational abilities. Even though grown-ups may accuse the parents of neglect, the child will not cease to experience them as personally defined and related figures; he will react to the inadequacy of his parents' attitude with personal resentment rather than with an impersonal orientation toward the "haveable."

Sometimes we find the child of creative parents prematurely being made into a passive or active partner of their inner life; or he witnesses from his early years onward the parents' almost contemptuous refusal to recognize their material condition as an objective problem requiring an objective solution; or he is being drawn into the turmoil that often is creative man's life within his environment, this life full of conflicts and tensions, full of aggressiveness and wounded pride. But in all these and many other situations the child does not experience that which he has not, as part of an external universe of the "haveable." Instead, he never ceases to see it as parts of his parental reality which is characterized by all-pervading feelings of ambivalence. This, too, prevents externalization.

When poverty becomes an incentive for ego transcendence through the assumption of *responsibility for changing social conditions in general,* a certain type of "fighter for principles" emerges, often of strongly adolescent tendencies and seldom aware of the personality factors that contribute to their transformations. It is this very unconsciousness of underlying motives that accounts for the frequent interventions of affects with thinking and deciding which we may witness in this type. Without going into the question of personality factors *being responsible for,* and *not resulting from,* the individual's reaction to poverty, it is safe to maintain that the conditions under which the child of such parents grows up are determined by these personality elements more than by their reactions to poverty.

He may be exposed to a number of equally harmful factors: the aggravation of poverty as the result of the parents' unwillingness to subordinate their ideals to their profane tasks as providers and educators; the immature and unrealistic approach to the solution of day-to-day problems which often characterize them and—understandably—decreases their value as objects of identification in the eyes of their children, particularly when this general immaturity combines with inability adequately to appreciate and react to, their children's needs. To the extent that the child, particularly when he is intelligent, *does* identify with his "fighter-parents," his personality development is bound to reflect some of the distortions that accompany their lack of realism and adolescent fanaticism. The results may be manifold, but all are likely to have one element in common, inner tension and uncertainty. Obviously, then, externalization is *not* to be expected in such cases.

The pattern of parental behavior described here and the impact it may have on the child's development is, of course, not the only possible way of transforming aggressiveness into social responsibility. There are ways better adapted to the objective goal, ways in which the immediate environment is *not* left out of the area of responsibility, and in which the principles are applied not only to mankind but also to the own family. This leads us to a discussion of the child's reactions to the last type of ego-transcendent attitudes toward poverty in their parents.

The Fourth-Level Reaction

There remains one question that requires at least a tentative answer: How does the child see his parents when conditions of want and poverty challenge them into initiative, parents for whom objects and persons do *not* belong to a "universe of the haveable" but are realistically related to specific needs, those of their children, whose guardians and servants they consider themselves?

Under such conditions the child can experience his parents as ego-transcending; they are near and reliable because they "come" to him from their rootedness in objective values, as separate individuals who direct their intentions toward him, who "mean" him and at the same time elicit his readiness to relate himself consciously to them and to the ideals and values for which they stand. It is this awareness of the parents as separate and reliable individuals that protects the child against the dangers of externalization, inherent in the very conditions of want in which he grows up. More: when the parents make the child feel that he is the center of their concern, poverty may become a stimulus for self-confrontation and self-reflection, and may thus set in motion processes of internalization, particularly in the learning phase. It is through the experience of his parents' ego transcendence that the child learns differentiation and that he is capable of making full use of his native abilities, whatever their level may be.

5. The School

When we speak of the quality of the child's learning facilities in his various life spheres outside the home (elementary, secondary and vocational school, apprenticeship, youth groups, etc.) as a factor influencing the process of his ego development and the growth of his consciousness, we should again distinguish between the objective and the subjective aspects of the problem: the availability of facilities and the individual's ability and readiness to utilize them.

Weakness or absence of such ability and readiness, however, can be regarded as a *symptom* of personality disorders rather than as a primary cause, although it should be remembered that it operates as a secondary, reinforcing factor as well, like any other symptom of an already extant pathological condition. Reversely, an adequate ability and readiness to make optimal use of the available learning facilities or even to enlarge them from within, through one's own initiative and productivity, indicate a positive personality constellation which, it is safe to assume, will find its expression in other symptoms of emotional and intellectual health as well.

In a discussion of negative social conditions emphasis is likely to be placed on the first rather than on the second aspect. On closer scrutiny, however, it will be discovered that the objective factor—availability of facilities—cannot be properly evaluated unless we include the second aspect: the relative failure of an individual adequately to utilize the learning facilities which society offers is not in every case indicative of a deep-lying personality disorder, but may be a perfectly logical and understandable reaction to an *inadequacy* of these facilities. It is relatively easy to understand why in a given society lack of opportunities for formal and informal learning diminishes the individual's chances of internalization by augmenting indirectly the attractiveness of external values. But when the available facilities do not meet the individual's needs, either for lack of differentiation or for lack of adaptation to a changing reality or for any other reason, the mere fact of their availability does *not* justify a diagnosis of "individual pathology" in every case in which a child fails to avail himself of the services he is offered.

This is not a problem of semantics but a matter of important practical consequences: In a later volume we shall try to answer the questions of education and treatment arising out of our present analyses: how an externalized individual can be helped toward internalization by way of social care, guidance of parents, and education; how neurotic distortions can be corrected (or prevented); how aggressiveness can be weakened through therapy and learning. Then, we shall also have to answer the question of what the school must do in the face of the ever-increasing number and intensity of factors obstructing internalization of learning in the development of many millions; to what extent and how methods of training and teaching should be adapted to prevent and to remedy the negative influence of pathogenic conditions prevailing today in so many societies, for a variety of different reasons; in other words, what should be done in order *to turn objective into subjective availability of learning facilities.*

In order to prepare the ground for answering these vital questions of educational practice we shall briefly analyze the functions of the school as an instrument of internalization of values and concepts. (Even in totalitarian, heteronomy-oriented regimes, it would be correct to call the school an instrument of internalization, although the contents of internalization are, of course, determined by the regime much more narrowly, rigidly, and definitely than in a nontotalitarian social order.) There will probably be general agreement to the following definition of the functions of the school on all levels:

The school must help the learner discover rule and law in the infiniteness of phenomena and of meaning hidden behind these surfaces.

The school must lead the learner from perceptions to concepts and from bewilderment at the experience of opposites as contradictions to recognition of their coexistence as a manifestation of the dynamic order of life.

The school must strengthen in the learner, through the very process of learning, the ability to leave a given phenomenon in its immediacy and to relate himself to more distant aims without misinterpretating as final the intermediary stations on the way.

Thus, the school should aim at developing and strengthening in the learner personal responsibility for his learning, a feeling of polarity between himself and the objective tasks and contents of his learning, so that in the end he will be able to face the non-ego everywhere both as an object and a subject, while experiencing himself both as a receptor of uniqueness and a discoverer of universalities.

So defined, the school is more than a mediator of skills and knowledge. Everything learned in school should strengthen not only the learner's ability to form concepts and to think abstractly (or to transfer what he has learned from one field to another), but also to feel more secure in his unforseeable encounters with the non-ego. This means that genuine classroom learning helps develop personal maturity and adequate behavior which, in turn, will then help enlarge not only the fields of action but also those of learnable contents and possible contents (*cf.* 37, pp. 76 *ff.*).

Thus, it could be said that the school is the representative and the delegate of the father or, better, of the "paternal principle of differentiation" (see pp. 22 *ff.*); and we should add that, although successful school learning *requires* maternal security, it is frequently—in fact, for an ever-increasing number of learners, should be—the most important and the most effective means of *establishing* this security. The importance of the school in our time grows to the extent that the parents, for a variety of reasons (personality defects or weaknesses, class-conditioned value systems and patterns of thinking and behaving), fail to provide the child with the basic experiences of trust and nearness, of autonomy and ambivalence, of differentiation and synthesis. When the school fails the child as well, that is, when it is not "adequately available," it is liable to become one of the most decisive pathogenic factors in his development (irrespective of class or culture).* The following is a short analysis of the elementary school of our time, quoted from another study (36, pp. 105 *ff.*):

"For a large proportion of our present-day elementary school population, and in certain social strata or cultural groups even for the majority of the pupils, teaching becomes meaningful only to the extent that it is based on a thorough integration of instructional methods and understanding of the cultural patterns and the family background which determine the child's associations and reactions, as well as on insight into the thought processes characteristic of the various age groups and the various cultures.

"We further maintain that, the vital contribution of mental hygiene in the classroom notwithstanding, the elementary school teacher of our generation—and particularly the one who has to teach children from so-called 'primitive' backgrounds or from socially underprivileged families—

---

* While it is self-evident that what we have said so far refers primarily to the elementary school, it is, with certain modifications, applicable to the vocational or the secondary school as well. True enough, the higher the age level, the greater the importance of the learner's autonomy and differentiation as *preconditions* of successful learning and problem solving. And yet, even at an advanced stage of objective learning it is one of the most important functions of the school to *strengthen* these conditions through the experience of the subject-object character of both the learner and the contents of his learning (polarity).

will be unable to fulfill his functions unless he understands, and takes cognizance of, the intimate connection that exists between what the psychologist may call the relational (interpersonal) ability, or lack of ability, of the child and his conceptual ability, or lack of ability. . . .

"The most important cultural factors which the educator of our times must take into consideration when setting out to determine the role of the elementary school, its aims and its methods, are:

"(a) The democratic ideal of all social strata participating equally in all courses of learning and in all social functions and areas of production.

"(b) The influence which technical progress has had on our value system, and in particular the preference for impersonal, anonymous, and specialized modes of operation and behavior as against the manifestations of individual identity, of emotional involvement, of phantasy or intuition.

"(c) The inability of many parents, particularly from the lower classes or from 'primitive' cultural groups, and the unwillingness of many others, particularly from the higher and middle classes, to cooperate with the school and to support the teacher's efforts. . . .

"What is the school's role in view of the ever-growing number of children who, upon entering school, either (a) do not bring with them that feeling of security which, as we said, is the precondition of autonomy and of the ability to form adequate concepts and to use them freely, or (b) cannot count on parental support of their learning experience at school?

"In order to explain what we understand by "parental support of the learning experience," we shall discuss briefly a number of social situations. Our first question will be: What happens to the middle-class child when he starts out on his school career?

"Psychoanalysis speaks of the 'passing of the oedipus complex' (48) at the age of six, the school-entrance age, when the struggle for the parents as libidinal objects is replaced by their introjection and by the crystallization of the superego. This does not mean that the emotional ties between the child and his parents are now loosened, or even replaced, by his interest in learning, on the one hand, and in the 'society of equals,' on the other. The contents of the child's relationships with his parents, however, do undergo a decisive change: instead of serving primarily as objects of his affective strivings, they are from now on expected to fulfill an additional function—to help him in the process of forming and expanding his spiritual world; they are expected to confirm, and to enlarge the area of, his learning. The child is not interested—as he may be at a later stage of his development—in a 'dethronement' of his parents; he does not want a complete separation between the agents of education, that is, the parents and the teacher. On the contrary, he wants his parents to remain the final and highest authority to confirm the truth of what he learns at school. We could perhaps speak of a process of spiritualization of the oedipal images, at least in the development of the middle-class child of 'our' society.

"Now, what happens when these parents fail to live up to their child's expectations? They may be unable to do so because of lack of education; they may be unwilling, because of egoistic or neurotic self-involvements, or because of intensive preoccupation with their work-functions, to accompany the child in his learning experience. The child is left alone with a world of contents which remain unconfirmed, as it were, by his parents. The disappointment which he is then bound to feel and the fear of becoming separated from his parents through the very process of learning may have a most disturbing influence on his scholastic achievements and, even more important, on the internalization of his concepts.

"Precisely because introjection of the parental images is one of the main functions of the post-oedipal phase in the development of the middle-class child, classroom learning requires confirmation by the parents to become internalized. Every concept, it is true, is already the result of a process of internalization; but when a middle-class child, growing up, as he does, in the intimacy of his family group, suddenly or gradually has to forego the emotional support of his parents in one of his most important activities, his learning, the knowledge and the concepts he acquires, are liable to remain, as it were, outside the area of his personal responsibility and initiative, taken over from the outside area of the classroom and the teacher, but not transformed into integral parts of his inner world. At best, the child may go on absorbing new material, but it is doubtful whether he will ever be able to use what he has learned in an autonomous, that is, in a critical, independent, and creative way.

"This is the fate of many children in our society. The learning processes have become too complicated for most parents to share in their children's experience beyond the first years of elementary school. It would, however, be sufficient to guarantee a continuity in the life of the child, from his early years to the pre-adolescent age—when autonomy of thinking and judging, once established, would continue to determine the learning processes—if the parents would accompany the child at least during the first years of schooling. But many middle-class parents fail to fulfill even this relatively easy function adequately; tensions and anxieties aroused by political dangers, on the one hand, and the (real or imagined) need for constant competition and achievement, on the other, make them forget and neglect their children's spiritual needs, even though they may take more or less adequate care of their physical needs.

"This seems to be one of the main reasons for the failure of so many middle-class children of our generation to learn how to think and act autonomously.

"It will probably be argued that a similar tendency on the part of parents to 'abandon' their child to the school may be noticed in other periods and in other cultures as well. It certainly happens in a 'tradition-directed' society (in Riesman's terms (112)) at least when this society uses settings of formal education as a means of socialization. It happens in culture-change situations—for instance, in immigrant transition, when the parent's values may clash with those transmitted by the school. And it happens, though for entirely different reasons, in the poverty-stricken family.

"The first case, that of children in traditional societies, does not disprove our thesis. Even when in such a society the parents delegate their educational power to the school and do not cooperate with the teacher in order to make the learning process more meaningful for the child, they nevertheless make themselves felt very strongly in every minute of his life as the guardians of that tradition in whose name the school operates. There is, therefore, at least by implication, very strong parental support of the school's teaching, although the parents may be unable or unwilling to share in the child's learning experience.

"On the other hand, the development of autonomy is not considered one of the major functions of the elementary school in a tradition-directed society. We may find differences—individually and groupwise—in the extent of internalization of traditional values and concepts; but autonomy is not the aim of school education in this type of society; on the contrary, heteronomy can be considered a necessary concomitant of tradition.

"Even when the values of tradition are internalized, they are, as a rule, not being used autonomously. Internalization means—here—conscious identification and ego involvement, but not individual decision and initiative. It may well be that the difference between internalized and externalized heteronomy in relation to the contents and values of tradition will be found in many cases to reflect a different degree of identification, on the part of the parents, with what the school is doing in order to transmit those values.

"That most immigrant parents are unable to participate in the school's activities is a commonplace. The reasons for this inability (loss of status, adjustment and language difficulties, resistance to the new culture, etc.) are too well known to require detailed discussion here. But what we should emphasize is the fact that the immigrant child's chances of scholastic achievement and of advance toward intellectual and social autonomy, including mastery of abstract thinking, improve when his parents feel neither superior nor inferior to the new culture. Only such parents are able to spare their child the crisis of value clash and tension, only they can remain for him representatives of values, objects of identification and internalization, hence also stimulating forces in his mental development. In a way, they do share in his learning experience to the extent that they supplement his learning meaningfully from their own cultural and personal experience which they do not distort affectively.

"When, on the other hand, the former culture has not been differentiated enough to prepare the parents for an understanding of the learning processes in the 'new' culture, the child is liable to grow up in an atmosphere of uncertainty, of lack of orientation, of a value vacuum, and learning is bound to remain externalized, unrelated to the synthesizing activity of the child's ego, because it remains unrelated to the parents' world. . . .

"In the third case, that of the child who grows up under the externalizing conditions of extreme poverty and parental neglect, the school has the function of preventing the loss of intelligence which is bound to result from lack of regularity, personal relationship, and parental stimulation, unless the school counteracts these environmental handicaps. Unless the school fulfills this preventive and rehabilitative function, it is bound to become a pathogenic factor in the life of an externalized child. Failure to arouse, strengthen, develop, and maintain in him an ability to think in abstract terms and to establish polar relationships with problems and with human beings (that is, failure to prepare the learner for equal participation in all social tasks and functions) causes not only disappointment or despair but also destruction of congenitally given potentialities until asocial or even antisocial behavior becomes the best substitute source of satisfaction. . . .

"These are, today, some of the social and cultural conditions in which the elementary school fails to fulfill its proclaimed functions, because it does not enjoy the parents' support and confirmation, whether they are unable or unwilling to give this support (see p. 220).

"But the time has passed when learning and the pursuit of knowledge, when guarding the values of society and directing its course, were considered the right and the duty of a few, coming from the small group of the socially privileged or the most intelligent, who, in any case, are less at the mercy of the hazards of inadequate schooling and lack of parental cooperation. During those times when social participation was governed by the principles of selectivity, the fact was more or less taken for granted that most graduates of elementary schools would not take an active and creative part in the life of society, but would remain heteronomous followers (although then, too, lip service was pain to autonomy as the highest value of education). Today, however, with the spread of 'the democratic ideal of all social strata participating equally in all courses of learning and in all areas of social production' (p. 220), the failure of the school to live up to this ideal becomes a cause of individual and social disorder, of frustration and despair in the life of millions, and a stumbling-block in the way of social advancement. . . .

"The child of immigrant parents who may be disoriented in the new society; the child from the urban slum quarter who grows up under conditions unfavorable to internalization of concepts and values, the frustrated middle-class child—all of them depend on the school for that support and stimulation which the parents have failed to give them; they rely on the school to implant in their ego structure that sense of basic security which is the precondition of autonomy. . . .

"The smaller the part of the parents in the total process of learning—of the mother as the agent of security and of the father as the agent of differentiation—the more urgent becomes the need for the school to replace the parents.

"Let us add that we are not dealing here with a problem of social discrimination. What we have in mind is the objective failure, resulting from inadequate parental education and schooling, of millions all over the world, in all classes and in all cultures, irrespective of whether or not some may be considered 'successful' by the external criteria of individualistic evalution. 'Objective' failure manifests itself in such symptoms as ineffective social behavior, faulty and unproductive thinking, rigidity of the ego, lack of courage, inability to change and to develop. When this failure becomes the fate of millions, it affects the life and limits the progress of any society, whatever its political order."

6. Leisure Time

The concept of "free" time is part of an individualistic compromise with a basically social definition of man. He is supposed to devote most of his time between infancy and old age, unless he is asleep or ill, to what society expects him to do according to his age. In other words, outside the limits set by biological needs, for sleep or for recovery from illness, or by the maturation process, man's time is defined by society as being divided into two parts, one devoted to what he *must* do and another to what he *wishes* to do.

The proportion between the two parts is often defined as a function of age and of the available means of subsistence, as if the young and the old and the rich had, by definition, more free time. This, however, is, so we claim, and shall try to explain, a fallacy.

When speaking of an infant, the concept of free time is meaningless, since his sole duty is growth, and no social demands are imposed on him. When learning and socialization processes start and duties *are* being imposed on the young child (in proportion to the progress of the structural ego-non-ego polarization), time begins indeed to be divided into two parts, one being free from outside pressure and free for observation, imagination, phantasy; one being devoted to conforming with more or less pleasant, more or less unpleasant, adult impositions. The latter grows into a substantial portion of the day when formal schooling begins with its increasingly impersonal learning tasks. The school system and society's expectations, at least in our society, and the personal ambitions of the child and of his parents now determine the amount of free time left entirely at the disposal of the child to do what he wants to do, that is, to be alone with himself, free from adult determination.

Other, self-imposed, limitations, however, through freely chosen peer-group activities or hobbies, for instance, may again deprive the child of his free time. This means that autonomy of choice is *not* the ultimate criterion of what is free time; that free time is not the time spent as one likes to spend it. The most decisive difference is that between the bulk of our time we spend on what we *must* do irrespectively of whether society, the family, a self-chosen group, or even a creative drive forces us into obedience and subordination under self-transcending duties, and that part of our time where we are entirely free from duties, whether imposed on us by others *or* by ourselves. Not only the slave, but creative man too, has little, if any, free time.

What, then, is the meaning of this concept? Free, really free, is only the time man spends *without* creating something objective (though something created may result!). Essentially, it does not make much difference whether this objective something is a piece of monotonous factory or office work, selling or farming, housework or child-rearing, thinking, planning and constructing or drawing, writing and composing, learning or praying. Wherever man is an active partner in a polar relationship with another person or a task, with nature or with God, an active partner conscious of his duty, he is not free. Free is the time man spends with himself dreaming or watching the clouds, talking to his neighbors without aim or purpose, moving the body as the body wishes or busying himself with some hobby without ambitions transcending that very moment of doing. When we *organize* our free time, in group work, in learning, in creative activity, we have already lost it, whether we do so on purpose in order to escape from ourselves, or let ourselves be drawn into it by some inner urge or by some extraneous call.

But this concept of freedom implies internalization. Dreaming, talking, moving, resting may just as well be symptoms of emptiness as they may indicate freedom and a life from within. Without this distinction all theoretical statements on the essence of leisure and, for that matter, all practical conclusions drawn from them, are unwarranted generalizations devoid of meaning.

To put it paradoxically: It is the degree of inner activity in the non-intentional process of relaxation that constitutes true leisure. And it is this ability and readiness to relax from a life defined in terms of objective duties that gives meaning also to those numerous activities and particpiations known as part of "leisure-time programs."

This is one of the reasons we cannot speak of free time in a life from without.

Unless man feels freedom from duty as an opportunity for experiencing his inner self freely, he will either spend his duty-free time in a way that will make him rigidly or even compulsively dependent on certain patterns of spending it, or he will try to "kill" it (particularly when he has too much of it, due either to lack of work or to abundance of means). In both cases, those of the compulsive "spender" and the empty "killer," it becomes as meaningless to speak of free time as in those cases of the age-conditioned absence of dichotomy between work and leisure that we have mentioned before, in infancy or in old age. Without the ever-recurring experience of such a dichotomy, the time dimension and, with it, freedom, are bound to be absent in early childhood as well as in old age, in the emptiness of a life in plenty as well as under conditions of extreme poverty.

To put it again, differently: When we do our duty, whether in work or in creation, whether in groups or alone, whether in relationships with others or with ourselves, we do so in the knowledge that we are subjected to ego-transcending laws; when we spend free time, and we spend it in

freedom, we feel ourselves somehow living opposite those laws whose binding existence we do not deny while we are momentarily free from their universal rule.

We have so far focused our discussion on the negative elements in the
definition of the concept of free time; we have said that free time is the time
which is *not* related to objective creation or achievement, which is relatively free from tension and intentionality, which is the opposite of time
spent on socially or individually imposed duties.

There is, however, a positive element as well in the definition, one that
becomes relevant in particular when we analyze the *contents* of man's free
time, the occupations of his mind. *We then find that these are characterized
by receptiveness and by a conflict-free unity feeling.* True enough, *escape*
from such receptiveness and unity feeling into tensions characterize modern
man's way of filling his free time, unless he transforms it into part of his
duty-bound and therefore "unfree" time. But this is only one of the many
distortions of the human image that are inevitable by-products of technol-
ogy and of the "organization man" (125). A few remarks on the essence of
these distortions will perhaps help us understand the meaning of those
positive elements in the definition of free time—receptiveness and unity
feeling.

Prima facie, it could be argued, modern methods of leisure-time con-
sumption increase man's receptiveness and foster unity feelings. For these
—seemingly contradictory, yet basically identical—methods are the creation of tensions and the subordination of the individual under some sort
of collective principle. In order to be capable of enjoying the tensions offered by modern society's so-called media of communication, man must
be receptive; and in order to find his place in one of the many group settings in which he is invited to spend his free time he must be capable of
responding to the call of unity feelings. But the argument is based on a
fallacy, a fundamental misunderstanding of what "receptiveness" and
"unity" really mean.

Tension created by newspaper reports on sexual violence, by crime and
sex literature, by films and television programs with their concretizations
of such topics, by watching and betting on races, *does not make man receptive* but arouses in him an illusion of activity either through identification with the hero or the victim (or alternately with both) or through
manipulation of fate, as it were. Genuine receptiveness in the face of the
non-ego precludes both such identifications and manipulations, which
transform the ego into a pseudo-subject and the non-ego into a pseudo-
object. These distortions, however, make man unfree, so that, in the end,
his time is divided not between work and leisure, but between two compulsions.

On the other hand, genuine receptiveness does *not* contradict what we have called *a conflict-free unity feeling.* Although it might be argued that the first requires clear boundaries between the ego and the non-ego, their existence by no means precludes a feeling of "being one" with an enjoyable part of the non-ego that is "there," in its objective separateness. Contact with nature, with one's own body-in-movement (to distinguish from competitive sports or gymnastics), with a love partner in erotic or sexual relationships; contact with one's children (beyond the sphere of intentional education), with neighbors and friends (without any social or societal ambitions or rivalries); talking, drinking, playing, observing; participating in communal, in religious, in national feasts or in events taking place in one's own or in a neighbor's family—in all of these occupations a feeling of oneness may be present, though, of course, always in different degrees only and never completely or irrevocably a feeling of oneness with the object of one's occupation. To the extent that man is capable of this experience, his time is really free; so is he, for some fleeting moments at least (as long as it lasts).

We maintain that it is this passing feeling or, better, the inner possibility of experiencing it, that gives meaning to all the other occupations as well with which man may choose to fill his free time, occupations that require relaxation *and* concentration, receptiveness *and* inner activity. We may watch, listen, or read, we may become involved in a game, a sport, a discussion, a technical hobby, a collection, in music or any other art; what makes these activities different from their professional counterparts, what allows us to distinguish between them as contents of leisure and as contents of work, is more than the simple fact that we are free *not* to undertake them; it is the absence of self-identification with the outcome, that is, the ability to see them as lying outside the core of our identity, or, in other words, the ability through them to "*play* at identity," that makes genuine receptiveness and the experience of unity and oneness possible (whereas, while working, man needs his identity to live in separateness and, through it, to become efficient, be this an efficiency of routine or an efficiency of ego involvement).*

Although we do not altogether agree with Huizinga's thesis (65) that play is the essence of all human creation, be that a philosophical thought, a legal or a religious system, a work of art or science, it would seem that he was right in emphasizing the elements of nondifferentiation, identity, and wholeness in play. None of the common-sense attitudes such as "nonserious," "voluntary," "superfluous," "pretending" seem adequate to reach the core of play. Time is "free" (from work, from study) to the extent that man is capable of experimenting with his identity, while experiencing his

---

* Man may keep his identity "outside" his work in order to be capable of putting up with the monotony of routine, or he may invest his identity in his work (that is, become identical with his work role and function), when he considers it a field suitable for the expression of his creativeness; in either case, however, he must endeavor to discover, to define, to foster the crystallization of, his identity but never "play at" being self-identical.

experiments as serious, as necessary (not as voluntary), as essential (not as superfluous), as representative (not as pretending).

The way in which man spends his free time is both a symptom of his personality and a factor in the causal equation of his development and behavior. Type conditions, intelligence, integrational ability, structural and functional preferences, somatic vitality and health—all are reflected in his so-called leisure-time activities (no less than they are reflected in his approach to work and relationships). When speaking of an adult we must add that the degree of internalization or externalization reached in the course of his life process certainly finds a clear expression in the way he spends his free time.

On the other hand, the law of circular causation, according to which every symptom is liable to become a cause in the continued development of the individual, is here very much in evidence: those leisure-time activities that *require* a high degree of ego participation, self-confrontation, polar relationships with objects and partners, also help *develop* these very qualities and, through them, may be conducive to internalization—or to neurotic escape. And those activities that are *symptomatic* of externality of behavior (as briefly defined in Chapter 7) *intensify* its manifestations. It is this second (the etiological and not the symptomatological) aspect of the problem that interests us here.

It is, of course, self-evident that the factor of leisure-time activity as such will never suffice to explain a behavioral outcome, be it internalization or externalization, neurotic escape or aggressive acting out. It is, in regard to this as to every causal factor, its configuration with other (personality, developmental and environmental) factors that accounts for its effects. But this general law of etiology does not preclude asking questions about the specific, at least reinforcing, contribution that the way in which man spends his free time may make to the crystallization of certain behavior patterns:

The lower the degree of ego involvement in all (but particularly in the less differentiated and less intentional) leisure-time activities, and the more distinct the occurrence character of life, the more difficult will it be for a thus "afflicted" individual to make a meaningful internal experience and to internalize his learning, even when the environment offers opportunities for such internalization, stimulates and fosters it. In other words, an abundance of low tensions or of external tensions in leisure-time activities is bound to weaken man's ability and readiness to react to the internalizing forces that may be active in his environment or in his personality, until these will cease to make themselves felt. It is the lack of structurality in what happens to the individual in his free time that then spreads to the other areas of his life, particularly when social conditions or personal indolence support such inductive processes.

(In this connection we should mention the reality of the city street with its multitude of tensions and fascinations, its habit-forming groups and its generally externalizing tendencies and effects; only specially planned measures of social and educational intervention and manipulation can, if at all, counteract the de-internalizing or externalizing influence of the street on the leisure-time activities of children and adults alike.)

What we have said about receptiveness and the passing experience of oneness being the essential elements of free time could also be said to be a definition of its internalizing effect, whereas in those forces that we have mentioned as symptomatic of, and conducive to, externalization, receptiveness is *not* accompanied by an experience of unity and oneness. This deficiency accounts for the lack of ego involvement and ego participation which presupposes the ability temporarily to lose the ego in a clearly separated non-ego, that is, the ability to experience oneness. Where the latter is absent, receptiveness loses it normative meaning, too, and becomes external and nonselective reactiveness only.

Where, on the other hand, oneness is not accompanied by receptiveness, the *former* is but an illusion. This is the case of reality distortion through neurotic escape. Man indulges in the illusion of being in unity contact with the non-ego when he invites or visits his friends, when he travels, when he participates in community affairs, when he "devours" crime stories or films. Even more serious and seemingly ego-transcending activities such as attending lectures, going to the theater, listening to music, collecting books or paintings, stones or stamps—even they may be but attempts to escape rather than to relax. The criterion of distinction between "genuine" and "false" is man's readiness and ability to relate objectively to the non-ego (of which all fields of interest are representative); that is, to see it in its independence, as a *source,* not as a *means* of stimulation.

Obviously, the neurotic escape type of leisure-time activity is a symptom and not a cause of personality disturbance. But on the other hand, it is one of the most potent and the most effective causal factors in the process of neurotic pattern formation. This difference—between the causal configuration leading to the emergence of a certain pathological condition, such as a character neurosis, and the reinforcement of that pathological condition through its symptoms—has not received sufficient attention in the literature dealing with the so-called psychodynamic aspects of normal and abnormal behavior. But it is undoubtedly a difference of great practical importance, since the type of therapy required for dealing with the patternizing effects of reinforcement through symptoms is different from that required for eliminating the primary pathogenic factors, as we shall try to show in a later study. (See also Chapter 5, in which the concept of structurization was applied to certain types of pathological conditions.)

A mild childhood neurosis or character neurosis may persist into adulthood without affecting the individual to such an extent that he could be diagnosed as unable to fulfill his social functions. But the manner in which he may learn to spend his free time is liable to reinforce and aggravate his neurotic syndrome until it will negatively affect his behavior in all other spheres of life as well. In this respect the crystallization of neurotic patterns resembles that of the patterns of externalized behavior: although both are fundamentally different forms of pathological conditions (so much so in fact that the one may be defined as the opposite of the other), they are both equally susceptible to the reinforcing effect of their symptoms.

Finally, we should mention here the aggressive type of leisure-time activity, the main purpose of which is to satisfy sadistic or masochistic needs: watching boxing matches or bullfights, highly competitive and record-oriented games and sports, crime films or other displays of aggressiveness— these and similar varieties of passing one's free time have in common the processes of avoiding relaxation and "dissolving" the ego in identification with either the aggressor or his victim. This may lead to an increase in the intensity of the motivating aggressive tendencies, or it may help to live out aggressiveness vicariously. In both cases, the activity plays the role of a *causal* factor in the behavior of the individual and should *not* be interpreted as a symptom only of a disordered personality.

10

Environmental Factors: The Family

1. THE FAMILY UNIT DISTURBED

When in an analysis of normal behavior and development, the "family" is being discussed as a causal factor, it is the normally functioning and complete family unit that is meant. This unit is, of course, composed differently under different cultural or historical conditions, and it certainly operates differently as a medium of socialization, transmitting different sets of values in each culture and in each social stratum. But these variations, which are the object of anthropological, sociological, and social-psychological studies, are variations *of*, not *from*, the norm. A *disruption* of the family unit, however the latter may have been defined, appears in the causal equation of behavior and development as a negative, a disintegrating, factor only, and there is practically no behavior disorder for which some sort of family disruption is *not* made responsible.

It is generally agreed upon that the susceptibility of the family to disrupting factors such as health, or repeated or prolonged absence of one or both parents, or separation or tension between the parents, or illegitimate birth, and the susceptibility of an individual child with regard to such events, are functions of the social order of which the family forms part (119). It is well known that there exist societies in which disruptions of this or any other kind are immediately corrected—for instance through the intervention of members of the extended family or the total community—and therefore have no ill effect on the development of the child.

But to the extent that socialization processes are being channeled through the family, any disruption of its unit is bound to produce certain difficulties for the child in his development and, as a rule, it is safe to assume that it operates as a pathogenic factor. What kind of difficulty or deviation will result depends not only on the specific variety of the disruption of the family unit, but also on the degree of internalization which is characteristic of a certain family type. Where intimate relationships between the child and his parents are part of the child's earliest experience, the result of any form of disruption of the family unit is bound to be different from what it will be where impersonal relationships prevail: it may have a neuroticizing effect in the first case, following intensive guilt and anxiety feelings (19); it may have an externalizing effect in the second case, following loss of external controls (and here again we shall have to distinguish between that form of impersonality that is characteristic of a life orientation toward the "haveable" and the other form which is characteristic of identification with a traditional value system).

Rarely, if ever, the question is being asked in a discussion of the causes of normal and abnormal development: Under which conditions does each of the abovementioned forms of family disruption operate, not only as a neuroticizing or as an externalizing factor, but perhaps also as an internalizing factor? To the extent that the question of such an alternative development does appear, the answer is that personality factors are the only relevant differentials. Constitution, maturation, and accumulation of experience are made responsible for the different outcomes of objectively similar factors.

In the following analysis of certain forms of family disruption we shall try to answer the question of "normal" *versus* "abnormal" reaction and behavioral outcome: why a situation that has a neuroticizing or an externalizing or any other pathological effect in certain cases may be an incentive to internalization and to normal development in others.

ILLEGITIMATE BIRTH

When we speak of illegitimate birth as one of the causes of a child's maladjustment, we have in mind the specific situation in which (1) an educationally incompetent, (2) economically handicapped, (3) socially discriminated against, and (4) often emotionally disturbed and/or (5) intellectually retarded mother (6) tries to bring up her child without the assistance of a husband, (7) often prejudicing her child, consciously or unconsciously, against his unknown father.

Each of these seven factors, alone or as an element in a different causal constellation, is capable of producing some kind of maladjustment in *any* child (not only in one born to an unmarried mother); but the specific characteristics of illegitimacy maladjustment will then *not* be present. We shall have an opportunity to discuss most of the abovementioned partial factors as isolated causes; we are concerned here, however, with their specific combination and their specific behavioral outcome only.*

* Mention should be made here of Bowlby's discussion (12) of illegitimate birth: When society does *not* discriminate against unmarried mothers, he says, and at the same

In what respects does the father's absence in the here-discussed case of illegitimacy mean something essentially different from what it means in other cases in which a mother is forced by acts of fate to bring up her child in a fatherless home (72)? We shall come back to this question when summing up what we shall have to say about desertion, divorce, death, prolonged absence of parents, and about family tension as perhaps the most dangerous form of family disruption. A few remarks, however, may well be added here about the impact on the child's development of an unmarried mother's possible attitudes toward motherhood.

Here again the second law of configuration, according to which the effect of a cause depends on *its* antecedents (see p. 86), is clearly in evidence: If the mother's pregnancy and the child's birth are chance results of her immaturity, she will be likely, in our society, at least, to give the child away for adoption or to an institution, and the child's development will then *not* be determined by the experience of the mother's personality. If mental deficiency has facilitated her yielding to sex impulses and falling victim to seductions without self-protection, it is the basic inability of such a defective woman to raise a child without a husband's help that will determine the end result (and we shall come back to this case when discussing the effect of parental subnormality in general on a child's development). No less, if not more, dangerous is the case of illegitimate birth due to neurotic distortions of motive and antiparental resentments. For, it is precisely this inner distortion and this resentment that may make an unmarried mother feel that she must "pay the price," "devote herself to motherhood," "punish her mother or father," or "show them" (whatever it may be that her unconscious has decided "to show them").

It is particularly this last-mentioned case of "fatherless childhood" that makes the use of the latter term meaningless: the difference between a widow whose emotional attachment to her deceased husband (in its positive *and* negative meaning) determines her reaction to the child, a divorced woman who feels either resentment for having been rejected or ambivalence toward the father of her children or disgust and even hatred for "that man" whose negative image she may have built up over a period of years, between a divorced and a deserted woman, between them and the one whose husband is forced by his occupation to absent himself from home frequently or for long periods—these and other

time the mother is neither emotionally disturbed nor intellectually retarded, and, in any case, does not feel resentment against the child's father but, on the contrary, continues to love him, and when, in addition, she is supported, morally and economically, by her own family, illegitimate birth is not a pathogenic factor. The presence of only one of those positive environmental and personality factors, however, is not sufficient to prevent the ill effects of illegitimacy.

differences are much too great to allow for a subsumption of all under the general term of "fatherless" families. It is the combination of accumulated resentment with external tensions and fears in the mother that we have in mind when we consider illegitimate birth a pathogenic factor.

What, then, is the psychological meaning of illegitimate birth for the child? The mother's affectivity—usually a mixture of anxieties and resentments—and the instability of her own and her child's life conditions are bound to reinforce the child's awareness of the absent father and of his being "different." His life course is liable to be determined by the category of incompleteness; hence the all-pervading doubt as to his own identity that makes itself felt as early as in the second phase of development, but certainly in the so-called oedipal phase, when the absence of a father image makes the child's relationship with his mother problematic.*

Here, however, it should be evident that illegitimate birth has an altogether different meaning for a boy and for a girl. In the development of a boy a self-contradictory pattern of behavior may emerge when uncertainty about his origins and ambivalence in his relationships with the "guilty" mother determine his reactions and feelings. Inner tensions may produce quasi-neurotic solutions, usually of the compulsive and addictive type; the ever-present and all-pervading experience of incompleteness, partiality, "absence," may give rise to drivenness and externalization, while, at the same time, intensifying tendencies toward fixation to the mother or to the mother substitutes. Internalization of learning, particularly in the more intelligent child, will then often show an impersonally rigid character, reflecting the relative absence of opportunities for ambivalence feelings and for identification with a personally relevant father figure. But even where weakness of differentiation (in less intelligent children) fosters the emergence of externality of behavior and thinking, signs of tension will not be absent.

It is this ambiguity of behavior and reaction patterns that in our society characterizes the development of the boy born out of wedlock in all phases of his development, whether he finally becomes an addict, a pervert, a criminal, or a passively driven, apathetic, indolent adult, whether he develops a neurosis or the ability to function more or less normally in his work and his interpersonal relationships. The same category of incompleteness which is responsible for the emergence of neurotic

* We have mentioned in the foregoing footnote (p. 232), Bowlby's hypothesis according to which the ill effects of illegitimate birth will not be felt as acutely where the society tolerates it as something more or less natural. Here we should add that where illegitimacy is not an unusual phenomenon, the psychological problem here raised will not be very acute either. It is then another factor, educational neglect and poverty, that will determine the child's development, irrespectively of whether his mother is married or unmarried, and not the child's unsuccessful quest for identity.

or externalized behavior patterns may also serve as an incentive for *creating* wholeness and synthesis, though probably never without the support of a highly developed intelligence and adequate learning facilities. But even in this case tension can always be felt.

For the girl, the absence of the father has a different significance altogether. It is not so much the quest of identity that may determine her development as it is the search for objects of relationship. Premature inner separation from the mother, and in any case weakness of identification with her, explains why so many daughters of unmarried mothers grow up to become women for whom the establishment of relationships with others, and particularly with men, is either "learned to be avoided" or, in any case, does not require ego involvement and self-definition. A life without identity, repression or diffusion of the relational ability, conception of the non-ego as "haveable"—these are typical manifestations of such a girl's reactions to the absence of a father figure and of her life without competition with the mother.*

Although illegitimate birth is usually being studied only as a negative force in the child's life, there are, as Bowlby has emphasized in his above-mentioned analysis of the factor (see p. 232), certain combinations of circumstances that allow for an undisturbed development of a child who is being brought up by an unmarried mother. Constitutional factors in personality undoubtedly play a most important role in preventing disorder (here as in any other case of growing up under the impact of a pathogenic environment. But the *mother's* personality is probably a still more decisive factor of determination—and this explains the relatively low incidence of *positive* developments: in most cases it is that very immaturity, mental retardation, or neurotic personality accounting for the illegitimate birth that will also prevent the unmarried mother from availing herself of such guidance and benefiting from such well-meaning advice as that offered by psychoanalysts and social workers with their typical middle-class orientation (see, for instance, 19, 21, 72).

PROLONGED ABSENCE OF THE FATHER OR OF THE MOTHER

Temporary and prolonged absence of the mother—usually as the result of her own or the child's physical or mental illness or for some personal reasons such as avoidance of an overt or latent conflict situation —is a less frequent occurrence than absence of the father, who may be absent not only for the same reasons but also when his work requires it or even when he serves a prison sentence. As regards the young child, only the mother's absence counts. Its ill effects in the personality de-

* Here, as in the case of the boy, we do *not* consider the ill effects of institutional care, usually without continuity, on the illegitimate child's development, since we shall devote a separate section (p. 246) to that problem of institutionalization.

velopment of the child have been studied by Bowlby (12), Burlingham and Freud (15), Goldfarb (56), Spitz (117), and others. While it affects the personality structure of the infant and the young child almost irrespectively of the factor that *caused* the absence of the mother, its effects on the development of an *older* child are largely determined by its causes: the stronger the child's ego, the less is the danger of regression or of reactivation of infantile fears and dependence, of withdrawal or of reactive aggressiveness—provided, of course, the child has no objective reason to feel neglected by an egotistic and egocentric mother.

The many studies of the effects of the child's separation from the mother have, strangely enough, neglected two important factors of differentiation: the causes of separation and the sex factor. Very little seems to be known from the available studies about the different reactions of boys and girls in the oedipal and latency phases of development to the disappearance of a mother who may have left the family for a more or less prolonged period for purely personal reasons. Such separations are fairly frequent occurrences in certain middle-class families, which as a rule make more or less adequate provisions for substitute care and maintenance of personal contact but nevertheless often fail to prevent damage to the personality of the growing child. It is obvious that boys and girls are differently affected by such conditions and that a number of personality factors and environmental factors must be included in the analysis to make its conclusions meaningful.

Prolonged and repeated absence of the father, in times of either war or peace, is liable to endanger the clarity and certainty of orientation which the child needs, particularly when he or she already has become dependent on the father, the boy needing him as an object of identification, the girl as an object of relationship, and both as a reliable source of guidance. Repeated changes in the family constellation, brought about by the father's return and leaving again, force the child into frequent reorientations and readjustments; these not only create energy-consuming tensions but also explain why identifications, introjections, and relationships are liable to become uncertain and noncommittal in such "provisional situations."

The young child is, of course, affected by the father's absence only through the medium of reactive tensions in the mother; in the oedipal phase of a middle-class child's development the father's absence acts primarily as a factor reinforcing ambivalence conflicts and intensifying existing feelings of anxiety and guilt. In latency, its weight may be felt, in the areas of learning and of behavior, as a cause of restlessness, doubt, uncertainty, and day-dreams. It is particularly this latency condition which may produce reactively a general orientation toward the external aspects of reality and thus set in motion processes of dedifferentiation.

Prolonged absence of the father means lack of reality support to the paternal principle of differentiation and internalization (see pp. 22 *ff.*), for which deficiency even adequate schooling cannot compensate except in part only. It may mean, at the same time, "irrealization" not only of the father image but also of those social values that are, as a rule, mediated and represented by him.

We are not considering here the case of a father's frequent or prolonged absence from home owing to imprisonment, since it is rarely the factor of absence that under such circumstances negatively affects the child's development, but rather the father's delinquency and its personality roots. Whether his offences are of an antisocial or of an ideological order, whether he is an egotist or an idealist, whether the child identifies with him or feels ashamed of him—it is *not* the fact of his physical absence that here determines the child's reactions.

But to the extent that absence of the father *does* play a decisive role in the causal equation of a child's development, irrealization is an essential element, whether the affected child is a boy or a girl, though we should add that for a girl the *emotional* aspects of a "dream life with the remote father" represents a greater danger than its *intellectual* implications.

On the other hand, where, as under conditions of extreme poverty and educational neglect, the child's intellectual and moral development is less determined by the father's active participation in his upbringing than by a combination of impersonal and often self-contradictory factors of environment, his frequent and prolonged absence is not as fateful as it is likely to be in many middle-class families. It may well reinforce the externalizing effect such conditions will have in any case; it may also contribute to the emergence of aggressive and delinquent behavior (whenever controls from without are preconditions of socialization); but it will not produce those tensions and conflicts that are liable to emerge in a middle-class child whose father is absent for a long time.

That a mother's unambiguous love and understanding of her children's needs may help a boy as well as a girl, in a lower class as well as in a middle-class family, to overcome the specific difficulties created by the father's absence, is a commonplace that certainly needs no elaboration.

DEATH OF THE FATHER OR THE MOTHER

The possible traumatic influences of this factor on the development of children of different ages have been analyzed frequently both in individual case studies and in surveys of emotional disorders (104) or delinquency (55). By way of summing up these studies, we may say that the death of one parent is liable to produce disturbances in the normal balance between masculine and feminine components within the structure of the growing child's personality. Thus, we find effemination or mother-fixation in fatherless boys, masculinity trends or promiscuity tendencies in fatherless girls, rejection of everything feminine or emotional shallowness in motherless boys, overstrong father-dependence in motherless girls, and many similar varieties of emotional confusion. Guilt feelings and anxiety are frequent reactions, particularly when the death of the father or of the mother occurred while the boy or the girl was in the oedipal stage. In addition, the child's mental development is exposed to the manifold dangers of insecurity and disorientation that characterize the incomplete family in general, at least in our culture.

Obviously, the differential effect of the factor here under discussion depends not only on the type and on the age of the child at the time of its occurrence, but also on the economic conditions of the family, on its culture-conditioned patterns of reaction and evaluation as well as on the personal—conscious and unconscious—reactions of the surviving parent. Only when considering these differential factors can we understand why death of a parent is sometimes the precipitating cause of regressive (and reactive) externalization, while in other cases it acts as a reinforcer of internalization, either accelerating the child's advance toward maturity or creating inner tensions and neuroses.

Thus, shallowness of feeling or promiscuity reactions may eliminate previous internalizations and set in motion processes of externalization when the surviving parent becomes preoccupied with material problems to the exclusion of unequivocal personal relationships; whereas the same reaction may lead to a neurotic disruption in the child's personality when the surviving parent struggles in vain to fulfill both his own and the opposite parental role and invariably becomes entangled in a web of anxieties and guilt feelings.

Fixation reactions may in one case operate as symptoms of an already existing neurosis or as indirectly and secondarily externalizing factors, particularly when the surviving parent "needs" the child's fixation, consciously or unconsciously.

In another case, those same reactions may intensify tendencies toward internalization (provided the child has already reached the age in which internalization becomes possible and meaningful), but only when cultural expectations include internalization as one of the essential "goods," and only when the surviving parent understands how to "handle" the child's fixational rigidity and how to alleviate the underlying anxieties. Needless to add, a constructive reaction of the surviving parent to the consequences of the death of his or her partner and consistently positive relationships with the child may transform even the disruption of the family by the parent's death into an additional factor of internalization. Here, it is in particular the surviving parent's readiness and ability to transform the image of the deceased, not only into part of a "living memory" but also into a challenge to the child's imagination and an object of realistic confrontation, that may help him internalize values and develop constructive attitudes of which the parent was representative.

DESERTION BY PARENTS

One may ask in what respect the situation arising in the child's life following the desertion of the family by one of the parents resembles, in what respect it differs from, that created by the parent's death. Is not in both cases the sudden disappearance of the parent the decisive factor? In answer, we should point to the tensions and the resentments often preceding, but invariably following, this form of family break-up and to their impact on the emotional climate in which the child is likely to be brought up under such conditions.

We shall consider the factor of interparental tensions and emotional ambiguity separately (see pp. 242 ff.). Here we are concerned with another aspect of the situation: After being deserted by his parent, a child who, at that time, has already reached the end of the oedipal phase, is liable to experience his parents as human beings independent of, and unrelated to, him; they apparently live their own life in which he, the child, plays no decisive role.

The critical age of susceptibility differs according to the degree of personal intimacy in the parent-child relationships and according to the sex of the child and the deserting parent. While either parent's desertion may mean only more neglect and want in a poverty-stricken family, irrespective of the age and the sex of the affected child, its meaning for the boy in a middle-class family with its intimacy and ambivalence patterns is essentially different from its meaning for the girl, and then again different in the various phases of the boy's or the girl's development. In the first stages only the mother's desertion counts, and it is likely to endanger the still precarious basic sense of trust (to the extent that it had been established before). With the oedipal phase the mother's desertion is likely to provoke as strong a feeling of guilt and anxiety in the girl as the father's desertion may provoke in the boy. The girl may react to desertion of the father, the boy to that of the mother, with feelings of deep disappointment and depression. Later, the father's desertion endangers the intellectual and moral development, particularly of the boy, not only because it deprives him of guidance but also because he may be overtaxed by a sudden confrontation with the feeling of being alone. In reaction, he may seek protection in unstructured groups and thereby lose whatever power of differentiation and introjection he may have had attained before; whereas the mother's desertion causes in both boys and girls loss of orientation and increases the danger of externalization. Adolescents are the least affected by parental desertion, to the extent at least that they live in "principles" (see pp. 166 *ff.*), and that they are not pathologically fixated to one of the parents.

Thus, we maintain that desertion of the family by one of the parents is liable to produce a variety of reactions in the child according to his age, sex, culture, social condition (apart from the always differentiating factor of constitutional dispositions which we must treat as "kept constant" in any analysis of environmental factors of causation). Positive, constructive solutions are rare exceptions, since the tensions and resentments that are bound to be produced by desertion of one parent in the family almost inevitably affect the latter's attitude toward the child.

Moreover, it is the element of sudden disappearance, of discontinuity, that is likely to damage almost every child's ability to integrate experience in the whole context of his growing identity. In other words, whatever the specific reaction of a boy or a girl in the various stages of their development and under the different conditions of their life may be, there will always be some damage to the process of identity formation.*

DIVORCE

There are three elements in divorce that are liable to affect the child's development unfavorably: the tensions between the parents prior to their divorce, which the child feels clearly, often even before the parents themselves have become aware of them; the parents' instrumentalistic attitude toward the child who is liable to become an almost anonymous factor in their interpersonal "strategy"; the ambiguity of relationships between the child and his divorced father and mother.

We shall deal with the first element separately in the following section, "Tensions between Parents." The second element, though a very common trait in the behavior of many divorced parents, is not an essential characteristic of divorce. All counseling and guidance services for disrupted families try to help such parents to give up their instrumentalistic attitudes and practices for the benefit of the child and his normal development. It is the personality disorder underlying their incompatibility that accounts for their selfish attempts to "draw away" the child from the other parent; but the same personality disorder may produce similar unwise attitudes in a married couple as well, when for some more or less objective reason they believe that they cannot trust each other.

---

* We suggest that the following hypothesis might well be tested by (longitudinal and/or retrospective) research: that many children who in their latency period experience desertion of the family by the father grow up to regard life as devoid of inner logic, and self-definition in terms of personal identity as dangerous; that many learn how to defend themselves against this danger and how to adjust themselves to a life without inner logic by giving up whatever autonomy and initiative they may have acquired earlier.

It is therefore primarily the third element, ambiguity of relationships with the father and the mother, that we should have in mind when speaking about the negative effects divorce may have on the child's development. The younger the child, the less will he be able or willing to accept as unalterable the fact that his father and mother cannot live together as do the parents of his friends. The child resists *any* attempt to reverse the accepted order of things, even when his emotional attachment to the absent parent had not been particularly strong, but of course his resistance is much more intensive when strong affective ties exist, of love or of hate, of fear or of guilt. Understandably, he resists being "left out"—which is exactly what happens when the parents part with each other for good. They may honestly try to make "satisfactory arrangements" for him, but all this cannot change the fact that he has ceased to be a *subject* of determination in the life of the family *unit*. Though he may not have been one before either, it is only now that he becomes aware of it, and this new awareness of being an "unessential" factor in such an essential event as his parents' separation means that he is alone.

It would seem that it is this painful discovery rather than a—no doubt equally painful but nevertheless more accessible—conflict of loyalties and of love feelings that may from now on determine the child's reactions and his development. Ambiguity of relationships means not only coexistence of mutually exclusive feelings, of love and hate for each of the frustrating parents, it also and essentially means doubt and uncertainty with regard to what the father and the mother represent structurally—the paternal principle (of differentiation and internalization) and the maternal principle (of unity and synthesis). Internalizations already achieved may become doubtful in the mind of the child since they are no longer supported by an unambiguous father figure; they may even vanish again, that is, be replaced by regressive externalizations. The learning process may become problematic, at least when the affected child is in the beginning of the phase of differentiation and synthesis, and again, not only because his mind may be distracted by confused thinking and phantasies about his parents (see the next section), but also because with the disappearance of the father-mother unit the structural basis of the functions required for adequate learning has become unstable.

A child of normal or above normal intelligence can, of course, overcome this basic learning difficulty and regain his original capacity by concentrating on content matter, but for some time after the traumatic experience of "aloneness" brought about by the parents' divorce he is liable to suffer from what might be called a structural (not functional) insecurity.

It goes without saying that these negative effects of parental divorce on the young child will be much less in evidence, or even completely absent, when cultural or social patterns preclude emotional dependence on intimate interrelatedness of father and mother and of the parents and the child. In other words, where a child grows up in an atmosphere of educational impersonality, divorce will affect his development much less traumatically. (The same applies to the effects of desertion, which, incidentally, is known to occur much more frequently than divorce in families characterized by relative impersonality of the educational climate.)

The reader will remember that we have mentioned "irrealization" of the father image and the social values represented by him as one of the possible outcomes of his prolonged absence (see p. 235). It is even more frequently observed in children of divorce (19). Idealization and phantasy distortion of an objectively unsatisfactory father (less frequently also a mother)—these forms of irrealization indicate a deep-rooted need which cannot be explained adequately in such terms of personalistic interpretation as "libidinal attachment" or "guilt reaction" or "overcompensation of inferiority feelings," but requires the use of structural, that is, transpersonal, categories.

The father, we have said in Chapter 2 (see pp. 22 ff.) normatively supplies the child with the experience, vital for his development, of a "stranger" gradually losing his character of strangeness, of remoteness, until, in the end, he becomes a suitable object of introjection (in contrast to the mother who has to lose her "part" character in order to enable the child to experience "nearness"). The father's "moving toward" the child is the prototype of the cognitive processes whose ultimate function is to help the "unknown" become known, not through conditioning but through differentiation and internalization. The father's disappearance, therefore, means danger, danger of regression to the infantile stage of remoteness and strangeness, without being protected by the "containing mother," as the infant was before the "transformation" of the father. It means danger of losing mastery over the paternal acquisitions of learning, of differentiation, of internalization.

What, then, is the difference, from the child's point of view, between desertion and divorce? Desertion, we have said, is liable to produce a feeling of discontinuity, of life being without inner logic; divorce, a feeling of being left out, of aloneness. The first is liable to affect the child's identity development and thereby to set in motion processes of externalization; the second is more likely to arouse feelings of depression and anxiety around the problem of self-definition and elicit attempts on the part of the child to maintain or to find his identity. The element of danger is much more acutely present in the second than in the first case.

TENSIONS BETWEEN THE PARENTS

The family unit can be disrupted much more radically through permanent tension between the parents than through any other factor.

There is practically no case of emotional disorders in which the tension factor did not play a prominent role as causal determinant, though of course in varying degrees of intensity. The insecurity, anxiety, and lack of orientation following the experience of interparental tensions may elicit, among other defenses, those of avoidance and escape, which in turn may lead to all kinds of phobic, hysteric, or compensatorily aggressive reactions.

A child growing up in an atmosphere of parental conflicts again and again is compelled to see, hear, and feel how the father is negated by the mother and the mother by the father. Thus, he is made aware of the negative more than of the positive aspects of each parent and becomes incapable of strong ambivalence feelings which normally form the basis of social, emotional, and intellectual developments. Exclusive reinforcement of the negative components is likely to externalize *every* intrapsychic conflict, to transform it, prematurely, into an external and more or less conscious conflict, a process which then is again bound to deprive ambivalence—to the extent that it does emerge later despite its weak "family foundations"—of its structural and developmental function as an incentive to introjection.* As a result, both positive and negative feelings may become "situationally conditioned," and externality of behavior may emerge.

This effect may be supported or "transformed" by another element of family tension: Under conditions of interparental conflicts both parents may either neglect or use the child for their own needs and purposes. In the first case, the possibly resulting externalization in the child's reactions and behavior differs from the "ideal type," which we shall describe and analyze in a future publication as the result of growing up under conditions of extreme poverty and educational neglect. Whereas, in the latter case, neglect is but a by-product of the parents' more or less exclusive orientation toward the "haveable," it reflects, in the first case, a kind of inability to love, the child losing his individuality in the minds of the embattled parents. As a result, there are liable to appear anxiety reactions, not so much to the frightening reality situation, in which the child may feel helpless and endangered, but rather to a life without love and to the loss of *inner* unity, which is represented by the parents' disunity.

The outcome of this existential fear, however, is not necessarily a neurotic development. Every neurosis is in some way a defense against one's *own* behavior, an attempt to avert the catastrophic effect this behavior may have on the immediate environment and to be on guard

---

* We are accustomed to consider this the function of ambivalence in childhood only and forget that introjection of relevant environmental figures occurs in every phase of man's development, at least until his late adult years, and that it is ambivalence again and again through which he is motivated to introject its human objects.

against the punishment that is bound to be inflicted on the sinner. In the case here under consideration, that of a child exposed to the ever-recurring evidence of his *parents'* "badness," as it manifests itself in the negation of the father by the mother and of the mother by the father, in this case of interparental tension neurotic developments will take place only when, for some reasons of his own, the child tends to interpret this tension as of his own making. Otherwise, fear of the parents' badness may set in motion processes of avoidance and escape or it may cause the child precociously or prematurely, successfully or unsuccessfully, to live "without" his parents, without receiving or even expecting from them the normally required support of his internalizations. The latter, positive, outcome of reactions to interparental tensions is undoubtedly due to structural more than to environmental factors.

But we should not forget cases in which a father's or a mother's constructive attitude toward the child, their love for him, remain almost unimpaired by their fight and by their mutual resentment. In these cases the child may preserve his integrational abilities and overcome the difficulties created by the tension factor without escape and without neurosis.

More frequent than neglect of the child or partial adequacy in the parents' attitude toward the child is what we have called their instrumentalistic attitude when they use the child for their own purposes and needs. While this attitude can be found in many parents as an expression of their own neurosis or character deformation, whether interparental tension is at its root (causally) or is only one of its results, the parents' tendency to draw the child away from each other has a different meaning when it appears in an embattled family or after the parents' divorce. The differentiating factor is the way in which the child understands or interprets his parents' intentions. As long as the family exists as a unity, at least in appearance, the child is liable to indulge in the illusion that by accepting his father's and his mother's favors separately he is holding together the weak remnants of this unit.

There is, of course, also the opposite case, that of the child who has learned how to exploit the advantages offered by his parents' instrumentalistic attitude, and by doing so not only develops *patterns of falsity* but also helps, wittingly or unwittingly, to intensify the tension. We find the same negative reaction and behavior quite frequently in children of divorced parents who spoil them because they feel that they have failed them.

STEP-PARENTS

The appearance of a step-father or a step-mother may have a traumatic effect on a child, not only because it aggravates or revives love conflicts and loyalty conflicts of a recent past (or even of the present) and reinforces feelings of resentment, envy, hatred, but also because it requires a reorientation in his introjective system. To the extent that the parent's image was already internalized before his (or her) death, the very fact of the step-parent's appearance, with its implied claim for acceptance, love, and identification, means that not only the remembered past but also the present ego is suddenly questioned. This, however, may be beyond the growing child's integrational abilities. (The introjection may not yet be sufficiently structurized, that is, detached from its personal elements, to allow for an "exchange" of images.)

As a result, the child may reject the step-parent aggressively or protest by transferring former identifications onto self-chosen, uncontrollable, and often negative substitutes. It is as if he wanted to say to his adult environment: "If *you* consider the internalized parental image exchangeable, why then should I identify with one only, why not with a number of 'ideals,' why only with such figures as *you* consider acceptable, why not, on the contrary, with representatives of opposite values?"

Another reaction may be submission at the expense of the already emerging identity. The child may accept the demands of his adults and may transfer his identifications onto the step-parent, but in doing so loses the relative autonomy which he may already have attained through his prior introjections.

In both cases, processes of dedifferentiation are liable to set in, although the manifestations will be different. Moreover, in the situation here under discussion, the strongly developed relatedness to personally defined objects that gave rise to each of the two reactions will in some cases continue to act as a neuroticizing factor. As a result, we then find neurotic delinquency with strong tendencies toward externalization as a reaction to the step-parent situation.

(We should add that the situation is often aggravated by the fact that the step-parent, too, is liable to reject the child, consciously or unconsciously, because he or she sees in him a representative of his (or her) partner's past. This rejection, however, must of necessity increase the child's confusion and disorientation, because it is the very process of normative identification with, and introjection of, the dead parent which here suddenly is being experienced as something objectionable and which now earns him the painful experience of rejection by the step-parent.)

But even where the child is helped by sensible adults in his adjustment to the new family and where none of the extreme situations here described emerges, we should be careful not to overlook the danger of increased vulnerability and of de-internalization, which is inherent in the step-parent condition.

We should again beware of simplifying the issue here under discussion. There are so many factors to be considered when we speak of the effects which a life with step-parents may have on a child's development —factors of age, sex, social and cultural patterns, the child's and the adult's personality structure, etc.—that no generalization should actually be allowed. Our remarks here, like those on each of the other forms of family disruption, have one purpose only: to formulate and emphasize some of the essential elements of the factor without analyzing its many reality implications.

REMOVAL OF THE CHILD FROM THE PARENTS

Where a child is removed from his home because of illness or physical or mental defects requiring special treatment, or because of the parents' inability to take care of him (due, in turn, to their ill health, personality deficiency, or social handicap), or because of such objective reasons as lack of safety under war conditions or after a natural catastrophe, the family unit is disrupted as far as the child is concerned.

We refer again to the separation studies which we have frequently mentioned (12, 15, 56, 117). We should distinguish between the following aspects of the problem for the purposes of our present discussion:

(a) *The aspect of constitutional changes.* In Chapter 5 we have mentioned as one of the forms of negative structurization the irreversible decrease of the child's congenitally given intellectual, relational, and physical dispositions, which is liable to occur when he is placed in a babies' home or a hospital for a considerable time at the beginning of his life. The impersonal routine atmosphere is responsible for the elimination or the non-development of the capacity for polar relationships.*

(b) *The aspect of regression.* It is a well known fact that removal of a young child from his mother for a considerable time is liable to elicit regression to earlier stages of development, with their greater need of dependence, their weaker "controls from within," and their lower level of differentiation. This proves that the relative autonomy, control, and differentiation reached by the young child depend for their development and structurization on the protective contact with the mother.

(c) *The aspect of quasi-neurotic reactions.* Older children often react to temporary or prolonged placement away from the home with increase in anxiety, day-dreaming, enuresis, and other signs of unhappiness. Although they may overcome their difficulties, at least outwardly, the resulting character formation nevertheless often shows traces of insecurity or emotional indifference or shallowness or demonstrated independence, all of which are rooted in the disappointing experience of their removal from the parents.

---

* This will be analyzed in a subsequent volume, to be published.

(d) *The aspect of negative fixation.* This is particularly evident in boys and girls who had to be removed because of their intolerable behavior at home, and who are unable to live without the parental environment as their field of ambivalence aggressions.

(e) *The aspect of parental guilt feelings.* This aspect may be present in each of the previous ones, though to a varying degree, according to the parents' personality. It is self-evident that guilt feelings in the parents not only do not alleviate the child's condition but rather aggravate it, as they are usually rooted in unconscious, hence irrational, reactions. It is also obvious that such feelings will necessarily act as additional factors of disruption in an already precarious family situation.

The most important outcomes of the various conditions here mentioned are the emotional and relational shallowness of the hospitalized infant and the regressive dedifferentiation of the institutionalized young child. They make normal internalization almost impossible, because of the low degree of ego participation and because of the relative lack of ambivalence so characteristic of these children. In addition, quasi-neurotic reactions and negative fixations are common to many institutionalized children, at least those who are placed out at a later stage of their development and following a history of doubt and tension at home. All cases of institutional care have, of course, one danger factor in common: *diffusion* of identifications may lead to a *weakening* of the identificational ability as such, that is, to a loss of structure. This loss of structure, however, makes the growing child more and more susceptible to externalizing factors that may be active in his environment.

There remains one question to be answered in our present discussion of the family unit and its disruptions as causal factors of development: Should we include the last case, that of the child's removal from his parents, among the varieties of family disruption only because the *child* is bound to experience it as such, or is the family unit itself objectively affected by it?

It would seem that only by seeing the basic identity of those two aspects will we be able correctly to understand the meaning of the concept of family "unit." We are not interested here in the relationship problems of childless couples but only in the family as a field of normal or abnormal *child* development. The way in which each of the family members sees this "field" and its components, different as this perception may be individually, constitutes the structure and the specific functions of the unit in every case. The exclusion of one of its members, in whatever way it may occur (including the removal of a child whom the unit is unable to tolerate or, anyway, to integrate), means an *objective* change of its structure and of the way in which each member now sees his own role within the changed unit as well as that of the others, parents and siblings alike.

It is through this change in role perception after the removal of a child from his parents no less than after the disappearance of any other members of the unit that the life course of the remaining (and/or substitute) member is liable to be changed at least until a new integration can take place. In other words: each family unity produces a specific pattern through which those of the social class or the ethnic culture present themselves to the individual. Any disruption of the family unit, we therefore claim, not only affects the child's development in one of the ways that we have briefly discussed in the present paragraph but may also interrupt the interaction between the family-specific pattern of experience and the flow of occurrences to which each member is exposed individually. This means that, whenever a member of the family unit disappears or is being removed (without general consent), the self-perception of every one of the others is being changed, so that reorientation becomes necessary. Failure in this respect means final disruption of the unit.

2. The Parental Environment

In Chapter 6 we have dealt with certain maternal or paternal deficiencies as related to certain structural differentials in the child. We now come back to discussing these deficiencies in greater detail and as related to the parents' personality. But first we must briefly analyze a number of more or less factual personality conditions, such as old age or age differences between the parents, low intelligence, chronic ill health, neurotic disorder, primitivity, asociality, externality, as determinants of their behavior in general and as parents. It is obvious that the way in which the family unit functions or fails to function when it is disrupted to no small extent depends on these and similar personality-determinants.

OLD AGE OF PARENTS

When we consider old age of one parent or both (in most instances, of course, the father) an *environmental* factor in the child's development, we should exclude the biological element of possible injury to his constitution through the parent's diminished vitality. Intrinsic elements of this factor are: the old parent's educational incompetence which may manifest itself as lack of interest in the child, as lack of understanding or lack of patience or as excessive indulgence; and the inability of an old parent to serve as a suitable object for identification and introjection, because he may not give rise to sufficiently strong ambivalence in the child.

Even when the latter chooses the way of compensatory identification with positive or negative substitute figures, these identifications and the thus crystallizing attitudes to the persons and the objective tasks confronting him risk being determined and "impregnated" by the basic experience of "remoteness" (the unreachability and the noncommital character of the parental "legislator"). It is in this way that the parent's old age may become an externalizing factor, particularly in a boy's development, as he depends more than the girl on identification with the father (who, we said, is more likely than the mother to be the old one).

On the other hand, the old father may become an archetypal representative of wisdom, law, and judgment. In this case, too, he remains remote, but it is his very remoteness that stimulates internalization. One of the dangers inherent in such a situation is that the child may grow up to become an adult with impaired autonomy. This danger is particularly evident in the development of a daughter who, through her fixation to the "old man," will later be unable to choose her partner without being determined, unconsciously and irrationally, by the father image.

For both sons and daughters there exists yet another danger in this condition of growing up under the impact of an archetypal representative of wisdom: the danger of becoming prematurely oriented toward the ideals of synthesis. Paradoxically, one could say that where the image of wisdom has been internalized too early (that is, without adequate preparation by the proper exercises in analysis and differentiation), an irrational element is being introduced into the process of intellectual and emotional maturation that, sooner or later, is bound to produce mental handicaps. The result may be deceptive: a seeming depth of thinking and feeling which, on closer scrutiny, will prove to be without foundation. (It should be evident that this behavioral outcome cannot be classified either as neurotic or as externalized or, for that matter, under any other clinical heading, although many forms of deviant behavior may *develop* out of it, according to the individually participating factors of determination, thresholds and structural preferences, traumatizations and cultural patterns.)

AGE DIFFERENCE BETWEEN THE PARENTS

Closely connected with the factor of old age (mostly of the father), is that of the age difference between an old father and a much younger mother. It is the mother's personality that determines the old father's impact on the children's development. The age discrepancy will have a different effect on the child according to the motives that led to the marriage: If the motive was an opportunistic consideration, the very egoism implied in it will frequently be felt in the mother's attitude toward the child as well, and the family atmosphere is likely to be tense or at least ambiguous. If a neurotic or quasi-neurotic fixation to her own (old) father motivated her choice, the mother will not be objective and rational in her attitude toward the child (who, in addition, will then be exposed to the dangers described in the foregoing paragraph).

If the marriage reflects a pattern of her cultural subgroup which is *not* in conformity with the norms prevailing in the general society, the elements of the situation are somewhat complex. To the extent that the cultural patterns of the subgroup are strong enough to represent values capable of competition with those of the dominant culture, it is not the age discrepancy but the total value system of the subgroup that determines the child's development; if, on the other hand, the mother experiences *her* value system as inferior, she is liable to depreciate —consciously and unconsciously—the father's image in the growing child's consciousness and thus prevent him from internalizing the father. In this case a strong orientation toward the "haveable" may take root in the child's personality, the "haveable" being the external goods and values of the dominant group.

But irrespectively of what led to the marriage between a young woman and a much older man, we often observe other undesirable results in the child's development: overstrong dependence of a boy on his mother, unhampered by the (normal) experience of conflict with the father; inability of a girl to identify with her mother, unaccompanied by guilt feelings; weakness of inner value tensions; demonstration of impersonal attitudes—these are some of the possible behavioral outcomes of the constellation here analyzed. Almost all these reactions are liable to set in motion processes of externalization.

But other basic reactions are not excluded. Wherever the mother succeeds not only in fulfilling her maternal functions in a natural and adequate manner but also in translating, as it were, the "old man's" image into the child's reality and in controlling the processes of internalizing this image, the factor of age discrepancy, far from endangering the normal development of the child, helps to actualize all that is positive in the father's old age.

CHRONIC ILL HEALTH OF PARENTS

Here, again, we should beware of interpreting the defensive escape as a neurosis, or the process of being conditioned into a specific susceptibility as externalization. The factor not only weakens the family's educational capacity and standard of living, but is also liable to create a climate of tensions, made up of fears and anxieties, of unnatural limitations of expression, suspiciousness and guilt feelings. To the extent that the child harbors such feelings, they are as a rule based on unconscious ambivalence and therefore tend to be irrational and uncontrollable. We therefore understand why he may try to escape from his internal and external tension into a "protecting" outside, where persons and objects, reactions and events are unambiguous, or, to put it more correctly, where he is able to *experience* them as unambiguous.

This, however, means that the child tries to avoid his own ego. Such avoidance is likely to lead—by way of induction, as it were—to a general *impersonalization* of relationships and of realities.

Escape from inner and from environmental (*intrapsychic* and *interpsychic*) tensions is an often used defense in other conditions as well; but its behavioral *results* differ according to its specific *causes*. Where it is chosen as a weapon against a parent's ill health, it is the experience of the adult's helplessness and dependence on uncontrollable factors that determines the "escaping" child's feeling and reactions. The experience may upset the child's trust in a reality capable of being determined and modified by personal initiative and effort; where the traumatic experience occurs earlier, this trust may not emerge at all.

His reactive escape into external realities will then be characterized by an ever-present expectation of something unforeseen and by a conscious and unconscious tendency to emphasize the impersonal character of life determinants. These characteristics can be interpreted finalistically, as defense against guilt feeling, and causally, as the gradually emerging result of a frequently experienced type of events: *In order* that he should not have to blame himself for having caused the parent's ill health by his conscious and unconscious aggressiveness, the child tries to eliminate, as it were, the categories of cause and personal responsibility altogether from his conception of the world. *Because* he lives in an atmosphere of helplessness, he becomes more and more susceptible to a certain type of occurrences, which confirm his impersonal life attitude (until he no longer needs defenses).

NEUROTIC DISTURBANCES IN THE PARENTS' PERSONALITY

The impact of parental neuroses on the child's personality development is not identical with that of interparental tensions (see pp. 242 *ff.*), though the latter may be a result of the former. For it is not so much the inevitable tension between parents, one or both of whom may be neurotics, as it is the irrationality of their behavior among themselves, toward the child, and toward life in general that here accounts for the pathogenic effect of the factor. More decisive than the neurotic parent's inability to establish adequate relationships and his ensuing failure as an educator of his children is this irrationality, that is, the unforeseeability, the lack of inner logic and consistency in his reactions.

Neurotic interaction in marriage often has already started with the choice of the mate (21, pp. 57 *ff.*) and is being maintained and reinforced by the satisfaction that each or one of the partners finds unconsciously in the marital bond (21, pp. 65 *ff*.); it invariably affects the child's development. Both parents may use him, may try to live out through him their neurotically distorted and distorting feelings, or one only may "mishandle" him, while the other remains normal enough to protect him, though he cannot prevent making him aware of the irrational basis in the other parent's attitudes.

Mittelman (94a) speaks of the reciprocal neurotic patterns in family relationships, "circular" and "complementary" reactions based on dependence or domination needs of one or both partners, fears and disappointments. He then goes on to describe the varieties of educational incompetence resulting from such neurotic tendencies (which we shall analyze separately)—anxiousness, overprotectiveness, rigidity, inconsistency, overambitiousness, seductiveness, etc. Each of these failures is liable to produce in the child a similar attitude toward his social, emotional, and intellectual tasks. In the end, a neurotic behavior pattern similar to that of the parent(s) may emerge, by way of induction, as it were, rather than as the end result of an individual neurotic development, that is, of a series of attempts to resolve problems of ambivalence, conscious and unconscious aggressiveness, or love, guilt and anxiety through repression and defense. But the interaction process goes on, insofar as the child's induced quasi-neurotic behavior binds the parents together still more closely, satisfies their unconscious needs (for punishment or domination, for anxiety or despair).

Not seldom will we see a child "living out," as it were, the drives and life goals which his parents repress, because they prefer the illusory safety of a neurosis to the dangers of self-recognition. The child will, of course, not be able to recognize the vicarious nature of his behavior; and the more it remains unconscious, the more frequently will his decisions and actions, his feelings and reactions "happen" to him "from without," as it were, and the less will they be anchored in his ego. But the unconscious identification of the child with his parents' unconscious drives and goals is responsible for the specific syndrome that is liable to emerge under such conditions: anxieties, obsessional ideas, and illogical ("stupid") actions along with aggressiveness and waywardness.

By way of summing up we can say that, although the behavior of a child growing up under the impact of a neurotic parent often resembles that of the parent, genuine introjection of the mother's or the father's image does *not* take place, since such introjection presupposes the existence, in the child's mind, of clearly definable, or at least identifiable, parents. The child's behavior may be full of quasi-neurotic traits or may be characterized by rebellious rejection of the parents, their values and their defenses—in any case it will be unstructured since it will lack ego-relatedness.

This does not mean, of course, that such a child may not develop a neurosis of his own, resulting, for instance, from his inability to cope with contradictory feelings and from his repressions. Neither is a development of asocial or antisocial conduct precluded, when structural dispositions and experience favor such development. But in the causal equation of such behavioral outcomes it will not be the parents' neurosis that accounts for the outcome (a serious complication in the clinical analysis of certain cases in which it seems obvious that the parents' neuroses are responsible for their children's disorders, in fact, so much so that the essential differences between the parents' and the children's disturbances are likely to be overlooked).

Here is not the place to discuss the numerous varieties of behavior that may become comprehensible when we consider the—direct or indirect—impact of the parents' neurosis on a boy or on a girl at different stages of their development. The factor obviously has a different causal meaning when the parents' neurosis is present from the start, or when it makes itself felt, suddenly or gradually, in a later phase only. But a detailed discussion of these varieties would require a clinical analysis of individual cases and therefore transcends the scope of our present study.

DISSOCIAL BEHAVIOR OF PARENTS

This factor has three aspects: dishonesty, waywardness, criminality.

In the first group we find such dubious or negative habits as cursing, lying, negligence, and indolence *vis-à-vis* the property of others and particularly of the community or the state, contradiction between the parents' demands and their conduct. The effect such habits and contradictions may have on the development of the child will be all the more harmful, the less the parents are aware of what their behavior means for the child. By imitating their dissocial habits and thus confronting the parents with their own, nonadmitted, dissociality, he antagonizes them and forces them into defense (which may take the form of rejecting the child); by accepting their commands he is liable to become compulsive in order to keep his "dark side" under control.

In the second group we find such symptoms of adult waywardness as drunkenness, sexual promiscuity, moral indolence; in the third, clearly criminal tendencies and actions.

The causal significance of parental dissociality, however, depends not only on the form and intensity of its manifestations but also on the family structure, that is (mainly), on the degree of its cohesion.

When the family remains a more or less unified field of relationships, the child may develop normally, at least in his first years, and the ground may be laid for identification and introjection. Only later, when the child begins to understand the contradiction between his parents' asocial or antisocial behavior and their functions as educators, the normal continuation of his development is interrupted, and his relationships with the parents become problematic. The *stronger* he feels attached to them, the more desperate will be his efforts to "save" their authority through imitating them. In this case a "negative" superego (51) may emerge. The *weaker* his attachments (because of the prevailing cultural or family patterns or because of personal peculiarities), the more likely will there be a tendency in the child to distantiate himself from his parents and to become independent prematurely by using all sorts of—inadequate—compensations. Neurotic development will be almost unavoidable in this case.

As a rule, however, dissocial parents tend to be dissocial towards their children as well (to be indolent, careless, or aggressive towards them), and the family does *not* function as a unified field of relationships. Whatever the constitutional, experiential, and developmental causes of dissociality may be, it includes among its symptoms, almost invariably, a tendency to judge the behavior of others, including that of the own child, by egoistic criteria. The child of dissocial parents cannot rely on them; they may perhaps be ready to accept his imitative behavior, but only until such time as it causes them some kind of inconvenience. Even when they protect him against the law and its representatives, they do it, as a rule, out of hate of society rather than out of love of the child.

In this way, the child very soon comes to see aggressiveness as the norm of behavior, and the generally accepted lack of personal and social relationships as directed against him. The place of introjection is then being taken by external imitation, that of conscience—by a set of opportunistic and instrumentalistic categories of evaluation. "Good" is: to escape the aggressiveness of others; "bad" is: to be defeated by them.

The aggressiveness that is bound to develop under the influence of dissocial parents is easily transferred from the parents to the outside world and back again from the world to the parents. In fact, the parents, too, represent in this case outside realities only. Inner tensions, as are directly or indirectly responsible for the emergence of neurotic traits in a behavioral picture, will be found in only a few exceptional cases; as a rule externalized behavior of the aggressive and—mostly—of the delinquent type is the outcome of a child's development under conditions as described here.

Our discussion would not be complete without mentioning those cases of children of dissocial parents, in whom a strongly developed tendency toward introversion prevents them from imitating their parents and thereby gliding into a similar behavioral pattern. The place of the *hostile* "outside" which provokes aggression is taken, in the introvert's consciousness, by a *threatening* "outside" which provokes anxiety and paralyzes all initiative. Such cases are, however, very rare, as the externalizing factors that operate in the life of children of dissocial parents necessarily weaken, impair, and corrupt introversive tendencies early in the child's development.

Another, even more exceptional, case is that of the ruthlessly aggressive fighter against the "bad" world, who can be destructive for the benefit of an idea, who avoids rejecting his parents by rejecting—like them, though for other reasons—the social reality.

LOW INTELLIGENCE OF PARENTS

This factor, again, does not concern us here as a possible cause of a constitutionally low level of intelligence in the child but only as one of the causes of parental incompetence.

The less developed the child's intelligence, and the more he therefore depends on environmental support and stimulation, the more harmful to his intellectual and emotional development becomes the parents' deficiency. For, feeblemindedness should be defined not only as low functional level but also as structural inability to make adequate use of the limited potentials; unless the environment takes the place of the (defective) integrational function of the ego, low intelligence risks to sink below its congenitally given level.*

For the intellectually normal child of feebleminded parents, their low intelligence has a different causal meaning: To the extent that these parents are unable to give adequate and convincing directives, the child depends for his orientation and adaptation on other adults. But these other adults will not, as a rule, be experienced as partners of relationship and objects of identification, at least not as intensively as parents are normally being experienced. One of the possible results of such a condition is the relative separation of intelligence from other ego functions and its relatively weak influence on the development of interpersonal abilities. While such limitations are by no means indicative of externalization, they do account for the fact that in these cases introjections are more of an intellectual than of a relational relevance. The contradiction between good intelligence and rather poor emotional and relational differentiation that we find not seldom in normal children of backward parents is an outcome of growing up without sufficient parental support.

Where, on the other hand, such support *is* given, at least by an emotionally warm and devoted mother, the developmental outcomes may be quite different. Inner contradictions between intelligence and feeling are in any case *not* typical of the normally intelligent child of a mentally

* See our earlier essays on feeblemindedness (38, 39, 39a). In these essays an attempt is made to analyze the various forms and types of feeblemindedness phenomenologically.

backward but emotionally satisfactory mother. (Which again proves that it is the emotional climate prevailing in a family, more than any other single factor, that determines the child's basic sense of trust, hence, his inner mobility and his individual degree of "normality.")

PRIMITIVITY OF PARENTS

Primitivity has a low level of differentiation in common with mental retardation, though it is a concept indicating a cultural rather than an individual pathology. We shall therefore have to devote a considerable part of a future study, dealing with the cultural varieties of externalization, to the different forms in which primitivity manifests itself. Here, in our discussion of the parental environment, we have in mind one aspect of the problem only: the parents' inability properly to recognize similarity and dissimilarity in seemingly dissimilar or similar situations and phenomena and to interpret to their children the complexity of life accordingly, that is, to help them become differentiated.

This inability may be rooted in a personality deficiency or in cultural disorientation.* Low intelligence, as already mentioned, is the most common of those individual deficiencies that produce primitive modes of functioning. But some of the other abovementioned factors of individual pathology, such as dissocial or neurotic behavior or old age, may have a similar effect secondarily, that is, as the end result of a process of dedifferentiation. Moreover, certain constitutionally or experientially conditioned personality traits, such as egocentricity, rigidity, aggressiveness, can be said to be *rooted* in a structural weakness of differentiation while at the same time *causing* inadequate differentiation in relational and cognitive tasks. Sudden transition from a simple to a complex and ambiguous society (from village to town, from a technically underdeveloped to a technically advanced society) and the conceptual and value disorientation that is liable to follow it, do not allow those processes of differentiation to take place that are indispensable for adequate cultural learning and adjustment. Under such conditions an already existing primitive mentality is liable to become now a pathogenic factor, whereas previously existing abilities to differentiate are liable to be lost.

As educators of their children such parents must fail, whatever the causes of their primitivity may have been. They are unable properly to understand, to evaluate, and to interpret the social and cultural forces that act upon their children, and they are liable to reject these forces affectively, to the extent that they feel they are helpless against them.

How then does the child react who is exposed to the impact of this form of parental inadequacy?

* We are concerned here *not* with the "original" primitivity of illiterate tribes whose patterns of education represent the subject of anthropological research, but with parental primitivity in modern society only.

He may negate his incompetent parents because he has fewer problems—so he believes—with his environment. Often enough, however, the reality which he understands and to which he is able to adjust himself is identical with some of its external aspects only, and he fails no less than his parents in reaching the "essentials"; but the feeling of superiority remains. The result is externality of behavior and thinking, reality being identical with its surface appearance behind which no meaning hides. Where he fails, something or someone in the external reality is to blame (including the negated parents). It is as if the child went on an excursion into a strange world; whenever he returns home he finds he has nothing in common with his primitive parents; the home has ceased to be a focus of relationship, the parents have ceased to be objects of introjection—though not of blame for his own failures. Thus, he remains "outside," between two worlds, and he does not belong either here or there.

The very externality of behavior and thinking that is characteristic of the child's reactions and development in this case may be accompanied by guilt feelings, where he is already tied to his parents in bonds of ambivalence, before he becomes aware of their primitivity and incompetence. Whether these guilt feelings will then express themselves in depression or in aggression depends on personality factors beyond those here under discussion.

But the parents' primitivity may also be passed on, as it were, to the next generation, without provoking protest, tension, or ambivalence and without the child making any serious attempts to come to terms with the complexity of the more differentiated environment. He remains anchored in his home, and the world maintains its character of absolute strangeness and outside-otherness.*

PARENTS' ATTITUDES TOWARD SOCIAL CONDITIONS

In the third and fourth sections of Chapter 9 we have tried to analyze, partly at least, the meanings of those factors known as social conditions. It had been our intention there to differentiate between the ways in which social conditions determine the child's development, further or hinder internalization or externalization according to the parents' reactions to the objective conditions of their life. It is true, the personality factors underlying, on the one hand, reactions of despair or hate, resignation or fear, egocentricity or apathy, tension or avoidance, and, on the other hand, reactions of constructive ego transcendence, undoubtedly determine the child's growth quite independently of the social conditions which may have elicited those reactions; but the parents' condition nowhere becomes more clearly evident as an *environmental* factor than here, that is, in connection with the social determinants of their personality. As far as the child is con-

* We shall come back to discussing these conditions in a subsequent book.

cerned, we should always ask to what extent the parents' reactions to the social conditions of their existence make them lose their identity in his eyes (for instance, when they give in to the forces of want or disappear, as it were in the fog of impersonal attitudes) or, on the contrary, make the child see their image imprinted on every part of his reality.

3. Parental Competence and Incompetence

The parents' attitude toward the child and toward themselves as his educators is an inseparable element of every environmental factor. Although it would be wrong to isolate this element and thus turn it into a factor of exclusive determination, we should never lose sight of the fact that, at least in a society in which the process of socialization takes place primarily through the medium of the family, it is the parents' attitude toward the child that determines the causal meaning of every other environmental factor and even of most structural conditions.

When we speak of normal development, and of normal transition from phase to phase, we imply that the parents fulfill their educational functions more or less adequately and objectively, that is, in accordance with the child's individual needs, and that they are not determined excessively or even exclusively by their own unconscious complexes or the patterns of their culture. True enough, the very concept of "normal" stages of development is an ideal type construct, which is represented in reality by degrees of normality only; and no parent will ever be able to relate to his child adequately in every respect and at every moment, since the distorting influences of his inner and outer non-ego on his relations can never be eliminated entirely (nor can the determinations of the child's needs and reactions through structural factors ever be calculated exactly by his parents). But the degree of normality in a child's development can nevertheless be said to depend on the extent to which, and on the manner in which, the parents are capable of transcending their own irrationality and of regulating their reactions realistically and naturally.

What we have said in Chapter 6 concerning the laws of causal configuration (that the determining influence of every partial factor depends not only on all the other partial factors with which it is configurated in the individual case but also on its specific causal antecedents and effects) can be demonstrated much more convincingly through cases of failure and deviation than through cases of normal development and behavior, and for quite obvious reasons: Normality implies ego transcendence, and ego transcendence means man's self-liberation from his own causal antecedents. It is therefore a form of human behavior whose effects depend much less on the specific way in which the individual has achieved it.*

---

* Although these effects are certainly codetermined by the object to which the ego-transcending individual relates himself—in our case the child to whom his adequately functioning parents are related.

Hence, an analysis of *normal* behavior that may result from adequate parental attitudes (provided, of course, no extreme constitutional or environmental deficiencies operate in the child's life) is much less illuminating for a differential understanding of environmental factors than a study of deviations, which cannot be understood adequately unless we analyze the causal configurations that are responsible for their emergence, both "horizontally" and "vertically," that is, both from the point of view of the child's and of the parents' life space and life history.

On the following pages, an attempt will be made to show in what way the main parental deficiencies—open rejection, overseverity, overprotectiveness, sexual overstimulation, inconsistency, overindulgence, indolence, and apathy—act differently on the child's development according to the various factors of parental personality and culture of which each of these deficiencies may be symptomatic in each individual case (factors that we have discussed in the foregoing section, dealing with the parental environment). This analysis will serve not only as an introduction to individual pathology, whose varieties will be dealt with in a later volume, or as an exemplification of the configurational approach to the problems of "cause" (see Chapter 6), but will also show what elements and what dangers of deficiency and deviation are present in even the most normal parental behavior.

REJECTION

When a child does not correspond to his *parents' expectations* of sex, temperament, intelligence, or behavior, and the parents are unable to free themselves of their rigid dependence on preconceived ideas and expectations, open rejection may result. The parents will, of course, be able to point out many "objective" facts (in the child's misbehavior or failures) that seem to justify the rejection. What they do *not* see is the fact that their lack of love and the very rigidity of dependence on their own expectations *force* the child into a reactive behavior (either of aggressiveness or of apathy) which then justifies their disappointment, confirms their ego position, and thus satisfies them.

Dependence on preconceived ideas and expectations in itself indicates lack of conscious control over feelings, that is, dominance of autonomous unconscious complexes. Such dominance may also produce a general readiness to *project* unlived parts of the own ego onto the environment, including the child. The parents may then reject him, because he represents an undesirable part of their own personality or of a rejected partner. This *projection* type of rejection is liable to produce different reactions in the child than the *expectation* type, because it is usually even more unconscious than the former and therefore may arouse anxieties in the rejected child, in addition to, or in the place of, other reactions.

Again different will be the child's behavior when the parent's rejective attitude serves as a kind of reaction formation to strong *unconscious sex desires.* There is a double threat implied in this condition: the child may not only suffer as the result of the parent's affectively negative attitude toward him, he may also feel the underlying desire which will be all the more frightening, the less the parent is aware of it. (Open, uninhibited sexual overstimulation by an oversexed parent has as we shall see later, a different effect on the child.)

Where parental rejection is the result of unconcealed *egoism*, it means for the child threat of annihilation, from which he may escape into psychopathic ego inflation or into autistic withdrawal from reality; that is, in any case, into some form of interruption of feeling-communication with the environment.

Where it results from an all-pervading sense of disappointment, helplessness in the face of a hostile, frustrating reality, and a *depressive attitude* toward life in general, the child (who is then being rejected as part of the rejected world, almost impersonally) is likely to be "infected" by his parents' attitude, and the experience of being rejected becomes a reinforcing factor in the development of his depressive reactions rather than a direct cause of aggressive reactions.

General *lack of affect control, sadistic impulses or tendencies, certain somatic conditions of tension and excitability*, are some of the remaining causes of parental rejection. Without going into details, it is obvious again that in each case the behavioral reaction of the child is likely to be different.

Another question arises out of the anthropological studies of educational patterns: Where rejection of the child—often of the daughter more than of the son, sometimes of the child *qua* child—*is part of a culture*, the resulting process of character formation will be relatively independent of individual factors such as the parents' personality (cultural patterns being in such cases an overriding cause). But when such a family migrates, and both the parents and the child are being exposed to *different* educational practices, the pattern of rejection becomes problematic and, as a result, the child will no longer—automatically, as it were—develop the expected character structure of his cultural group. The result will then be tension and counter-rejection of the parents, whom the child will now experience as aggressive individuals.

Perhaps with the exception of the last-mentioned form of rejection, this manifestation of parental incompetence does *not* seem to be conducive to externalization in the development of the child. There is too much of the parents' personal problems involved in a true rejection pattern; hence, the child experiences the rejecting parents "as persons" and remains, consciously or unconsciously, related to them to an extent that precludes externalization.

This, however, does not mean that in all the other cases here discussed (in which rejection of a child by his parents or by one of them results from disappointment or projection, from unconscious desires or pervert tendencies, from egoism or depressiveness, from organic overexcitability or from any other factor in their personality) the child will be likely to display reactions of aggressiveness, or of apathetic withdrawal, or of neurotic defenses. His development may be, or at least may appear to be, quite normal, and not only under the impact of strong compensatory and integrational forces that may operate in *his* personality, but also because the parents' rejectiveness may be compensated, at least partly, by *their own* endeavors to control or to change their attitude, to come to terms with it, to protect the child against them (that is, to transcend the boundaries of their ego). Besides that, we should never lose sight of the ambiguity of the child's position between his two parents and of the resulting ambivalence feelings and identification processes. It would therefore be hopeless to look for correlations between parental rejectiveness as an isolated factor and the child's behavior.

OVERSEVERITY

Overseverity is not identical with rejection, although many of the factors that are responsible for rejection can be found as causal antecedents of overseverity as well. It is essentially different, insofar as it implies much more intentionality and directedness to the child. The oversevere parent "means" the child, the rejecting parent "means" himself (at least as long as he is not aware of the meaning of his attitudes and does not try to cope with it).

Overseverity may be a method of preventing the child from developing character traits and weaknesses similar to those of a negative image, a relative, a husband or wife, even a fictional figure, but also similar to those of the parent himself. While these are conscious reasons for the educational practice, it will not be too difficult to discover behind them an unconscious tendency to *project* own weaknesses onto the child. The usually irrational fear, lest the child may come to resemble some negative image, is in itself an indication and a proof of the fact that unconscious factors participate in the crystallization of overseverity.

The same applies to those cases in which the attitude is based on *principles*, whose character-neurotic roots are often quite evident (even, or better: particularly, when they form parts of a rigid system and of a *Weltanschauung* which may seem unassailable objectively).

In these cases a child, while conforming to his oversevere parents' demands, may lose his identity and develop the same character neurosis that is at the root of the parents' educational philosophy, or he may, reactively and aggressively, develop precisely those character traits that the parents wanted to suppress in him (and repress in themselves).

Where the attitude is rooted in *cultural patterns*, the resulting character structure will invariably show clear indications of compulsiveness. These compulsive character traits, however, will cause serious adjustment problems only when the individual is exposed to a different culture with different ideals, expectations, and educational practices and attitudes.

Again, we find externalization as a result of overseverity only in the last case, where it may lead the child to escaping from the unpleasant atmosphere of his parental environment into the unstructured and incomprehensible world at large. In the other cases, overseverity may have a neuroticizing effect on the child's personality and will not in any way allow him naively to respond to the conditioning influence of external stimulation; but it may also leave the personality intact, particularly where and to the extent that the overseverity has become part of the parents' rationality and remains controllable.

OVERPROTECTION

A third form of parental aggressiveness is overprotection. Most studies refer only to *maternal* overprotection of the *son* (89). The fact that the daughter is only in exceptional cases the object and victim of the mother's overprotection can be explained in two—complementary, not alternative —ways: as an outcome of individual pathological conditions and as a reflection on our culture.

Psychoanalysis has elaborated the first aspect only: A woman's unsolved oedipal conflicts not only may determine her irrational choice of a husband and thus cause her emotional and sexual dissatisfaction, but may also decisively influence her attitude toward her children in general and toward her son in particular. Her *unconscious aggressiveness against the frustrating males* in her life may turn the son into a representative figure. The defense mechanism raised against her dangerous destructive tendencies is overprotection. The son must be protected against all kinds of dangers, says her consciousness; he must be prevented from growing into an independent male, says her unconscious mind. And she succeeds in "killing" his masculinity by overprotection.

In another case, she *projects her own infantility* onto her children, and by overprotecting them maintains the illusion of being a competent grownup person. But as infantility in women is again rooted in unresolved oedipal conflicts, it will be once more the son rather than the daughter who is liable to fall victim to her projective overprotection.

To the extent that unconscious *incest wishes* determine her attitude, it is obviously the son who "needs" overprotection and thus is turned into his mother's lover (to follow Lawrence's argument (89)).

But in order to understand the relative frequency of overprotection in our time, we should ask: What *cultural* factors are at work today to cause so many women to be dissatisfied with their male partners? It would seem that it is first and foremost man's inability to maintain his autonomy in the face of omnipotent technical and political forces (of his own making) that explain why her disappointment in the way man "lives" his structural role, and why her aggressive reaction (which is being repressed for the sake of her biological needs) occur today more frequently than in other times.

We shall discuss, in another book, this cultural situation as one of the varieties of externalization. Here, it may suffice to point out the possible differences in the reactions of children to the *causes* of their mothers' tendency to overprotect them: Effemination, overdependence and infantility, sexual deviations and inefficiency are the most important of these reactions. None of them is conducive to the development of externalized behavior (the "haveable" can never be primarily material and external as long as the *mother* is "haveable"!).

To the extent that the *father* is overprotecting, an analysis of his personality will show that in many cases incestuous wishes or homosexual tendencies are at work to determine his behavior (either unconsciously or half-consciously), while in some cases projection of unresolved childhood conflicts and fears produces his overprotectiveness.

SEXUAL OVERSTIMULATION

Sexual overstimulation, of a boy by his mother, of a daughter by her father, and of either one of them by the total environment, may accompany overprotection as a by-product or as a means of *intensifying the child's dependence;* but it may also be a direct expression of *sexual tension or dissatisfaction* in the parent or of thoughtlessness and *negligence.*

And again, we understand that the child's behavioral reaction will differ according to what causes the parents to overstimulate their children sexually. The less they are aware of the meaning and the implications of their doings, but indulge in the illusion that they love their child, the stronger will be the anxiety that is liable to be aroused in him, since he may feel threatened by the ambiguity of relationships which characterize in this case the family atmosphere. The more directly and egotistically the sexual motives of the parent are being expressed and experienced, the greater will be the danger either of precocious sexualization or of fear and unhappiness. Apart from constitutional peculiarities and the child's primary relationships with the mother, it is particularly the time factor that determines the differential outcome.

Externalization is more likely to be found in the development of *girls* that are being overstimulated either directly (by seduction) or indirectly (by too much physical care), and particularly by living in an oversexed environment. The girl may become addicted to sexual tension and pleasure which she will seek outside her family in protest against a father who may have used her in a brutally instrumental manner. She may escape in panic into an "outside" area in which she will find herself unsupported, drifting from occurrence to occurrence, with all sorts of material values becoming substitute sources of satisfaction.

A sexually overstimulated *boy*, on the other hand, is much more likely to become a sexual pervert than a wayward delinquent with his typical externality of behavior, irrespectively of whether he was a victim of, or a passive witness to, sexual promiscuity or brutality in his home and neighborhood.

The limit between acceptable and traumatic manifestations of parental attitudes cannot, it is true, be determined objectively with regard to *any* of the so far mentioned and still to be discussed peculiarities: What is too much (strictness or leniency, protection or indolence) for one child, may be quite within the limits of the "tolerable" for another. But it is particularly difficult to define as objectively measurable the factor of sexual stimulation. The child's susceptibility of sexual stimuli depends on so many somatic dispositions, cultural patterns, family relationships, and psychodynamics of individual development that we need not be surprised when we see the most different outcomes of seemingly similar or even equally intensive experiences.

INCONSISTENCY

When *egoistic thoughtlessness* makes parents inconsistent in their educational attitudes and actions, the child's reactive behavior will be different from what it is likely to be in case the parents' inconsistency reflects the *deep insecurity of a conflict-ridden ego*. Again different will be the effect on the child's development when general *indolence* or loss of orientation in a process of *culture change* or *mental retardation* are at the root of this manifestation of parental incompetence.

Thus, the child may feel not only isolated and left to himself in the ambience of self-centered parents but also free to exploit their lack of consistency when this is the specific manifestation of their *egocentricity*. The same lack of consistency, however, when betraying *insecurity* and deep-lying conflicts, may produce in the child bewilderment, anxiety, and inability to establish genuine interpersonal relationships. In the end, we may find in both cases relational inability; but while it indicates in the first case a tendency in the child to exploit to his own advantage any environmental weakness—in response, as it were, to the parents' egoistic thoughtlessness—it indicates in the second case inner tensions, in response to the parents' insecurity. It is obvious that only in the first case the experience of the parents as "absent" may set in motion processes of externalization and turn the mind toward the "haveable" to compensate for human relationships that are not available.

Where the parents' inconsistency is an outcome of loss of orientation in culture change or is an outcome of their mental retardation, what we have previously said about these two factors (see pp. 194 *ff*. and 255 *f*.) applies; where inconsistency is an epiphenomenon of indolence, it is again the latter factor which is responsible for the child's reactions and development (see p. 266).

OVERLENIENCY

Some parents are overindulgent and spoil a child when they feel *guilty* over some real or imaginary omission, or when they are *afraid* of some real or imaginary threat to the child's health and welfare; others are overlenient because they are *too weak* physically or mentally to resist the child's demands, and again others because the *patterns* of their culture demand of them extreme leniency, either in general, toward the child *qua* child, or under specific conditions only, for instance, of age or sex.

While *guilt and fear* indicate, *prima facie*, concern with the child's needs, it is the very irrationality and uncontrollability of these feelings that prove the participation of other, unconscious, motives and forces. When we analyze these elements we often find that the parents are, consciously and unconsciously, concerned much more with their own problems than with the child's needs which they distort by way of projecting their own complexes onto him. The child, then, feels that he is not really "meant" by his parents when they give in to each of his demands (which often may only serve to cover his real needs for unambiguous direction and limitation).

While in this case character-neurotic (under certain conditions of structure, psychopathic) developments are the outcome, exploitation of a parent's *physical or mental weakness* is likely to produce not only egocentricity but also delinquent behavior, when the child comes to experience the difference between his home and the wider environment and the pattern of exploitation has already taken root in his personality. *Culture-conditioned* overleniency, on the other hand, produces either the "average-expected" type of behavior and reaction that characterizes the specific cultural group of subgroup, or, in a change situation, causes again one of those conflicts that are found whenever an individual is exposed to the experience of norm contradictions. (In this specific case it is the fixation to the conveniently indulgent parents and the ensuing inability and unwillingness to participate in any other, more exacting and less protective, social context which explains maladjustment, unhappiness, "avoidance" or protest reactions that characterize many of such children.)

It may be of interest to compare the effects of parental inconsistency with those of overleniency. Both may be exploited by the child, and both may provoke relational inability in the child. But there exists an essential difference between the two forms of exploitation, on the one hand, and between the two forms of relational inability, on the other.

When the exploitation pattern is based on an early experience of the parents as self-contradictory (in case of egocentric inconsistency), we are likely to find in it a strong element of reality orientation. High intelligence will then help the child adapt himself to contradictory situations without being hindered by feelings of identity, while low intelligence will turn the reality orientation into an additional source of constant failure.

When the exploitation pattern is based on an early experience of parental impotence (in the case of leniency out of weakness), the child is liable to overlook the objective facts and data of his reality so that he is bound to fail, irrespectively of the degree of his intelligence.

When relational inability is the result of experiencing not only the (insecure and therefore inconsistent) parents but also the world as such, the material and social non-ego, as ambiguous (and thus *causing* the parental insecurity!), it means that the child did not learn the law of mutuality and polarity, because his environment did not offer him sufficient opportunity for identification or for recognition of regularity, rule, and law.

When, on the other hand, relational inability results from prematurely experiencing weak and *therefore* overlenient parents as being determined by unconscious, irrational, and uncontrollable forces which paralyze and eliminate their activity and willpower, the developmental defect will be of a more irrational, neurotic or quasi-neurotic character.

INDOLENCE AND APATHY

This factor, although present in some of the others as well, differs from them essentially insofar as its main manifestation—neglect—is not accompanied by any form of personal emphasis. This, however, means that the child of indolent parents grows up in an atmosphere of utter *impersonality*. Indolence may be the result of physical or mental weakness, of constitutional apathy, of natural or cultural conditions, of psychotic withdrawal, or of conditions of poverty. In the last-mentioned case it is one of the factors that account for the externalizing effect of poverty.*

There is no need to emphasize again that the causal meaning of parental indolence in the development of the child depends not only on the latter's constitutional dispositions and environmental and cultural conditions and experiences, but also—as in all other here discussed manifestations of parental failure—on its roots in the parents' personality. This is particularly evident when we compare the development of a child who grows up in the ambience of a psychotic mother, whose withdrawal from reality expresses itself also in her complete lack of interest in her child, with the development of a child growing up under the externalizing conditions of poverty and educational neglect.

* To be analyzed in a future book.

11

Environment and Development: Summary

We now come back to the questions raised above (see p. 83): How is the causal effect of environmental factors determined by the developmental phase in which a child or an adult may be exposed to their impact? And how can the essentials of a certain phase of development be distorted by the impact of certain environmental factors?

Both questions obviously have different meanings when we consider *a traumatic event*, an "act of fate" (104) such as the death of a parent, divorce, appearance of a step-parent, placement of a child in an institution, etc., or *a parental quality or attitude* such as old age of the father, age differences between the parents, low intelligence of one or both of them, their educational incompetence, etc., or a general *life condition* such as cultural patterns, culture clash, social and educational defects, etc. Some factors may make themselves felt in the life of the child from a certain phase on only, irrespectively of whether they had been *potentially present before or not* (*e.g.*, neurotic disorders or ill health in the parents); others become causally relevant only *when life conditions change* (*e.g.*, primitivity after transition to a more differentiated culture).

It is self-evident that the first of our two questions (about the influence of the developmental phase on the specific effect of a certain factor) refers to traumatic events or to change situations, whereas our second question (about the distortion of the phase essentials through the influence of a certain factor) refers to parental qualities and attitudes or to cultural patterns, that is, to factors that are responsible for the educational climate in which a child grows up. Some factors belong to both groups: Neurotic or dissocial disorders in the parents' personality, ill health, tension, and certain inadequate attitudes may make themselves felt in the child's life from the "start" (in which case they act as patternizing factors), but they may also emerge, more or less suddenly, at a later stage of the child's development (in which case they have the meaning of traumatizing factors).

1. ACTS OF FATE

The causal effect of every "act of fate" depends, as we have emphasized several times, on the age of the affected child. Thus, *a father's death* may re-

main without immediate consequences for a small child (although indirectly, that is, through the mother's reactive loss of spontaneity, the infant, too, will be exposed to the ill effects of the father's death). But when
the child, boy and girl alike, begins to discover the "parents as a couple"
(101), the father's sudden disappearance may be experienced as a traumatic,
anxiety- and guilt-provoking event and may set in motion processes of
defense or despair. Later, the learning child needs the father's image (even
more than his actual guidance) as a protection against regressive tendencies
and as an incentive to experiment with "remoteness," this precondition of
abstraction; his death is then liable to jeopardize the development of abstractive abilities. The adolescent's reaction to the father's death is again
different: the unpredictability and the coexistence of contradictory reactions, lifeless intellectualizations together with abandonment of identity,
and both without genuine involvement—these are frequently found characteristics of adolescent reaction to the father's death, at least in a Western
middle-class family. (It goes without saying the personality variables must
be kept constant in order to make any statement about the differential
influence of developmental phases meaningful. Our short remarks in this
chapter must therefore be understood as a contribution to clinical differentiation rather than as an attempt to construct laws of causal connection.)

The mother's death is known to set in motion catastrophic regressions in
every phase of the child's development, at least until the middle of the
learning phase when the ego becomes an agent of synthesis and, according
to Piaget (106), acquires relative autonomy of thinking and of moral judgment. The initiative to manipulate and to explore the environment and
thereby to learn how to anticipate the future depends on the experience
of maternal regularity and reliability and may therefore be damaged seriously, if not irreparably, when the infant loses his mother and a fully adequate and acceptable substitute is not made available immediately.

Ambivalence, this most important achievement of the second phase, "is
rooted in the child's experience that the good adult is bad, the beloved
one, hateful; that the object of his own aggressiveness, of his own badness,
is identical with the object of his own love" (pp. 153 *ff.*). The mother's sudden and final disappearance during this second phase, therefore, is liable
to leave the child without a basis for being good and bad at one and the
same time, and thus to make him develop into a rigid, nonadjustable "all-
or-nothing" personality, repressive or aggressive, overstatic or overexpan-
sive. Communication difficulties that often appear in a thus traumatized
child are not only due to regressions or to lack of adequate stimulation
through the environment but are also rooted in that inner weakness of
differentiation that results from defective ambivalence.

In the so-called oedipal phase, the mother's death is liable not only to
aggravate anxieties and guilt feelings—as emphasized in every psycho-

analytically oriented textbook on emotional disorders in childhood (see, for instance, 27, 104)—but also to deprive the father of his structural function, that of supporting the child's ability to differentiate and to internalize (which dynamically depends on ambivalence).

In the learning phase, the quality as well as the intensity of the ill effects produced by the mother's death depend on the child's intelligence more than on any other single factor of determination. The average child needs communication with the family and the feeling of togetherness in the family circle, so we have said (p. 164), to make his now acquired knowledge and skills meaningful for his total life experience (and this in spite of the fact that learning now takes place in less familiar, less personal, more anonymous settings, in the classroom or in the play group). Hence, the mother's death is liable to disturb the learning processes by forcing the child prematurely into a *paternal* world of impersonal objectivity, which he may use as a defense against anxieties. Only when the child is of high intelligence will this impersonality of learning *per se* be a source of satisfaction and a means of compensation, not a defense against fear.

The reaction of middle-class adolescents to the mother's death may be very similar in essence to their reaction to the father's death (always bearing in mind the differential factors of sex and personality). In their "life with principles" death is likely to lose its personal meaning.

We have already mentioned the age factor in our discussion of other traumatic acts of fate such as *desertion, divorce, step-parents* and *removal of the child from his family* (see pp. 239 ff.). By way of summing up what we have said there or, better, of finding a common denominator for the various age modifications of the different factors we could say:

Whereas each environmental factor has its specific causal significance (which we can describe in general terms), it is the structurally given and definable sequence of phasal achievements that determines the differential impact of each of these factors on the child's development. Any traumatization following a disturbance of the "normal" family unit must be evaluated against the background of these achievements. The more the child advances toward autonomy, the more rational and controllable are his reactions to acts of fate likely to be. The stronger his dependence on non-ego forces (within and without), the more disruptive will these reactions be.*

This is only another way of saying that early traumatization through disruptive environmental factors is liable to produce irreversible structure changes which then influence the whole life course, whereas the same in-

---

* We should not forget that we have so far not included in our discussion traumatic changes in the child's organism due to illness, devitalization, accidents, sensory limitations, etc., or neurotic developments due to a variety of environmental factors. All these will be analyzed in a later book.

juries when occurring in a later phase only, that is, after a more or less normal start, do not affect the ego's power of compensation and integration. A child who has experienced maternal regularity and who has learned the secrets of intentionality, anticipation, ambivalence, and mutuality, will never be affected by later anxieties and disappointments through separation experiences as radically as a child who finds himself exposed to them unprepared by earlier normality.

With these remarks we have already touched on the second of our two questions: how the phase essentials are likely to be distorted by certain parental qualities or attitudes, by cultural patterns or other factors responsible for the creation of a negative educational climate.

2. NEGATIVE CONDITIONS OF GROWTH

We have mentioned the father's old age, a large age difference between the parents, low intelligence of the parents, their educational incompetence (whatever its causes may have been)—but also illegitimacy—as factors conducive to the emergence of negative growth conditions. Other factors, such as parental dissociality, neurosis, ill health, or tension—but also frequent and prolonged absence of the father and primitivity in transition from one culture to another—may belong to either one of our two categories.

When discussing the factors of *the father's old age* and *age discrepancy between the parents* (pp. 248 *ff.*), we have emphasized in particular the difficulties a child may encounter in his endeavors to identify with, to introject, ideal images: Under such conditions all objects of identification are liable to remain too "remote" to arouse total involvement; as a result, the child will grow up to become an adult whose intellectual and moral vigor may be rather weak and who may show signs of rigidity and lack of spontaneity in his emotions and relationships with objects and with persons (even though he may be of high intelligence and of moral integrity).

This, however, relates to what is likely to happen to such a child in the so-called post-oedipal phases only, in those years when identifications become the source of learning and character development. Even when we mentioned the old father's inability to serve as a suitable object of identification, "because he may not give rise to sufficiently strong ambivalence in the child" (p. 248), we did not refer to that second phase of development, of which ambivalence is a structural element, but rather to the oedipal conflict area. It would therefore seem legitimate to ask here, how the *earliest* development of the child is liable to be affected by the father's old age.

In the second half of the first year, when normally the father acquires meaning for the infant to the extent that he enters into the orbit of his slowly expanding consciousness as part of a familiar environment, an *old* father may remain irrelevant. As a result, the child will experience the alternation of nearness and remoteness as an element of his *maternal* universe only. This partiality, and not the weakness of the oedipal conflict, lies at the root of his inadequate experience of ambivalence and, consequently, may also result in relational weakness. Though he may learn, in the second phase of development, everything a child normally learns— mutuality, relative autonomy, aggressive self-assertion—he will do so through his relationship with the mother only, hence will not be properly prepared for active differentiation in the third phase. The child is liable to suffer from an "overdose" of maternal unity feelings, as it were.

(It is certainly not necessary to add that this is not the only possible development. We refer the reader to what we have said above (pp. 249 *ff.*) about the archetypal significance of the "old man.")

When discussing the influence of *the parents' low intelligence* on a normal child's development we have mentioned the relative disconnection between his (normal) intelligence and his (weak) ability to establish meaningful relationships, that is, his relative inability to learn from the latter, as one of the typical handicaps of such a child (unless an emotionally warm family climate compensates for lack of guidance). It is particularly the learning phase which is liable to be distorted by parental insufficiency based on their mental retardedness, since the child is then forced to learn from "strangers" only and without parental confirmation. Moreover, the preceding period often shows much less tension than we find ordinarily in a child of intellectually normal parents, and this, in turn, because there is less intensive involvement with the parents, less ambivalence, less danger of regression, hence also less need for defenses. Thus, impersonality of learning and relative paucity of emotional bonds characterize this child in his later phases of development as well (*cf.* our discussion dealing with the father's death, pp. 237 *ff.*).

All forms of *parental incompetence*, though they may be antithetical in their manifestations, have one element in common: they do not allow the child to develop a genuine sense of security and independence. Other phase-essential achievements may be more or less normal,* in spite of the parents' consistent failure; but the basic insecurity and heteronomous dependence on the outer or the inner non-ego are bound to make themselves felt as distorting factors in every phase of the individual's development. This is the reason why we so often find similar pathological conditions resulting from the most different forms of parental inadequacy, and why it is possible to discover common traits in the most different behavior entities, of the aggressive or of the neurotic variety, of the ex-

---

* See, however, in Section 3, Chapter 10, our remarks on the specific deviations that may result from the experience of a specific faulty attitude in the parents (aggressiveness or leniency, overprotection or indolence, inconsistency or sexual overstimulation, etc.).

ternalization type or the delinquency type (see Chapter 7). When the parents fail to enable the child to synthesize the contradictory experiences of presence and absence into that of nearness, he will be unable to proceed from nearness to ambivalence. These basic limitations, however, will reflect themselves in his later processes of differentiation and learning, irrespectively of how the parents (one or both of them, jointly or in different directions) "mishandle" the growing child in the various phases of his development. In other words: the impact of parental incompetence on *later* phases of development is determined by the basic deficiencies which have been produced by that incompetence at the beginning of his life, provided they are not eliminated or compensated by subsequent improvements in the parents' attitudes and in the educational climate in which the child grows up.

This, however, does not mean that the causal connection between a specific parental deficiency and the child's reaction to it in a certain phase of his development is negligible. The distortion of the essentials of this (and any other) phase is not adequately accounted for by reduction to the primary deviation from the norm at the beginning of life.

Let us mention one factor only of the many that could and should be mentioned here, *inconsistency*. It not only produces those patterns of insecurity and heteronomy that will make themselves felt in every phase of development and in every task area, but it also affects very specifically such phasal achievements as ambivalence or differentiation or synthesis or abstraction or adolescent illusions of staticness and finality. Under the impact of parental inconsistency we find the following distortions of "phasal achievements":

Instead of ambivalent *coexistence* of contradictory feelings there is vacillation from one feeling modality to another without interrelatedness or integration, in imitation, as it were, of the experience of parental unreliability and changeability.

Instead of dissolution of units (including the parental unit) into their components (father and mother as individual partners of personal relationship, for instance), there is undifferentiated relatedness to chance manifestations of these—undefined—units.

Instead of synthesis in cognitive task areas, there is a conception of life being regulated by different and often mutually exclusive "laws" which do not form part of an all-comprising system.

Instead of abstraction, there is a tendency to relate to the universe of changing phenomena rather than to generalizations and concepts (although highly intelligent individuals will, here as in any other task area, overcome this—modifiable—limitation).

Instead of the adolescent's illusions resulting from his "life with principles," there is elevating instability of phenomena to the level of a "pseudo-principle"; denial of finality and staticness, since there is no logical necessity for things to be as they appear to be.

We could, of course, go on and show how every phase and every subphase bears the stamp of inconsistency; or how every other negative pattern of parental attitudes produces specific deviations from the norm in every phase of the individual's development. This, however, would mean writing a treatise about clinical phenomena on a level of abstract constructions only. We prefer to confine ourselves here to these few remarks which should serve as illustration of a principle rather than as a substitute for clinical analyses.

The same applies to *illegitimacy* and its impact on the various phases in the development of a boy or a girl. We have defined the conditions under which illegitimacy can be considered a definable causal factor (pp. 232 *ff*.). We excluded from our definition the child born out of wedlock who is placed out in an institution or with a family and therefore is not exposed to the impact of maternal tensions that characterize illegitimacy. These tensions, and not not only the anonymity and the unknownness of the father, account in the second and third phases for the often considerable delay in the development of differentiation and for a corresponding avoidance of rational exploration. The third phase in particular is characterized by an ever-increasing fear of the unknown, together with an almost compulsive tendency to generalize unknownness, as it were. Needless to add, the learning process is bound to suffer where the ego invests so much of its energies in an unconscious quest for the father.

On the other hand, it is extremely difficult to inquire into the essence of this factor, since most children born out of wedlock are being raised either by adoptive parents or in an institution or with their extended family (particularly where illegitimacy is not an unusual occurrence, such as in certain Catholic rural communities in South America), whereby other causal factors become much more decisive than illegitimacy.

3. TRAUMA OR PATTERN

We are now going to discuss briefly a number of factors which, we have said, may belong to either one of the two groups, acts of fate or negative conditions of growth. Dissocial or neurotic behavior of the parents, their chronic ill health, or tension between the father and the mother may be present when the child is born, so that he is forced to grow up under the impact of these pathological conditions; but they may also appear in a certain phase of his development only, as the result of some critical events in the parents' life, and then act as traumatizing factors on the further development of the child. The same applies to prolonged absence of the father or to cultural transition, particularly from an undifferentiated to a more differentiated environment.

Thus, a *parent's criminality* may fundamentally change the oedipal guilt-anxiety ratio in the child if—for instance—the father's antisocial behavior makes its first appearance when the child passes through the oedipal stage. It will lead to the emergence of negative identifications in that same phase of development if it forms part of the general family climate in which the child grows up. In adolescence, sudden confrontation with criminal acts committed by a parent may provoke irrealistic escape into oversevere moralism or equally irrealistic identifications, whereas a child brought up in an atmosphere of criminality until he has reached adolescence is likely to have been conditioned into a similar behavior.

It goes without saying that, even when comparing equally intelligent children, a father's or a mother's dishonesty, associality, or antisociality modifies the phases of development of a boy or of a girl in different ways. General dishonesty of a mother, for instance, is liable to harm the intellectual development of her daughter much more than that of her son, particularly in the learning phase. Asocial behavior of a mother makes itself felt as an externalizing factor in the *first* phases of her son's and her daughter's development rather than later (when it may provoke defensive reactions).

A detailed discussion of all possible combinations of factors and of all varieties of resulting behavior disorders would again require a comprehensive clinical analysis of cases and must therefore be excluded. For the same reason it would be impossible fully to discuss the different impacts of the various forces of *neurotic disturbance in the parents' personality,* or of *chronic ill health* in one or both of the parents, on each of the child's developmental phases.

The main difference between the effect on the child's personality of a permanent *tension* climate and a suddenly emerging tension between the parents is again one between conditioning and traumatization (that is, "de-conditioning," as it were). The trust-shattering experience of the two most important objects of relationship and identification being negated by each other brings about disorientation and anxiety which, in turn, are liable to reverse certain phasal achievements. The disintegrating effect of traumatic tension experience depends to no small degree on whether the child is affected by them when passing through a phase of structural consolidation or of expansion. It is particularly in the first case that an experience of interparental tension is liable to set in motion regressions, that is, processes of dedifferentiation and of partial loss of identity.

Thus, the aggressiveness at the end of the second phase, which normally serves to protect the precarious beginnings of autonomy against adult interference, is liable to turn into a vehicle of resentment directed against the parents whose tension and tenseness make them forget their parental functions; as a result, autonomy, which may have begun to emerge, is being replaced by dependence on an undefinable environment (basically a dependence on the inner non-ego, the universe of uncontrollable affects and inner tensions). Synthesis, normally the achievement of the first part of the learning phase, is liable to be replaced—under the impact of suddenly appearing tensions between the parents—by a tendency, often reminiscent of hysterical denials, to disregard and ignore these tensions. Post-adolescent return to the adults' world will be made almost impossible when these adults lose their identifiability, their unambiguity, under the influence of interparental tensions.

As a last example we choose the impact of the *parents' primitivity* in cultural transition on the various phases of the child's development. In another book we shall try to define and analyze the essentials of transition from various forms of primitivity to a modern world. We shall then see that one of the common characteristics of a child's development under conditions of transition is his painful awareness of the fact that his parents encounter greater difficulties in adjusting themselves to the new environment than he, the child, does (or at least believes he does). This in turn, accounts, as we have pointed out (see pp. 256 *ff.*), for the almost unavoidable processes of externalization in the life of these children: Why should they introject a parental image in which personal insecurity and social incompetence are so much in evidence? But not being supported in their adjustment and learning processes by the parents, neither from within nor from without, the children will be incapable of experiencing or of understanding the *meaning* behind the external manifestations of the new culture.

Here, the phase differences will obviously be decisive. When a child is *born* to parents who immigrated from a "primitive" environment and failed to internalize the new culture, he is, from the start, exposed to the ambiguity of an educational situation in which he is confronted with contradictory value directions. The same applies to a child coming to the new culture with his "primitive" parents at an early age (although here other factors, such as the individual cohesiveness of the family and cultural patterns of early child-rearing, will determine, no less than the age factor *per se*, to what extent the little child will already have identified with the "original" values). But the older the child at the time of the family's immigration—in other words, the more advanced the culturally conditioned identification and socialization process had been—the more likely it is that he will reject, or at least feel ambivalent toward, the learning demands of the new society.

In concluding our analysis of "Environment and Development," as it pertains to our study of the "Roots of the Ego," let us remark that we have offered questions rather than answers, hypotheses rather than evidence on which to base empirical research. We are also well aware of the frag-mentary character of these hypotheses. The entire study is but an attempt to define a number of concepts which we consider fruitful when applied to an interpretation of human behavior. We shall try to show some of these applications in subsequent studies on externalization. But the frag-mentary, nonsystematic form of our analysis is an essential characteristic of the configurational approach to etiology and genesis as well as to struc-ture and structurization; for, configuration means—infinity.

References

1. Abraham, K.: *Selected Papers*. London, Hogarth Press, 1928.
2. Adler, A.: *Problems of Neurosis*. New York, Cosmopolitan Book Corporation, 1930.
3. Aichhorn, A.: *Wayward Youth*. London, Putnam & Company, Ltd., 1936.
4. Ainsworth, M. D.: The effects of maternal deprivation. In *Deprivation of Maternal Care—a Re-assessment of Its Effects*. Geneva, World Health Organization, 1962.
5. Alexander, F.: The neurotic character. Int. J. Psychoanal., *11*: 292–313, 1930.
6. Allport, G.: *Personality*. New York, Henry Holt & Company, 1937.
7. Bellwald, J.: *Der Erlebnisraum des Gebirgskindes*. Freiburg (Schweiz), Universitätsverlag Freiburg, 1960.
8. Bender, L.: Psychopathic behaviour disorders in children. In *Handbook of Correctional Psychology*, edited by R. M. Lindner and R. V. Seliger. New York, The Philosophical Library, 1947.
9. Benedict, R.: *Patterns of Culture*. New York, A Mentor Book, 1946.
10. Bettelheim, B.: *Truants from Life*. Glencoe, Ill., The Free Press, 1955.
11. Bovet, L.: *The Psychiatric Aspects of Juvenile Delinquency*. Geneva, World Health Organization, 1950.
12. Bowlby, J.: *Maternal Care and Mental Health*. Geneva, World Health Organization, 1950.
13. Bowlby, J.: *Forty-Four Juvenile Thieves*. London, Bailliére, Tindall & Cox, 1947.
14. Bühler, C.: *Kindheit und Jugend*. Leipzig, S. Hirzel, 1928.
15. Burlingham, D., and Freud, A.: *Infants without Families*. New York, International Universities Press, 1944.
16. Cannon, W.: *The Wisdom of the Body*. New York, W. W. Norton & Company, 1932.
17. Davis, A.: American status system and the socialization of the child. American Sociological Review, *6*: 345–354, 1941.
18. Davis, A., Gardner, B. B., and Gardner, M. R.: *Deep South*. Chicago, University of Chicago Press, 1941.
19. Despert, L.: *Children of Divorce*. New York, Doubleday & Company, Inc., 1962.
20. Drever, J.: *A Dictionary of Psychology*. Baltimore, Penguin Books, 1955.
21. Eisenstadt, V. (ed.): *Neurotic Interaction in Marriage*. New York, Basic Books, 1956.
22. Eissler, K. R.: Some problems of delinquency. In *Searchlights on Delinquency*, edited by K. R. Eissler, London, Imago Publishing Company, Ltd., 1949.
23. Erikson, E. H.: *Childhood and Society*. London, Imago Publishing Company, Ltd., 1950.
24. Erikson, E. H.: Growth and crises in the healthy personality. In *Personality in Nature, Society and Culture*, edited by C. K. Kluckholm and H. A. Murray, New York, Alfred A. Knopf, Inc., 1953.

25. Erikson, E. H.: *Identity and the Life Cycle*. New York, International Universities Press, 1959.
26. Federn, P.: *Ego Psychology and the Psychoses*. New York, Basic Books, 1952.
27. Fenichel, O.: *The Psychoanalytic Theory of Neuroses*. London, Routledge and Kegan Paul, Ltd., 1946.
28. Frankenstein, C.: *Die Fehlentwicklung der sozialen Funktionen* (in Hebrew translation). Jerusalem, Szold Foundation, 1947.
29. Frankenstein, C.: Structural factors in the anxiety of children. Acta Psychol., *12:* 201–325, 1956.
30. Frankenstein, C.: The psychodynamics of social behaviour disturbances. Arch. Criminal Psychodynamics, *2:* 82–106, 1957.
31. Frankenstein, C.: The structural meaning of aggressiveness. Acta Psychol., *14:* 253–280, 1958.
32. Frankenstein, C.: Das Unbewusste und die Tiefenzone des Seelischen. Zeitschrift für diagnostische Psychologie und Persönlichkeitsforschung, *6:* 185–210, 1958.
33. Frankenstein, C.: *Die Äusserlichkeit des Lebensstils*. Amsterdam, J. M. Meulenhoff, 1959.
34. Frankenstein, C.: *Psychopathy*. New York, Grune & Stratton, Inc., 1959.
35. Frankenstein, C.: Einige Bemerkungen zum Problem des Traumes. In *Horizons of a Philosopher*, edited by J. Frank, *et al.* Leiden, E. J. Brill, 1963.
36. Frankenstein, C.: School without parents. In *Scripta Hierosolymitana: Studies in Education*. Jerusalem, The Hebrew University Press, 1963.
37. Frankenstein, C.: *Persönlichkeitswandel durch Fürsorge, Erziehung und Therapie*. München, Urban & Schwarzenberg, 1964.
38. Frankenstein, C.: Impaired intelligence. Israel Ann. Psychiat., *2:* 209–227, 1964.
39. Frankenstein, C.: The development of the feebleminded child and the concept of "mental age." Acta Psychol., *24:* 167–204, 1964.
39a. Frankenstein, C.: Environmental varieties of mental retardation. Acta Psychol., *24:* 283–313, 1965.
40. Frazier, E. F.: *The Negro Family in the United States*. Chicago, University of Chicago Press, 1939.
41. Freud, A.: *The Ego and the Mechanisms of Defence*. London, Hogarth Press, Ltd., 1937.
42. Freud, S.: Drei Abhandlungen zur Sexualtheorie. Ges. Werke, *5:* 1948.
43. Freud, S.: Das Unbewusste. Ges. Werke, *10:* 1948.
44. Freud, S.: Einige Charaktertypen aus der psychoanalytischen Arbeit. Ges. Werke, *10:* 1948.
45. Freud, S.: Vorlesungen zur Einführung in die Psychoanalyse. Ges. Werke, *11:* 1948.
46. Freud, S.: Jenseits des Lustprinzips. Ges. Werke, *13:* 1948.
47. Freud, S.: Das Ich und das Es. Ges. Werke, *13:* 1948.
48. Freud, S.: Der Untergang des Ödipuskomplexes. Ges. Werke, *13:* 1948.
49. Freud, S.: Die Zukunft einer Illusion. Ges. Werke, *14:* 1948.
50. Freud, S.: Über die Weibliche Sexualität. Ges. Werke, *14:* 1948.
51. Friedlander, K.: *Psychoanalytical Approach to Juvenile Delinquency*. London, Routledge & Kegan Paul, Inc., 1947.
52. Fromm, E.: *The Art of Loving*. London, George Allen and Unwin, Ltd., 1964.
53. Garner, A. a.o.: *The Mother-Child Interaction in Psychosomatic Disorders*. Urbana, Ill., University of Illinois Press, 1959.

54. Gesell, A., *et al.: Child Development.* New York, Harper & Brothers, 1949.
55. Glueck, S., and Glueck, E.: *Unraveling Juvenile Delinquency.* New York, The Commonwealth Fund, 1950.
56. Goldfarb, W.: Various papers (1943–1949). Amer. J. Orthopsychiat., *14*: 441–447; *15*: 247–255; *19*: 624–633.
57a. Goldstein, K.: *The Organism.* Boston, Beacon Press, 1963.
57b. Goldstein, K., and Scheerer, M.: Abstract and concrete behavior. Psychol. Monog., *53*: 1941.
58. Hartmann, H.: *Ego Psychology and the Problem of Adaptation.* New York, International Universities Press, 1958.
59. Hartmann, H. a.o.: Comments on the formation of psychic structure. Psychoanal. Stud. Child, *2*: 1956.
60. Hartmann, H.: Comments on the psychoanalytic theory of the ego. Psychoanal. Stud. Child, *5:* 74–96, 1950.
61. Heiss, R.: *Allgemeine Tiefenpsychologie.* Bern, Hans Huber, 1956.
62. Hellpach, W.: *Geopsyche.* Leipzig, W. Engelmann, 1935.
63. Hollingshead, A., and Redlich, F. C.: *Social Class and Mental Illness.* New York, John Wiley & Sons, Inc., 1958.
64. Horney, K.: *Our Inner Conflicts.* New York, W. W. Norton & Company, 1945.
65. Huizinga, J.: *Homo Ludens.* Boston, Beacon Press, 1955.
66. Huntington, E.: *Mainsprings of Civilization.* London, Chapman & Hall, Ltd., 1945.
67. Inhelder, B., and Piaget, J.: *The Growth of Logical Thinking from Childhood to Adolescence.* New York, Basic Books, 1958.
68. Isaacs, S.: *Intellectual Growth in Young Children.* London, Routledge & Kegan Paul, Ltd., 1930.
69. Isaacs, S.: *Social Development in Children.* London, Routledge & Kegan Paul, Ltd., 1933.
70. Isaacs, S.: *Childhood and After.* New York, International Universities Press, 1949.
71. James, W.: *Varieties of Religious Experience.* New York, Longmans, 1902.
72. Jones, E.: *Raising Your Child in a Fatherless Home.* Glencoe, Ill., The Free Press, 1963.
73. Jung, C. G.: *Psychologische Typen.* Zürich, Rascher, 1930.
74. Jung, C. G.: *Seelenprobleme der Gegenwart.* Zürich, Rascher, 1933.
75. Jung, C. G.: *Wirklichkeit der Seele.* Zürich, Rascher, 1934.
76. Jung, C. G.: *Integration of the Personality.* London, Routledge & Kegan Paul, Inc., 1941.
77. Jung, C. G.: *Über die Psychologie des Unbewussten.* Zürich, Rascher, 1943.
78. Jung, C. G.: *Von den Wurzeln des Bewusstseins.* Zürich, Rascher, 1954.
79. Kafka, F.: Vor dem Gesetz. In *Erzählungen und kleine Prosa.* Berlin, Schocken, 1935.
80. Kanner, L.: Problems of nosology and psychodynamics of early autism. Amer. J. Orthopsychiat., *19:* 416–426, 1949.
81. Kant, J.: *Die Kritik der reinen Vernunft.* Leipzig, F. Meiner, 1926.
82. Kardiner, A.: *The Psychological Frontiers of Society.* New York, Columbia University Press, 1945.
83. Kerr, M.: *The People of Shipstreet.* London, Routledge & Kegan Paul, Inc., 1958.
84. Klein, M.: *The Psychoanalysis of Children.* London, Hogarth Press, 1933.
85. Klein, M.: *Contributions to Psychoanalysis.* London, Hogarth Press, 1948.
86. Koos, E. L.: *Families in Trouble.* New York, Columbia University Press, 1946.

87. Kretschmer, E.: *Hysteria.* New York, Nervous and Mental Disease Publishing Company, 1926.

88. Kris, E.: The recovery of childhood memories. Psychoanal. Stud. Child, *11:* 54–88, 1956.

89. Lawrence, D. H.: *Sons and Lovers.* Penguin Books, Baltimore, 1956.

90. Levy, D. M.: *Maternal Overprotection.* New York, Columbia University Press, 1943.

91. Levi-Brühl, L.: *Les Fonctions Mentales dans des Sociétés Inférieures.* Paris, Presses Universitaires de France, 1951.

92. Loosli-Usteri, M.: *Die Angst des Kindes.* Bern, Hans Huber, 1948.

93. Mead, M.: *Sex and Temperament in Three Primitive Societies.* New York, A Mentor Book, 1950.

94. Mead, M.: *Male and Female.* New York, W. Murrow & Co., 1949.

94a. Mittelman, B.: Analysis of reciprocal neurotic patterns in family relationships. In *Neurotic Interaction in Marriage,* edited by V. Eisenstadt. New York, Basic Books, 1956.

95. Murphy, G.: *Personality.* New York, Harper & Brothers, 1947.

96. Neumann, E.: *Zur Psychologie des Weiblichen.* Zürich, Rascher, 1953.

97. Neumann, E.: *The Origins and History of Consciousness.* London, Routledge and Kegan Paul, Inc., 1954.

98. Neumann, E.: Leonardo da Vinci und der Mutterarchetyp. In *Kunst und schöpferisches Unbewusstes.* Zürich, Rascher, 1964.

99. Neumann, E.: *Das Kind.* Zürich, Rhein Verlag, 1963.

100. Oberndorf, C. P., Greenacre, P., and Kubie, L.: Symposium on the evaluation of the results of psychoanalytic therapy. Int. J. Psychoanal., *29:* 7–33, 1948.

101. Ophuijsen, J. H. W. van: Primary conduct disturbances. In *Modern Trends in Child Psychiatry,* edited by N. D. C. Lewis and B. L. Pacella. New York, International Universities Press, 1950.

102. *Oxford Dictionary,* Ed. 4 (revised), 1952.

103. Parsons, T., and Bales, R.: *Family, Socialization and Interaction Process.* Glencoe, Ill., The Free Press, 1955.

104. Pearson, G. N. J.: *Emotional Disorders in Children.* New York, W. W. Norton & Co., 1949.

105. Piaget, J.: *The Moral Judgment of the Child.* Glencoe, Ill., The Free Press, 1948.

106. Piaget, J.: *The Origins of Intelligence in Children.* New York, International Universities Press, 1952.

107. Portmann, A.: *Biologische Fragmente zu einer Lehre vom Menschen.* Basel, Benno Schwabe & Company, 1944.

108. Radin, P.: *Primitive Man as Philosopher.* New York, Dover Publications, 1957.

109. Redl, F.: *Children Who Hate.* Glencoe, Ill., The Free Press, 1952.

Index